EGYPT

CANARY ISLANDS

BERLITZ TRAVEL GUIDES

* in preparation / ○ country guides 192 or 256 p.

BERLITZ PHRASE BOOKS

World's bestselling phrase books feature not only expressions and vocabulary you'll need, but also travel tips, useful facts and pronunciation throughout. The handiest and most readable conversation aid available.

Arabic	French	Portuguese
Chinese	German	Russian
Danish	Greek	Serbo-Croatian
Dutch	Hebrew	Spanish
European (14 languages)	Hungarian	Latin-American Spanish
	Italian	
European Menu Reader	Japanese	Swahili
	Norwegian	Swedish
Finnish	Polish	Turkish

BERLITZ CASSETTEPAKS

The above-mentioned titles are also available combined with a cassette to help you improve your accent. A helpful 32-page script is included containing the complete text of the dual language hi-fi recording.

BERLITZ®

EUROPEAN
Menu Reader

By the staff of Berlitz Guides

Revised edition
6th printing 1989

Printed in Switzerland

Berlitz Trademark Reg. U.S. Patent Office
and other countries—Marca Registrada

Berlitz Guides
Avenue d'Ouchy 61
1000 Lausanne 6, Switzerland

Contents

What's for dinner?

That's an easy enough question at home. But on a trip, the answer might not come as quickly. Menus are often untranslatable; you've seen the humorous mistakes when restaurant owners try.

What help is the waiter? Often, little. The dish may be so local it can't be described, much less translated. The waiter may not know enough English. In fact, he may be a foreigner himself with only the faintest idea of what the dish is all about.

Faced with this challenge, Berlitz has prepared this menu reader for use in 14 basic language areas of Europe. Then, acknowledging the profound problem of British vs. American terminology, we added a condensed, dual menu reader to help English speakers understand one another's cookery.

Whenever we found it possible to translate a foreign expression into an exact English equivalent, we did—with relief! There's little more to be done with the word *rosbif*.

But when the dish was untranslatable, we went into as much description of ingredients as we thought necessary to convey its appearance and taste. Sauces and dressings were subject to particular scrutiny and culinary debate. The ingredients of soups occasionally brought manuscript editing to a halt—yes or no to the marjoram? The result of this dedication: a handy glossary of the cuisines of Europe.

Obviously, Berlitz believes in gastronomic experimentation while you're abroad. To make it easier and more fun, we've organized the listings by language area. The sections on France, Germany, Holland, Italy, Portugal and Spain also include dishes from Belgium, Switzerland, Austria and Latin America—depending upon the language.

As a supplement to each food section, we've added a section on drinks including local beverages.

Each food and drink list is preceded by a pronunciation guide along with some of the most common expressions you'll use in a restaurant or bar.

Menus written in Greek or Russian will be all the more exotic. But through a simplified transliteration system, we help you to pronounce these languages. An alphabetical index at the back of the book also makes it easier for you to find in the Greek and Russian lists a particular dish you've heard of or know. Anyone really interested in a particular language is well advised to obtain a Berlitz phrase book or pocket dictionary.

Bon appétit and *à votre santé!*

Danish

Guide to pronunciation

Letter	Approximate pronunciation
Consonants	
b, c, f, h, l, m, n, v	as in English
d	1) when at the end of the word, or between two vowels, like **th** in **th**is 2) otherwise, as in English
g	1) at the beginning of a word or syllable, as in **go** 2) when at the end of a word after a long vowel or before unstressed **e**, like **ch** in Scottish lo**ch**, but weaker and voiced 3) usually mute after **i, y** and sometimes mute after **a, e, o**
j, hj	like **y** in **y**et
hv	like **v** in **v**iew
k, p, t	1) when at the beginning of a word, as in **k**ite, **p**ill and **to** 2) otherwise, like **g, b, d** in **go**, **b**it and **do**

DANISH

l	always as in leaf, never as in bell
r	pronounced in the back of the throat
s	always as in see
sj	like sh in sheet
w	for Danes this is the same as v
z	like s in so

Vowels

A vowel is generally long in stressed syllables when it's the final letter or followed by only one consonant. If followed by two or more consonants, or in unstressed syllables, the vowel is generally short.

a	1) when long, like a in car; it can also be pronounced like a in bad, but longer 2) when short, like long a
e	1) when long, the same quality as a in plate, but longer, and a pure vowel, not a diphthong 2) when short, somewhere between the a in plate and the i in hit 3) when short, also like e in met 4) when unstressed, like a in about
i	1) when long, like ee in bee 2) when short, like ee in meet
o	1) when long, like aw in saw, but with the tongue higher in the mouth; quite like u in put 2) when more or less the same quality of sound 3) when short, also like o in lot
u	1) when long, like oo in pool 2) when short, like oo in loot
y	put your tongue in the position for the ee of bee, but round your lips as for the oo of pool; the vowel you pronounce like this should be more or less correct
æ	1) when long, like the first part of the word air 2) when short, like e in get, but next to r it sounds more like the a of hat
å	1) when long, like aw in saw 2) when short, like o in on
ø	like ur in fur, but with the lips rounded; can be long or short

Diphthongs

av	like **ow** in n**ow**
ej	like **igh** in s**igh**
ev	like **e** in g**e**t followed by a short **u** as in p**u**t
ou	like **o** in g**o**t followed by a short **u** as in p**u**t
øi	like **oi** in **oi**l
øv	like **ur** in h**ur**t followed by a short **u** as in p**u**t

Note

1. Many Danish speakers put a glottal stop in or after vowels (like the Cockney pronunciation of **t** in *wa'er*). Although it has a certain distinctive role, you'll be understood perfectly well if you don't use it.
2. **dd** and **gg** between vowels are pronounced like **d** in **d**o and **g** in **g**o.
3. The letter **d** isn't pronounced in **nd** and **ld** at the end of a word or syllable or before unstressed **e** or before **t** or **s** in the same syllable.

Some useful expressions

Hungry

I'm hungry/I'm thirsty.	**Jeg er sulten/Jeg er tørstig.**
Can you recommend a good restaurant?	**Kan De anbefale en god restaurant?**
Are there any good, cheap restaurants around here?	**Er der en god, billig restaurant i nærheden?**
I'd like to reserve a table for … people.	**Jeg vil gerne reservere et bord til … personer.**
We'll come at … o'clock.	**Vi er der klokken …**

Asking

Good evening. I'd like a table for … people.	**Godaften. Jeg vil gerne have et bord til … personer.**
Could we have a table…?	**Kan vi få et bord…?**
in the corner	**i hjørnet**
by the window	**ved vinduet**
outside	**udenfor**
on the terrace	**på terrassen**

DANISH

May I please have the menu?	**Må jeg få spisekortet?**
What's this?	**Hvad er dette?**
Do you have…?	**Har De …?**
a set menu	**en fast menu**
local dishes	**specialiteter fra egnen**
a children's menu	**en ret til børn**
Waiter/Waitress!	**Tjener/Frøken!**
What do you recommend?	**Hvad kan De anbefale?**
Could I have (a/an)… please?	**Må jeg få …?**
ashtray	**et askebæger**
another chair	**en ekstra stol**
finger bowl	**en skylleskål**
fork	**en gaffel**
glass	**et glas**
knife	**en kniv**
napkin	**en serviet**
plate	**en tallerken**
pepper mill	**en peberkværn**
serviette	**en serviet**
spoon	**en ske**
toothpick	**en tandstikker**

Ordering

I'd like a/an/some…	**Jeg vil gerne have …**
aperitif	**en aperitif**
appetizer	**en appetitvækker**
beer	**en øl**
bread	**noget brød**
butter	**noget smør**
cheese	**ost**
chips	**pommes frites**
coffee	**kaffe**
dessert	**en dessert**
fish	**fisk**
french fries	**pommes frites**
fruit	**frugt**
game	**vildt**
ice-cream	**is**

lemon	**citron**
lettuce	**grøn salat**
meat	**kød**
mineral water	**en mineralvand**
milk	**mælk**
mustard	**sennep**
noodles	**nudler**
oil	**olie**
olive oil	**olivenolie**
pepper	**peber**
potatoes	**kartofler**
poultry	**fjerkræ**
rice	**ris**
rolls	**rundstykker**
saccharin	**sødetabletter**
salad	**salat**
salt	**salt**
sandwich	**en sandwich**
seafood	**skaldyr**
seasoning	**krydderier**
soup	**suppe**
starter	**en forret**
sugar	**sukker**
tea	**te**
vegetables	**grønsager**
vinegar	**eddike**
(iced) water	**(is)vand**
wine	**vin**

DANISH

VELBEKOMME!
ENJOY YOUR MEAL!

---

baked	**bagt**
baked in parchment	**bagt i folie**
boiled	**kogt**
braised	**grydestegt**
cured	**lagret**
fried	**stegt på panden**
grilled	**grillstegt**
marinated	**marineret**

poached	**pocheret**
roasted	**ovnstegt**
sautéed	**sauteret**
smoked	**røget**
steamed	**dampkogt**
stewed	**kogt over svag ild**
underdone (rare)	**rødstegt**
medium	**mellemstegt**
well-done	**gennemstegt**

SKÅL!
CHEERS!

DANISH

glass	**et glas**
bottle	**en flaske**
red	**rød**
white	**hvid**
rosé	**rosé**
very dry	**meget tør**
dry	**tør**
sweet	**sød**
light	**let**
full-bodied	**fyldig**
sparkling	**mousserende**
neat (straight)	**tør**
on the rocks	**med isterninger**

The bill

I'd like to pay.	**Jeg vil gerne betale.**
We'd like to pay separately.	**Vi vil gerne betale hver for sig.**
You've made a mistake in this bill, I think.	**Jeg tror, De har lavet en fejl i regningen.**
What's this amount for?	**Hvad dækker dette beløb?**
Is service included?	**Er det med betjening?**
Is everything included?	**Er alt inkluderet?**
Do you accept traveller's cheques?	**Tager De imod rejsechecks?**

Thank you. This is for you.	**Mange tak, dette er til Dem.**
Keep the change.	**Behold småpengene.**
That was a very good meal.	**Det var et dejligt måltid.**
We enjoyed it, thank you.	**Vi har nydt det.**

Complaints

That's not what I ordered.	**Det er ikke det, jeg bestilte.**
I asked for...	**Jeg har bestilt ...**
May I change this?	**Kan jeg få noget andet?**
The meat is...	**Kødet er ...**
overdone	**stegt for meget**
underdone	**stegt for lidt**
too rare	**for råt**
too tough	**for sejt**
This is too...	**Dette er for ...**
bitter/salty/sweet	**bittert/salt/sødt**
The food is cold.	**Maden er kold.**
This isn't fresh.	**Dette er ikke friskt.**
What's taking you so long?	**Hvorfor varer det så længe?**
Where are our drinks?	**Hvor bliver vore drinks af?**
This isn't clean.	**Dette er ikke rent.**
Would you ask the head waiter to come over?	**Vil De kalde på overtjeneren?**

DANISH

Numbers

1	**en, et**	11	**elleve**
2	**to**	12	**tolv**
3	**tre**	13	**tretten**
4	**fire**	14	**fjorten**
5	**fem**	15	**femten**
6	**seks**	16	**seksten**
7	**syv**	17	**sytten**
8	**otte**	18	**atten**
9	**ni**	19	**nitten**
10	**ti**	20	**tyve**

Food

Please note that Danish alphabetical order is a-z, æ, ø, å.

aborre perch
abrikos apricot
aftensmad dinner
agerhøne partridge
agurk cucumber
agurkesalat sliced cucumber in vinegar dressing
ananas pineapple
and duck
ansjos 1) marinated sprat 2) anchovy
appelsin orange
artiskok artichoke
asie kind of large cucumber, seeded and pickled
asparges asparagus
bagt kartoffel baked potato
banan banana
bankekød beef stew
benløse fugle thin slices of veal or beef wrapped around a stuffing of bacon, parsley and chopped onions
betjening iberegnet service included
biksemad diced meat fried with potatoes and onions
blodpølse black pudding (US blood sausage)
blomkål cauliflower
blomme plum
blødkogt æg soft-boiled egg
blåbær bilberry (US blueberry)

bolle 1) bun 2) meat or fish ball
bondepige med slør dessert made from stewed apples, rye-bread crumbs toasted in butter and sugar, topped with whipped cream
brasede kartofler sliced, sautéed potatoes
brisler sweetbreads
brombær blackberry
brun kage brown, spicy biscuit (US cookie)
brunede kartofler boiled, caramelized potatoes
brunet smør browned butter sauce
brød bread
budding pudding
bøf (beef) steak
~ **sandwich** hamburger
~ **tatar** steak tartare; finely chopped raw beef, served on rye bread with egg-yolk, onion, horse-radish and capers
bønne bean
børnemenu children's menu
chalotteløg shallot
champignon mushroom
citron lemon
~ **fromage** lemon blancmange, mousse (pudding)
daddelblomme persimmon
dadler dates

DANISH

dagens middag set menu
dagens ret day's special
dampet steamed
Danablue Danish blue cheese
Danbo mild, firm cheese, sometimes flavoured with caraway seed
dild dill
diætmad diet food
due pigeon (US squab)
dyrekølle haunch of venison
dyresteg roast venison
eddike white vinegar
Elbo cheese with mild flavour
engelsk bøf steak and onions
Esrom mild, slightly aromatic cheese
fasan pheasant
fersken peach
fisk fish
fiskefilet fillet of fish (usually plaice)
fiskefrikadelle fried fishball, served hot, or cold on *smørrebrød*
fjerkræ fowl
flamberet flamed
flute kind of French bread
flæskesteg roast pork with crackling
flæskeæggekage thick omelet with fried bacon, tomatoes and chives, served with rye bread
fløde cream
　~kage pastry topped with whipped cream
　~ost cream cheese
　~skum whipped cream
forloren hare type of meatloaf of pork and veal, served with apple halves filled with redcurrant jelly, together with potatoes and red cabbage
forret first course, starter

forårsrulle (Chinese) spring roll, egg roll
franskbrød white bread
frikadelle meatball of minced pork and veal
frisk fresh
friturekogt, -stegt deep fried
frokost lunch
　~bord buffet of cold and hot specialities to make your own *smørrebrød*
　~platte hot and cold specialities to make your own *smørrebrød*, served on a tray
fromage blancmange, mousse (pudding)
frugt fruit
frølår frogs' legs
fyld stuffing
fyldt stuffed
　~hvidkål cabbage stuffed with minced pork and veal
Fynbo mild, rich cheese similar to *Samsø*
fårekød mutton
gedde pike
gennemstegt well-done
grapefrugt grapefruit
gratin baked casserole
gravad laks, gravlaks salt and dill-cured salmon, served with a creamy mustard sauce
grillstegt grilled
gryderet stew of meat and vegetables
grydestegt braised
grøn bønne French bean (US green bean)
grøn salat lettuce
grønlangkål creamed kale
grøn(t)sager vegetables
grønært green pea
grønærtesuppe pea soup
gule ærter med flæsk split-pea

soup served with boiled, salt
pork and sausages
gulerødder carrots
gås goose
gåselever(postej) goose liver
(paté)
gåsesteg roast goose
~ **med æbler og svesker** stuffed
with apples and prunes
hakkebøf med løg hamburger
steak served with fried onions
hakket chopped, minced
halv, halvdel half
hamburgerryg slightly smoked
loin of pork
haresteg roast hare
hasselnød hazelnut
Havarti semi-hard cheese with a
piquant flavour
havregrød oatmeal
helleflynder halibut
helstegt roasted whole
hindbær raspberry
hjemmelavet home-made
hjerte heart
hjerter i flødesovs hearts, usually
of pork, served in a cream
sauce
honning honey
hornfisk garfish
hovedret main dish
hummer lobster
hvidkål cabbage
hvidløg garlic
hytteost cottage cheese
høne hen
hønsebryst chicken breast
hønsekødsuppe chicken broth
hårdkogt æg hard-boiled egg
ingefær ginger
~ **brød** gingerbread
is ice-cream, ice
italiensk salat mayonnaise mixed
with peas, chopped carrots and

asparagus, served with ham on
smørrebrød
jomfruhummer Norway lobster
jordbær strawberry
~ **grød** kind of strawberry
purée, served with cream
julesalat chicory (US endive)
kage cake
kalkun turkey
kalvebrisler sweetbreads
kalvekød veal
kantarel chanterelle mushroom
kapers capers
karamelrand caramel custard
karbonade breaded minced steak
of pork or veal
karpe carp
karry curry
karse cress
kartoffel potato
~ **mos** mashed potatoes
~ **salat** potato salad (hot or
cold)
kastanie chestnut
kaviar caviar
kiks biscuit (US cookie)
kirsebær cherry
klar suppe consommé, clear soup
~ **med boller og grønsager**
consommé with meat balls and
vegetables
klipfisk dried salt cod
kogt boiled
~ **torsk (med sennepssovs)**
steamed cod (with mustard
sauce)
kold cold
koldt bord a wide variety of open
sandwiches, small warm dishes,
salads and cheeses
kotelet cutlet, chop
krabbe crab
kransekage pyramid of almond
macaroons

krebs freshwater crayfish
kringle variety of Danish pastry
krydder toasted bun
krydderi spice
kryddersild pickled herring
kryddersmør herb butter
kræmmerhus med flødeskum
  pastry cone filled with whipped
  cream and topped with jam
kuvertbrød (French) roll
kvæde quince
kylling chicken
kærnemælkskoldskål chilled
  buttermilk soup, served with
  rusks (US zwieback)
kød meat
  ~ **bolle** meatball
  ~ **fars** forcemeat, stuffing
kørvelsuppe chervil soup
kål cabbage
labskovs lobscouse; casserole of
  potatoes, meat and vegetables
lagkage layer cake, usually filled
  with whipped cream, jam, fruit
  purée or custard
laks salmon
lammebov shoulder of lamb
lammebryst breast of lamb
lammekød lamb
lammekølle leg of lamb
legeret suppe cream soup
lever liver
  ~ **postej** liver pâté
linse 1) lentil 2) custard pastry
løg onion
majs maize (US corn)
  ~ **kolbe** corn on the cob
makrel mackerel
makron macaroon
mandel almond
Maribo soft, mild cheese
marineret marinated
  ~ **sild** marinated herring
medisterpølse pork sausage

melbolle dumpling
mellemstegt medium (done)
millionbøf minced meat in cream
  sauce
Molbo a yellow, pressed cheese
  similar to Edam
morgencomplet continental
  breakfast
morgenmad breakfast
musling mussel
Mycella cheese similar to Danish
  blue, but milder
mørbrad fillet of meat (US tenderloin)
  ~ **bøf** small round pork fillet
  ~ **steg** porterhouse steak
måltid meal
nye kartofler new potatoes
nyre kidney
nød nut
oksebryst brisket of beef
oksefilet fillet of beef (US tenderloin)
oksehalesuppe oxtail soup
oksekød beef
  ~ **suppe** broth, consommé
oksemørbrad fillet of beef
oksesteg roast beef
olie oil
oliven olive
omelet med kyllingelever chicken
  liver omelet
ost cheese
osteanretning cheese board
Othellokage layer cake filled with
  custard, topped with chocolate
  sauce and whipped cream
ovnbagt baked
ovnstegt roasted
pandekage pancake
paneret breaded
pariserbøf hamburger on toast
  with egg-yolk, chopped onions
  and capers

parisertoast toasted ham-and-cheese sandwich

pattegris suck(l)ing pig

peber black pepper

~ **bøf** (beef)steak with peppercorns

~ **frugt** pimiento

~ **rod** horse-radish

persille parsley

pighvar turbot

pillede rejer shelled shrimps

pocheret poached

pommes frites chips (US French fries)

porre leek

purløg chive

pære pear

pølse sausage

pålæg cold meat, sausage, salad, fish or cheese as a garnish for *smørrebrød*

rabarber rhubarb

radise radish

regning bill (US check)

reje shrimp

remoulade mayonnaise flavoured with finely chopped pickles, capers, onions and mustard

ribbenssteg rib-roast of pork with crackling, often served with red cabbage

~ **med æbler og svesker** rib-roast of pork stuffed with apples and prunes

ribs currant (red or white)

~ **gelé** redcurrant jelly

ris rice

~ **à l'amande** rice pudding with grated almonds, served with hot cherry sauce

risengrød rice boiled in milk, served with cinnamon and butter

rosenkål brussels sprouts

rosin raisin

roulade 1) meat roll 2) Swiss roll

rugbrød rye bread

rullepølse kind of sausage made of rolled veal and pork, sliced and served on *smørrebrød*

rundstykke poppy-seed roll

rødbede beetroot

rødgrød kind of thickened red fruit juice, served with cream

rødkål red cabbage

rødspætte plaice

~ **filet** fillet of plaice

rødstegt underdone (US rare)

røget smoked

~ **sild** smoked herring on rye bread garnished with chopped hardboiled eggs, onions, radishes and chives

rørt smør creamed butter

røræg scrambled eggs

rå raw

~ **kost** uncooked vegetables or fruit

salat 1) salad 2) lettuce

saltet salted, cured

sammenkogt ret stew of meat and vegetables

Samsø mild, firm cheese with a sweet flavour

selleri celery

sennep mustard

sigtebrød bread made of rye and wheat flour

sild herring

sildesalat herring and beetroot salad

skaldyr shellfish

skinke ham

~ **med spejlæg** ham and eggs

skipperlabskovs lobscouse; thick stew of beef, carrots and onions

skive slice

skrubbe flounder
slankekost low calorie food
smeltet smør melted butter
smør butter
smørrebrød slices of buttered rye (or wheat) bread with any of a variety of garnishes, such as shrimps, herring, ham, roast beef, cheese and salads
småkage biscuit (US cookie)
snittebønne sliced French bean
solbær blackcurrant
sovs sauce
spegepølse kind of raw sausage, salami
spejlæg fried egg
spinat spinach
spisekort menu, bill of fare
steg joint of meat, roast
stegt fried, roasted
stikkelsbær gooseberry
stuvet creamed
sukker sugar
suppe soup
surkål sauerkraut
sursød sweet-and-sour
sveske prune
svinekam med svesker roast loin of pork stuffed with prunes
svinekød pork
svinemørbrad fillet of pork (US tenderloin)
sylte brawn (US head cheese)
syltede agurker gherkins (US pickles)
syltetøj jam
sød sweet
søtunge sole
tatar see *bøftatar*

tebirkes type of bun with poppy seeds
timian thyme
tomatsuppe tomato soup
torsk cod
torskerogn cod roe
tranebær cranberry
tunfisk tunny (US tuna)
tunge tongue
tykmælk kind of junket, thin yoghurt
tyttebær mountain cranberry, red whortleberry
tærte cake, tart
vaffel wafer, waffle
vagtel quail
valnød walnut
vandmelon watermelon
varm warm
vildand wild duck
vildt game
vindrue grape
vinkort wine list
wienerbrød Danish pastry
ymer kind of sour milk
æble apple
  ~ **flæsk** fried apples and bacon
  ~ **grød** stewed apples
  ~ **kage** kind of apple charlotte
  ~ **mos** apple sauce
  ~ **skive** kind of fritter, served with jam
æg egg(s)
æggeblomme egg-yolk
ært pea
ørred trout
østers oyster
ål eel
  ~ **i gelé** jellied

DANISH

Drink

akvavit aquavit, spirits distilled from potatoes or grain, often flavoured with aromatic seeds and spices

alkoholfri non-alcoholic

appelsinjuice orange juice

appelsinvand orangeade

bordvin table wine

Carlsberg a renowned Danish brewery

Cherry Heering see *Peter Heering*

chokolade hot chocolate (drink)

citronvand lemonade

danskvand soda water

dessertvin dessert wine

elefantøl also known as *exportøl* or *luksusøl:* beer with a high alcoholic content

fadøl draught (US draft) beer

fløde cream

frugtjuice fruit juice

gløgg mulled wine (Christmas speciality)

hedvin fortified wine

husets vin open wine

hvidvin white wine

irsk kaffe Irish coffee

kaffe coffee

   ~ med fløde with cream

   ~ med mælk with milk

kærnemælk buttermilk

lagerøl dark lager

letmælk partially skimmed milk

likør liqueur, cordial

lyst øl light beer

mineralvand mineral water

mousserende vin sparkling wine

mælk milk

mørkt øl dark beer

Peter Heering a renowned Danish cherry liqueur

pilsner lager; light beer

porter stout

portvin port (wine)

påskebryg beer with a high alcoholic content, brewed at Easter

rom rum

rødvin red wine

saft juice

saftevand squash (US fruit drink)

skummetmælk skim milk

snaps see *akvavit*

sodavand fruit-flavoured soda water

sødmælk full milk

te tea

   ~ med citron with lemon

   ~ med mælk with milk

Tuborg a renowned Danish brewery

vand water

varm mælk hot milk

vin wine

æblemost apple juice

øl beer

Dutch

Guide to pronunciation

Letter	Approximate pronunciation
Consonants	
c, f, h, k, l, m, n, p, q, t, v, y, z	as in English
b	as in English, but when at the end of a word, like **p** in cu**p**
ch	1) generally like **ch** in Scottish lo**ch** 2) in words of French origin like **sh** in **sh**ut
chtj	like Dutch **ch** followed by Dutch **j**
d	as in English, but when at the end of a word like **t** in hi**t**
g	1) generally like **ch** in Scottish lo**ch**, but often slightly softer and voiced 2) in a few words of French origin, like **s** in plea**s**ure
j	like **y** in **y**es
nj	like **ni** in o**ni**on
r	always trilled, either in the front or the back of the mouth

s	always like **s** in si**t**
sj, stj	like **sh** in **sh**ut
sch	like **s** followed by a Dutch **ch**
th	like **t**
tj	like **ty** in hi**t you**
w	something like **v**, but with the bottom lip raised a little higher

Vowels

In Dutch a vowel is *short* when followed by two consonants or by one consonant at the end of a word. It's *long* when it's at the end of a word, before a consonant followed by a vowel or when written double.

a	1) when short, between **a** in c**a**rt and **u** in c**u**t 2) when long, like **a** in c**a**rt
e	1) when short, like **e** in b**e**d 2) when long, like **a** in l**a**te, but a pure vowel 3) in unstressed syllables, like **a** in **a**bove
eu	long, like **eu** in French f**eu**; approximately like **u** in f**u**r, said with rounded lips
i	1) when short, like **i** in b**i**t 2) when long (also spelt **ie**), like **ee** in b**ee** 3) sometimes, in unstressed syllables, like **a** in **a**bove
ij	sometimes, in unstressed syllables, like **a** in **a**bove
o	1) when short, like a very short version of **aw** in l**aw**n 2) when long, something like **oa** in r**oa**d, but a pure vowel and with more rounded lips
oe	long, like **oo** in m**oo**n and well rounded
u	1) when short, something like **u** in h**u**rt, but with rounded lips 2) when long, like **u** in French s**u**r or **ü** in German f**ü**r; say **ee** and without moving your tongue, round your lips. The resulting "rounded **ee**" should be the correct sound.

Diphthongs

ai	like **igh** in s**igh**
ei, ij	like **a** in l**a**te
au, ou	Dutch short **o** followed by a weak, short **u** sound; can sound very much like **ow** in n**ow**

The following diphthongs have a long vowel as their first element:

aai	like **a** in c**a**rt followed by a short **ee** sound
eeuw	like **a** in l**a**te followed by a short **oo** sound
ieuw	like **ee** in fr**ee** followed by a short **oo** sound
ooi	like **o** in wr**o**te followed by a short **ee** sound
oei	like **oo** in s**oo**n followed by a short **ee** sound
ui	like **u** in f**u**r followed by a short Dutch **u** sound as described in **u**, example 2)
uw	like the sound described in **u**, example 2) followed by a weak **oo** sound

Note

1. When two consonants are next to each other, one will often influence the other even if it isn't in the same word, e.g., the **z** in *ziens* is pronounced like the **z** in *zoo*, but in the expression *tot ziens*, it's pronounced like the **s** in sit under the influence of the **t** before it.
2. In the **-en** ending of verbs and plural nouns, the **n** is generally dropped in everyday speech.

Some useful expressions

Hungry

I'm hungry/I'm thirsty.	**Ik heb honger/Ik heb dorst.**
Can you recommend a good restaurant?	**Kunt U een goed restaurant aanbevelen?**
Are there any good, cheap restaurants around here?	**Zijn hier ook goede, niet te dure restaurants in de buurt?**
I'd like to reserve a table for ... people.	**Ik wil graag een tafel reserveren voor ... personen.**
We'll come at ... o'clock.	**We komen om ... uur.**

Asking

Good evening. I'd like a table for ... people.	**Goedenavond. Een tafel voor ... personen, alstublieft.**
Could we have a table...?	**We willen graag een tafel...**
in the corner	**in de hoek**
by the window	**bij het raam**

outside	**buiten**
on the terrace	**op het terras**
May I please have the menu?	**Mag ik de menukaart, alstublieft?**
What's this?	**Wat is dit?**
Do you have…?	**Hebt u…?**
a set menu	**een dagschotel**
local dishes	**plaatselijke specialiteiten**
a children's menu	**een kindermenu**
Waiter/Waitress!	**Ober/Juffrouw!**
What do you recommend?	**Wat kunt U ons aanraden?**
Could I have (a/an)… please?	**Mag ik een…, alstublieft?**
ashtray	**asbak**
another chair	**stoel erbij**
fork	**vork**
glass	**glas**
knife	**mes**
napkin	**servet**
plate	**bord**
pepper mill	**pepermolen**
serviette	**servet**
spoon	**lepel**
toothpick	**tandenstoker**

Ordering

I'd like a/an/some…	**Ik wil graag …**
aperitif	**een aperitief**
appetizer	**een voorgerecht**
beer	**een bier**
bread	**brood**
butter	**boter**
cheese	**kaas**
chips	**patates frites**
coffee	**koffie**
dessert	**een nagerecht**
fish	**vis**
french fries	**patates frites**
fruit	**fruit**

game	**wild**
ice-cream	**ijs**
lemon	**citroen**
lettuce	**stoofsla**
meat	**vlees**
mineral water	**mineraalwater**
milk	**melk**
mustard	**mosterd**
noodles	**noedels**
oil	**olie**
olive oil	**olijfolie**
pepper	**peper**
potatoes	**aardappels**
poultry	**gevogelte**
rice	**rijst**
rolls	**broodjes**
saccharin	**saccharine**
salad	**sla**
salt	**zout**
sandwich	**een boterham**
seafood	**schaal- en schelpdieren**
seasoning	**specerij**
soup	**soep**
starter	**een voorgerecht**
sugar	**suiker**
tea	**thee**
vegetables	**groenten**
vinegar	**azijn**
(iced) water	**(ijs)water**
wine	**wijn**

SMAKELIJK ETEN!
ENJOY YOUR MEAL!

---

baked	**in de oven gebakken**
baked in parchment	**gebraden in perkamentpapier**
boiled	**gekookt**
braised	**gesmoord**
cured	**gedroogd**

fried	**gebakken**
grilled	**geroosterd**
marinated	**gemarineerd**
poached	**gepocheerd**
roasted	**gebraden**
sautéed	**zacht gebakken**
smoked	**gerookt**
steamed	**gestoomd**
stewed	**gestoofd**
underdone (rare)	**licht gebakken**
medium	**half doorbakken**
well-done	**goed doorbakken**

GEZONDHEID!
CHEERS!

---

glass	**glas**
bottle	**fles**
red	**rood**
white	**wit**
rosé	**rosé**
very dry	**zeer droog**
dry	**droog**
sweet	**zoet**
light	**licht**
full-bodied	**zwaar**
sparkling	**mousserend**
neat (straight)	**puur**
on the rocks	**met ijs**

The bill

I'd like to pay.	**Mag ik afrekenen?**
We'd like to pay separately.	**We willen graag apart betalen.**
You've made a mistake in this bill, I think.	**Ik geloof dat u een fout gemaakt hebt in de rekening.**
What's this amount for?	**Waarvoor is dit bedrag?**
Is service included?	**Is de bediening inbegrepen?**
Is everything included?	**Is alles inbegrepen?**

Do you accept traveller's cheques?	**Accepteert u reischeques?**
Thank you. This is for you.	**Dank u, dit is voor u.**
Keep the change.	**Houd het wisselgeld maar.**
That was a very good meal.	**Het heeft ons prima gesmaakt.**
We enjoyed it, thank you.	**Het was lekker, dank u.**

Complaints

That's not what I ordered.	**Dat heb ik niet besteld.**
I asked for...	**Ik heb... gevraagd.**
May I change this?	**Kan ik hier iets anders voor krijgen?**
The meat is...	**Het vlees is...**
overdone	**te gaar**
underdone	**te rauw**
too rare	**te rood**
too tough	**te taai**
This is too...	**Dit is te...**
bitter/salty/sweet	**bitter/zout/zoet**
The food is cold.	**Het eten is koud.**
This isn't fresh.	**Dit is niet vers.**
What's taking you so long?	**Waarom duurt het zo lang?**
Where are our drinks?	**Waar blijven onze drankjes?**
This isn't clean.	**Dit is niet schoon.**
Would you ask the head waiter to come over?	**Wilt u de chef kelner vragen even hier te komen?**

Numbers

1	één		11	elf
2	twee		12	twaalf
3	drie		13	dertien
4	vier		14	veertien
5	vijf		15	vijftien
6	zes		16	zestien
7	zeven		17	zeventien
8	acht		18	achttien
9	negen		19	negentien
10	tien		20	twintig

Food

aalbes redcurrant
aardappel potato
  ~puree mashed potatoes
aardbei strawberry
abrikoos apricot
amandel almond
  ~broodje a sweet roll with almond-paste filling
ananas pineapple
andijvie endive (US chicory)
  ~stamppot mashed potato and endive casserole
anijs aniseed
ansjovis anchovy
appel apple
  ~beignet fritter
  ~bol dumpling
  ~flap puff-pastry containing an apple slice
  ~gebak cake
  ~moes sauce
Ardense pastei rich pork mixture cooked in a pastry crust, served cold in slices
artisjok artichoke
asperge asparagus
  ~punt tip
aubergine aubergine (US eggplant)
augurk gherkin (US pickle)

avondeten dinner, supper
azijn vinegar
baars perch
babi pangang slices of roast suck-(l)ing pig, served with a sweet-and-sour sauce
bami goreng a casserole of noodles, vegetables, diced pork and shrimps
banaan banana
banketletter pastry with an almond-paste filling
basilicum basil
bediening service
belegd broodje roll with a variety of garnishes
belegen kaas pungent-flavoured cheese
biefstuk fillet of beef
  ~ van de haas small round fillet of beef
bieslook chive
bitterbal small, round breaded meatball served as an appetizer
blinde vink veal bird; thin slice of veal rolled around stuffing
bloedworst black pudding (US blood sausage)
  ~ met appelen with cooked apples

bloemkool cauliflower
boerenkool met worst kale mixed with mashed potatoes and served with smoked sausage
boerenomelet omelet with diced vegetables and bacon
bokking bloater
boon bean
borrelhapje appetizer
borststuk breast, brisket
bosbes bilberry (US blueberry)
bot 1) flounder 2) bone
boter butter
boterham slice of buttered bread
bouillon broth
braadhaantje spring chicken
braadworst frying sausage
braam blackberry
brasem bream
brood bread
~ **maaltijd** bread served with cold meat, eggs, cheese, jam or other garnishes
~ **pudding** kind of bread pudding with eggs, cinnamon and rum flavouring
broodje roll
~ **halfom** buttered roll with liver and salted beef
~ **kaas** buttered roll with cheese
bruine bonen met spek red kidney beans served with bacon
Brussels lof chicory (US endive)
caramelpudding caramel mould
caramelvla caramel custard
champignon mushroom
chocola(de) chocolate
citroen lemon
cordon bleu veal scallop stuffed with ham and cheese
dadel date
dagschotel day's special
dame blanche vanilla ice-cream

with hot chocolate sauce
dille dill
doperwt green pea
dragon tarragon
drie-in-de-pan small, fluffy pancake filled with currants
druif grape
duif pigeon
Duitse biefstuk hamburger steak
Edam, Edammer kaas firm, mild-flavoured yellow cheese, coated with red wax
eend duck
ei egg
eierpannekoek egg pancake
erwt pea
erwtensoep met kluif pea soup with diced, smoked sausage, pork fat, pig's trotter (US feet), parsley, leeks and celery
exclusief not included
fazant pheasant
filet fillet
~ **américain** steak tartare
flensje small, thin pancake
foe yong hai omelet with leeks, onions, and shrimps served in a sweet-and-sour sauce
forel trout
framboos raspberry
Friese nagelkaas cheese made from skimmed milk, flavoured with cloves
frikadel meatball
frites, frieten chips (US french fries)
gaar well-done
gans goose
garnaal shrimp, prawn
gebak pastry, cake
gebakken fried
gebonden soep cream soup
gebraden roasted
gedroogde pruim prune

gehakt 1) minced 2) minced meat
~**bal** meatball
gekookt boiled
gekruid seasoned
gemarineerd marinated
gember ginger
~**koek** gingerbread
gemengd assorted, mixed
gepaneerd breaded
gepocheerd ei poached egg
geraspt grated
gerecht course, dish
gerookt smoked
geroosterd brood toast
gerst barley
gestoofd braised
gevogelte fowl
gevuld stuffed
gezouten salted
Goudakaas, Goudse kaas a renowned Dutch cheese, similar to *Edam*, large, flat and round; it gains in flavour with maturity
griesmeel semolina
~**pudding** semolina pudding
griet brill
groente vegetable
Haagse bluf dessert of whipped egg-whites, served with redcurrant sauce
haantje cockerel
haas hare
hachee hash of minced meat, onions and spices
half, halve half
hardgekookt ei hard-boiled egg
haring herring
hart heart
havermoutpap (oatmeal) porridge
hazelnoot hazelnut
heilbot halibut
heldere soep consommé, clear soup
hersenen brains

hete bliksem potatoes, bacon and apples, seasoned with butter, salt and sugar
Hollandse biefstuk loin section of a porterhouse or T-bone steak
Hollandse nieuwe freshly caught, filleted herring
honing honey
houtsnip 1) woodcock 2) cheese sandwich on rye bread
hutspot met klapstuk hotch-potch of mashed potatoes, carrots and onions served with boiled beef
huzarensla salad of potatoes, hard-boiled eggs, cold meat, gherkins, beetroot and mayonnaise
ijs ice, ice-cream
inclusief included
Italiaanse salade mixed salad with tomatoes, olives and tunny fish
jachtschotel a casserole of meat, onions and potatoes, often served with apple sauce
jonge kaas fresh cheese
jus gravy
kaas cheese
~**balletje** baked cheese ball
kabeljauw cod
kalfslapje, kalfsoester veal cutlet
kalfsrollade roast veal
kalfsvlees veal
kalkoen turkey
kapucijners met spek peas served with fried bacon, boiled potatoes, onions and green salad
karbonade chop, cutlet
karper carp
kastanje chestnut
kaviaar caviar
kerrie curry
kers cherry
kievitsei plover's egg
kip chicken

ippeborst breast of chicken
ippebout leg of chicken
nakworst small frankfurter sausage
noflook garlic
oek 1) cake 2) gingerbread
oekje biscuit (US cookie)
offietafel light lunch consisting of bread and butter with a variety of garnishes, served with coffee
okosnoot coconut
omijnekaas cheese flavoured with cumin seeds
omkommer cucumber
onijn rabbit
oninginnesoep cream of chicken
ool cabbage
  ~**schotel met gehakt** casserole of meatballs and cabbage
otelet chop, cutlet
oud cold
  ~ **vlees** cold meat (US cold cuts)
rab crab
rabbetje spare rib
rent currant
roepoek large, deep-fried shrimp wafer
roket croquette
ruiderij herb, seasoning
ruidnagel clove
ruisbes gooseberry
wark fresh white cheese
wartel quail
weepeer quince
amsbout leg of lamb
amsvlees lamb
angoest spiny lobster
Leidse kaas cheese flavoured with cumin seeds
ekkerbekje fried, filleted haddock or plaice
endestuk sirloin
ever liver

linze lentil
loempia spring roll (US egg roll)
maïskolf corn on the cob
makreel mackerel
mandarijntje tangerine
marsepein marzipan
meikaas a creamy cheese with high fat content
meloen melon
menu van de dag set menu
mossel mussel
mosterd mustard
nagerecht dessert
nasi goreng a casserole of rice, fried onions, meat, chicken, shrimps, vegetables and seasoning, usually topped with a fried egg
nier kidney
  ~**broodje** roll filled with kidneys and chopped onions
noot nut
oester oyster
olie oil
  ~**bol** fritter with raisins
olijf olive
omelet fines herbes herb omelet
omelet met kippelevertjes chicken liver omelet
omelet nature plain omelet
ongaar underdone (US rare)
ontbijt breakfast
  ~**koek** honey cake
  ~**spek** bacon, rasher
ossehaas fillet of beef
ossestaart oxtail
oude kaas any mature and strong cheese
paddestoel mushroom
paling eel
  ~ **in 't groen** braised in white sauce garnished with chopped parsley and other greens
pannekoek pancake

~ **met stroop** pancake served with treacle (US syrup)

pap porridge

paprika green or red (sweet) pepper

patates frites chips (US french fries)

pastei pie, pasty

patrijs partridge

peer pear

pekeltong salt(ed) tongue

pekelvlees slices of salted meat

peper pepper

  ~ **koek** gingerbread

perzik peach

peterselie parsley

piccalilly pickle

pinda peanut

  ~ **kaas** peanut butter

pisang goreng fried banana

poffertje fritter served with sugar and butter

pompelmoes grapefruit

portie portion

postelein purslane (edible plant)

prei leek

prinsessenboon French bean (US green bean)

pruim plum

rabarber rhubarb

radijs radish

rauw raw

reebout, reerug venison

reine-claude greengage

rekening bill

ribstuk rib of beef

rijst rice

  ~ **tafel** an Indonesian preparation composed of some 30 dishes including stewed vegetables, spit-roasted meat and fowl, served with rice, various sauces, fruit, nuts and spices

rivierkreeft crayfish

rode biet beetroot

rode kool red cabbage

roerei scrambled egg

roggebrood rye bread

rolmops Bismarck herring

rolpens fried slices of spiced and pickled minced beef and tripe, topped with an apple slice

rookspek smoked bacon

rookworst smoked sausage

roomboter butter

roomijs ice-cream

rosbief roast beef

rozemarijn rosemary

runderlap beefsteak

rundvlees beef

Russische eieren Russian eggs; hard-boiled egg-halves garnished with mayonnaise, herring, shrimps, capers, anchovies and sometimes caviar; served on lettuce

salade salad

sambal kind of spicy paste consisting mainly of ground pimentos, usually served with *rijsttafel*, *bami* or *nasi goreng*

sardien sardine

saté, sateh skewered pieces of meat covered with a spicy peanut sauce

saucijzebroodje sausage roll

saus sauce, gravy

schaaldier shellfish

schapevlees mutton

scharretong lemon sole

schelvis haddock

schildpadsoep turtle soup

schnitzel cutlet

schol plaice

schuimomelet fluffy dessert omelet

selderij celery

sinaasappel orange

sjaslik skewered chunks of meat, grilled, then braised in a spicy sauce of tomatoes, onions and bacon

sla salad, lettuce

slaboon French bean (US green bean)

slagroom whipped cream

slak snail

sneeuwbal kind of cream puff, sometimes filled with currants and raisins

snijboon sliced French bean

soep soup

~ **van de dag** soup of the day

sorbet water ice (US sherbet)

speculaas spiced almond biscuit

spek bacon

sperzieboon French bean (US green bean)

spiegelei fried egg

spijskaart menu, bill of fare

spinazie spinach

sprits a kind of shortbread

spruitje brussels sprout

stamppot a stew of vegetables and mashed potatoes

steur sturgeon

stokvis stockfish (dried cod)

stroop treacle (US syrup)

suiker sugar

taart cake

tarbot turbot

tartaar steak tartare

~ **speciaal** extra-large portion, of prime quality

tijm thyme

tjap tjoy chop suey; a dish of fried meat and vegetables served with rice

toeristenmenu tourist menu

tomaat tomato

tong 1) tongue 2) sole

tonijn tunny (US tuna)

toost toast

tosti grilled cheese-and-ham sandwich

tournedos thick round fillet cut of prime beef (US rib or rib-eye steak)

truffel truffle

tuinboon broad bean

ui onion

uitsmijter two slices of bread garnished with ham or roast beef and topped with two fried eggs

vanille vanilla

varkenshaas pork tenderloin

varkenslapje pork fillet

varkensvlees pork

venkel fennel

vermicellisoep consommé with thin noodles

vers fresh

vijg fig

vis fish

vla custard

vlaai fruit tart

Vlaamse karbonade small slices of beef and onions braised in broth, with beer sometimes added

vlees meat

voorgerecht starter or first course

vrucht fruit

vruchtensalade fruit salad

wafel wafer

walnoot walnut

warm hot

waterkers watercress

waterzooi chicken poached in white wine and shredded vegetables, cream and egg-yolk

wentelteefje French toast; slice of white bread dipped in egg batter and fried, then sprinkled with cinnamon and sugar

wijnkaart wine list

wijting whiting
wild game
~ **zwijn** wild boar
wilde eend wild duck
witlof chicory (US endive)
~ **op zijn Brussels** chicory rolled in a slice of ham and oven-browned with cheese sauce

worst sausage
wortel carrot
zachtgekookt ei soft-boiled egg
zalm salmon
zeekreeft lobster
zeevis saltwater fish
zout salt
zuurkool sauerkraut
zwezerik sweetbread

Drink

advocaat egg liqueur
ananassap pineapple juice
aperitief aperitif
bessenjenever blackcurrant gin
bier beer
bisschopswijn mulled wine
bittertje bitter-tasting aperitif
boerenjongens Dutch brandy with raisins
boerenmeisjes Dutch brandy with apricots
borrel shot
brandewijn brandy
cassis blackcurrant liqueur
chocolademelk, chocomel(k) chocolate drink
citroenbrandewijn lemon brandy
citroenjenever lemon-flavoured gin
citroentje met suiker brandy flavoured with lemon peel, with sugar added
cognac brandy, cognac
donker bier porter; dark sweet-tasting beer
druivesap grape juice

frisdrank soft drink
gekoeld iced
genever see *jenever*
Geuzelambiek a strong Flemish bitter beer brewed from wheat and barley
jenever Dutch gin
jonge jenever/klare young Dutch gin
karnemelk buttermilk
kersenbrandewijn kirsch; spirit distilled from cherries
koffie coffee
~ **met melk** with milk
~ **met room** with cream
~ **met slagroom** with whipped cream
~ **verkeerd** white coffee; equal quantity of coffee and hot milk
zwarte ~ black
Kriekenlambiek a strong Brussels bitter beer flavoured with morello cherries
kwast hot or cold lemon squash
licht bier lager; light beer
likeur liqueur

limonade lemonade
melk milk
mineraalwater mineral water
oude jenever/klare Dutch gin aged in wood casks, yellowish in colour and more mature than *jonge jenever*
oranjebitter orange-flavoured bitter
pils general name for beer
sap juice
sinas orangeade
spuitwater soda water
sterkedrank liquor, spirit
tafelwater mineral water

thee tea
~ **met citroen** with lemon
~ **met suiker en melk** with sugar and milk
trappistenbier malt beer brewed (originally) by Trappist monks
vieux brandy bottled in Holland
vruchtesap fruit juice
warme chocola hot chocolate
wijn wine
droge ~ dry
rode ~ red
witte ~ white
zoete ~ sweet
wodka vodka

Finnish

Guide to pronunciation

Letter	Approximate pronunciation
Consonants	

k, m, n, p, t, v	as in English
d	as in rea**d**y, but sometimes very weak
g	only found after **n**; **ng** is pronounced as in si**ng**er
h	as in **h**ot, whatever its position in the word
j	like **y** in **y**ou
l	as in **l**et
r	always rolled
s	always as in **s**et

Vowels	
a	like **a** in c**a**r, but shorter
e	like **a** in l**a**te

i	like **i** in p**i**n
o	like **aw** in l**aw**, but shorter
u	like **u** in p**u**ll
y	like **u** in French s**u**r or **ü** in German **ü**ber; say **ee** as in s**ee** and round your lips while still trying to pronounce **ee**
ä	like **a** in h**a**t
ö	like **ur** in f**ur**, but with the lips rounded

Note

The letters **b, c, f, q, š, sh, x, z, ž** and **å** are only found in words borrowed from foreign languages, and they're pronounced as in the language of origin.

Diphthongs

In Finnish, diphthongs occur only in the first syllable of a word, except for those ending in **-i** which can occur anywhere. They should be pronounced as a combination of the two vowel sounds represented by the spelling. The first vowel is pronounced louder in the following diphthongs: **ai, ei, oi, ui, yi, äi, öi, au, eu, ou, ey, äy, öy, iu**; the second vowel is louder in **ie, uo, yö**.

Double letters

Remember that in Finnish *every* letter is pronounced, therefore a letter written double is pronounced long. Thus, the **kk** in kukka should be pronounced like the two **k** sounds in the words thi**ck c**oat Similarly, the **aa** in kaatua should be pronounced long (like **a** in English c**a**r). These distinctions are important, not least of all because kuka has a different meaning from kukka and katua a different meaning from kaatua.

Stress

A strong stress always falls on the first syllable of a word.

Some useful expressions

Hungry

I'm hungry/I'm thirsty.	**Minulla on nälkä/Minulla on jano.**
Can you recommend a good restaurant?	**Voitteko suositella hyvää ravintolaa?**
Are there any good, cheap restaurants around here?	**Onko täällä lähellä halpaa ja hyvää ravintolaa?**
I'd like to reserve a table for ... people.	**Haluaisin varata pöydän ... henkilölle.**
We'll come at ... o'clock.	**Tulemme kello ...**

Asking

Good evening. I'd like a table for ... people.	**Hyvää iltaa. Haluaisin pöydän ...henkilölle.**
Could we have a table...?	**Voisimmeko saada...?**
in the corner	**nurkkapöydän**
by the window	**ikkunapöydän**
outside	**pöydän ulkoa**
on the terrace	**pöydän terassilta**
May I please have the menu?	**Saisinko ruokalistan?**
What's this?	**Mitä tämä on?**
Do you have...?	**Onko teillä...?**
a set menu	**päivän ateria**
local dishes	**paikallisia erikoisuuksia**
a children's menu	**lasten ateria**
Waiter/Waitress!	**Tarjoilija/Neiti!**
What do you recommend?	**Mitä suosittelette?**
Could I have (a/an)... please?	**Voisinko saada ...?**
ashtray	**tuhkakupin**
another chair	**vielä yhden tuolin**
finger bowl	**huuhdekupin**
fork	**haarukan**
glass	**lasin**
knife	**veitsen**

napkin	**lautasliinan**
plate	**lautasen**
pepper mill	**pippurimyllyn**
serviette	**lautasliinan**
spoon	**lusikan**
toothpick	**hammastikun**

Ordering

I'd like a/an/some...	**Haluaisin...**
aperitif	**aperitiivin**
appetizer	**alkupalat**
beer	**olutta**
bread	**leipää**
butter	**voita**
cheese	**juustoa**
chips	**ranskalaisia perunoita**
coffee	**kahvia**
dessert	**jälkiruokaa**
fish	**kalaa**
french fries	**ranskalaisia perunoita**
fruit	**hedelmiä**
game	**riistaa**
ice-cream	**jäätelöä**
ketchup	**tomaattisosetta**
lemon	**sitruunaa**
lettuce	**lehtisalaattia**
meat	**lihaa**
mineral water	**kivennäisvettä**
milk	**maitoa**
mustard	**sinappia**
noodles	**nauhamakaroneja**
oil	**öljyä**
olive oil	**oliiviöljyä**
pepper	**pippuria**
potatoes	**perunoita**
poultry	**siipikarjaa**
rice	**riisiä**
rolls	**sämpylöitä**
saccharin	**sakariinia**
salad	**salaattia**

salt	**suolaa**
sandwich	**voileivän**
seafood	**kaloja ja äyriäisiä**
seasoning	**mausteita**
soup	**keittoa**
starter	**alkupalat**
sugar	**sokeria**
tea	**teetä**
vegetables	**vihanneksia**
vinegar	**etikkaa**
(iced) water	**(jää)vettä**
wine	**viiniä**

**NAUTTIKAA
ATERIASTANNE!**
ENJOY YOUR MEAL!

---

baked	**uunissa paistettu**
baked in parchment	**unnissa paistettu voipaperiin käärittynä**
boiled	**keitetty**
braised	**hauduttaen kypsennetty**
cured	**suolaveteen säilötty**
fried	**paistettu**
grilled	**pariloitu**
marinated	**marinoitu**
poached	**upotettuna keitetty**
roasted	**paahdettu**
sautéed	**voissa paistettu**
smoked	**savustettu**
steamed	**höyryttäen kypsennetty**
stewed	**muhennettu**
underdone (rare)	**vähän paistettuna**
medium	**puolikypsänä**
well-done	**kypsänä**

FINNISH

TERVEYDEKSI!
CHEERS!

glass	lasi
bottle	pullo
red	punaviini
white	valkoviini
rosé	roséviini
very dry	hyvin kuiva
dry	kuiva
sweet	makea
light	kevyt
full-bodied	täyteläisen makuinen
sparkling	helmeilevä
neat (straight)	sekoittamaton
on the rocks	jään kera

The bill

I'd like to pay.	Haluaisin maksaa.
We'd like to pay separately.	Maksamme kukin erikseen.
You've made a mistake in this bill, I think.	Luulen että tähän laskuun on tullut virhe.
What's this amount for?	Mitä tämä summa tarkoittaa?
Is service included?	Sisältyykö palvelumaksu laskuun?
Is everything included?	Sisältyykö siihen kaikki?
Do you accept traveller's cheques?	Otatteko vastaan matkašekkejä?
Thank you. This is for you.	Kiitos, tämä on teille.
Keep the change.	Pitäkää vaihtoraha.
That was a very good meal.	Se oli erinomainen ateria.
We enjoyed it, thank you.	Nautimme siitä.

Complaints

That's not what I ordered. I asked for...	En tilannut tätä. Pyysin...
May I change this?	Voinko vaihtaa tämän?

The meat is…	**Liha on…**
overdone	**liian kypsää**
underdone	**liian vähän paistettua**
too rare	**liian raakaa**
too tough	**liian sitkeää**
This is too…	**Tämä on liian…**
bitter/salty/sweet	**kitkerää/suolaista/makeaa**
The food is cold.	**Ruoka on kylmää.**
This isn't fresh.	**Tämä ei ole tuoretta.**
What's taking you so long?	**Miksi tarjoilu on näin hidasta?**
Where are our drinks?	**Missä ovat juomamme?**
This isn't clean.	**Tämä ei ole puhdas.**
Would you ask the head waiter to come over?	**Pyytäisittekö hovimestarin tänne.**

Numbers

1	**yksi**	11	**yksitoista**
2	**kaksi**	12	**kaksitoista**
3	**kolme**	13	**kolmetoista**
4	**neljä**	14	**neljätoista**
5	**viisi**	15	**viisitoista**
6	**kuusi**	16	**kuusitoista**
7	**seitsemän**	17	**seitsemäntoista**
8	**kahdeksan**	18	**kahdeksantoista**
9	**yhdeksän**	19	**yhdeksäntoista**
10	**kymmenen**	20	**kaksikymmentä**

FINNISH

Food

Please note that Finnish alphabetical order is **a-z, ä, ö**.

aamiainen breakfast
ahven perch
alkupala appetizer, starter
ananas pineapple
anjovis marinated sprats
ankerias eel
ankka duck
annos portion
appelsiini orange
aprikoosi apricot
aromivoi herb butter
ateria meal
Aura blue cheese
avokado avocado (pear)
banaani banana
blini buckwheat pancake
borssikeitto borscht; beetroot
    soup consisting of chopped
    meat, cabbage and carrot,
    served with sour cream
broileri broiler, chicken
dieettiruoka diet food
dippikastike dip sauce
donitsi doughnut
etana snail
etikka white vinegar
    ~**kurkku** gherkin
    ~**sienet** pickled mushrooms
eturuoka warm first course
fasaani pheasant
fenkoli fennel
filee fillet
forelli trout

friteerattu deep-fried
graavi/lohi salmon cured with
    salt, sugar, pepper and dill
    ~**siika** salt- and sugar-cured
    whitefish
    ~**silakat** cured and marinated
    Baltic herrings
grahamleipä graham bread
gratiini gratin
gratinoitu gratinéed
greippi grapefruit
grillattu grilled
grilli/makkara grilled sausage
    ~**pihvi** grilled steak
halstrattu barbecued (fish)
hampurilainen hamburger
hanhenmaksa goose liver
    ~**pasteija** goose-liver pâté
hanhi goose
hapan/imelä sweet-and-sour
    ~**kaali** sauerkraut
    ~**kerma** sour cream
    ~**korppu** very thin rye crisp
    bread (US hardtack)
    ~**leipä** rye bread
hasselpähkinä hazelnut
haudutettu braised
hauki pike
hedelmä fruit
    ~**hilloke** stewed fruit
    ~**salaatti** fruit salad
herkkusieni button mushroom
herne (pl **herneet**) pea

~**keitto** thick pea soup with pork
hienonnettu mashed, minced
hiillostettu barbecued
hiivaleipä yeast bread
hillo jam
  ~**munkki** jam (US jelly) doughnut
  ~**sipuli** pickled pearl onion
hirven/käristys roast elk served in cream sauce
  ~**liha** elk meat
  ~**seläke** saddle of elk
hirvipaisti roast elk
hummeri lobster
hunaja honey
  ~**meloni** cantaloupe
hyvin paistettu well-done
hyytelö jelly
hyytelöity jellied
härän/filee fillet of beef
  ~**häntäkeitto** oxtail soup
  ~**kyljys** rib steak
  ~**leike** porterhouse steak
  ~**liha** beef
  ~**paisti** roast joint of beef
illallinen supper
inkivääri ginger
italiansalaatti boiled vegetables in mayonnaise
Janssonin kiusaus baked casserole of sliced potatoes, onions and marinated sprats in cream sauce
jauheliha minced meat
  ~**pihvi** hamburger steak
  ~**sämpylä** hamburger
jauhettu minced
joulu/kinkku baked ham covered with mustard and breadcrumbs
  ~**pöytä** buffet of Christmas specialities
jugurtti yoghurt
Juhla kind of Cheddar cheese

juomaraha tip
juottoporsas suck(l)ing pig
juurekset root vegetables
juusto cheese
  ~**kohokas** cheese soufflé
  ~**tanko** cheese straw
  ~**tarjotin** cheese board
jälkiruoka dessert
jälkiuunileipä rye bread baked in a slow oven
jänispaisti roast hare
jäädyke water ice (US sherbet)
jäätelö ice-cream
kaali cabbage
  ~**keitto** cabbage soup with mutton or pork
  ~**kääryleet** cabbage leaves stuffed with minced meat and rice
  ~**laatikko** layers of cabbage and minced meat
kahvi/aamiainen continental breakfast
  ~**leipä** coffee cake; generic term for cakes, sweet rolls and pastries
kakku cake
kala fish
  ~**keitto** fish soup
  ~**kukko** pie made of small whitefish and pork, baked in rye dough
  ~**mureke** fish mousse
  ~**pulla**, ~ **pyörykkä** fish ball
  ~**ruoka** fish course
  ~**vuoka** fish gratin
kalkkuna turkey
kampela flounder
kana hen
kanan/koipi chicken thigh
  ~**maksa** chicken liver
  ~**muna** egg
  ~**poika** spring chicken
  ~**rinta** chicken breast

kaneli cinnamon
kantarelli chanterelle mushroom
kapris caper
karhun/liha bear meat
 ~ **paisti** roast bear
 ~ **vatukka** blackberry
karitsanliha lamb
karjalan/paisti stew of beef, mutton, pork, kidneys, liver and onions
 ~ **piirakka** a thin and crisp rye-pastry shell filled with rice or mashed potatoes, served with finely chopped hard-boiled eggs mixed with butter
karpalo cranberry
karviaismarja gooseberry
kastanja chestnut
kastike sauce, gravy
kasvis (pl **kasvikset**) vegetable
 ~ **ruoka** vegetable course
katajanmarja juniper berry
kateenkorva sweetbread
katemaksu cover charge
katkarapu shrimp
kaura/keksi oatmeal biscuit
 ~ **puuro** oatmeal
kauris deer
kaviaari caviar
keitetty boiled, cooked
keitetyt perunat boiled potatoes
keitto soup, cream
keksi biscuit (US cookie)
keltasieni chanterelle mushroom
kerma cream
 ~ **juusto** cream cheese
 ~ **kakku** sponge layer cake with cream and jam filling
 ~ **kastike** cream sauce
 ~ **leivos** cream pastry
 ~ **vaahto** whipped cream
 ~ **viili** kind of sour cream
Kesti hard cheese flavoured with caraway seeds

kesäkeitto spring vegetable soup
ketsuppi catsup
kevyt/kerma coffee cream
 ~ **viili** low-calorie yoghurt
kieli tongue
kiisseli dessert of berry or fruit juice thickened with potato flour
kinkku ham
kirjolohi salmon trout
kirsikka cherry
kohokas soufflé
kokojyväleipä whole-meal bread
kolja haddock
korppu rusk (US zwieback)
 ~ **jauhotettu** breaded
korva/puusti cinnamon roll
 ~ **sieni** morel mushroom
kotiruoka home cooking, plain food
kotitekoinen home-made
kovaksi keitetty muna hard-boiled egg
Kreivi semi-hard cheese, mildly pungent
kuha pike-perch
kuivattu luumu prune
kukkakaali cauliflower
kukkoa viinissä chicken stewed in red wine
kulibjaka pie stuffed with salmon, rice, hard-boiled eggs and dill, served in slices with melted butter
kumina caraway
kuoriperunat potatoes in their jacket
kuorrutettu oven-browned
kuorukka croquette
kurkku cucumber
kurpitsa gourd, pumpkin, squash
kutunjuusto goat's cheese, brown in colour
kyljys chop

kylkipaisti spare-rib
kylmä cold
kypsä well-done
kyyhkynen pigeon
kääre/syltty kind of brawn
  (US head cheese)
  ~torttu Swiss roll
kääryle thin slice of meat, stuffed
  and rolled
köyhät ritarit French toast; slices
  of bread dipped in egg batter,
  fried and served with jam
laatikko casserole, gratin
lahna bream
lakka Arctic cloudberry
lammas mutton
  ~kaali Irish stew; lamb and
  cabbage stew
  ~muhennos lamb stew
lampaan/kyljys lamb chop
  ~liha lamb
  ~paisti leg of lamb
lankkupihvi steak served on a
  board (US plank steak)
lanttu swede
  ~laatikko oven-browned
  swede purée
lapa shoulder
lasimestarinsilli pieces of herring
  fillets marinated in sweetened
  vinegar with onion, carrot,
  black and white peppercorns
  and bay leaves
laskiaispulla bun filled with
  almond paste and whipped
  cream
lasku bill, check
lasten ruokalista children's menu
lautanen plate
lehti/pihvi very thin slice of beef
  ~salaatti lettuce
leike cutlet
leikkeleet cold meat (US cold
  cuts)

leikkelelautanen plate of cold
  meat
leipä (pl leivät) bread
leivitetty breaded
leivos (pl leivokset) cake, pastry
lenkkimakkara ring-shaped sausage, eaten grilled, fried, baked
  or as an ingredient in stews and
  soups
liekitetty flamed
liemi broth
liha meat
  ~keitto beef and vegetable
  soup
  ~liemi meat broth, consommé
  ~mureke meat-loaf
  ~piirakka pie stuffed with rice
  and minced meat
  ~pulla, ~pyörykkä meat ball
  ~ruoka meat course
limppu sweetened rye bread
Lindströmin pihvi hamburger
  steak flavoured with pickled
  beetroot and capers
linnapaisti pot roast flavoured
  with brandy, molasses and
  marinated sprats
linturuoka fowl course
lipeäkala specially treated stockfish poached and served with
  potatoes and white sauce
lohi salmon
  ~piirakka pie stuffed with salmon, rice, hard-boiled eggs and
  dill, served in slices with
  melted butter
loimu/lohi salmon grilled on an
  open fire
  ~siika whitefish grilled very
  slowly on an open fire
lounas lunch
luu bone
luumu plum
luuydin bone marrow

FINNISH

lämmin warm
~ **ruoka** (pl **lämpimät ruoat**) main course, hot dish
länsirannikon salaatti seafood salad
maa-artisokka Jerusalem artichoke
maapähkinä peanut
made burbot
maissi maize (US corn)
maissintähkä corn on the cob
majoneesi mayonnaise
makaroni macaroni
~ **laatikko** baked macaroni
makea sweet
makkara sausage
~ **kastike** diced sausages stewed in a sauce
makrilli mackerel
maksa liver
~ **laatikko** liver and meat-loaf flavoured with molasses, onions and raisins
~ **makkara** liver sausage
~ **pasteija** liver paste
mandariini mandarin (US tangerine)
mansikka strawberry
~ **kakku** sponge layer cake with strawberries and whipped cream
~ **leivos** strawberry pastry
~ **torttu** strawberry flan
manteli almond
marenki meringue
marinoitu marinated
marja berry
marmelaati, marmeladi marmalade
mateenmäti burbot roe
mauste (pl **mausteet**) spice, condiment
~ **silli** spiced, marinated herring

meetvursti kind of salami
mehukeitto dessert of berry or fruit juice slightly thickened with potato flour
meloni melon
meriantura sole
merimiespihvi sliced beef, onions and potatoes braised in beer
mesimarja Arctic raspberry
metso capercaillie, wood-grouse
metsämansikka wild strawberry
metsästäjänleike veal scallop with mushroom sauce
muhennettu stewed, mashed
muhennos stew, purée
muikku vendace (small whitefish)
~ **pata** vendace casserole
muikunmäti vendace roe
multasieni truffle
muna egg
munakas omelet
munakoiso aubergine (US eggplant)
munakokkeli scrambled eggs
munariisipasteija egg and rice pasty
munavoi finely chopped hardboiled eggs mixed with butter
munkki (jam) doughnut
munuainen (pl **munuaiset**) kidney
munuaishöystö kidney stew
mureke 1) fish or meat mousse 2) forcemeat, stuffing
murot breakfast cereals
musta viinimarja blackcurrant
mustikka blueberry
~ **keitto** dessert of blueberry juice thickened with potato flour
~ **piirakka** blueberry pie
muurain (pl **muuraimet**) Arctic cloudberry
mämmi dessert pudding of malted rye and rye flour flavoured

with orange rind, served cold
with cream and sugar
äti fish roe
ahkiainen lamprey
akki (pl **nakit**) frankfurter
audanliha beef
äkkileipä crisp bread (US hardtack)
hrasämpylä barley roll
hukaiset small thin pancakes
liivi olive
~ **öljy** olive oil
meletti omelet
mena apple
~ **hilloke** stewed apples
~ **paistos** baked apple
~ **sose** apple sauce
opperavoileipä toast topped with
a hamburger steak and a fried
egg
steri oyster
aahdettu toasted, roasted
aahto/leipä toast
~ **paisti** roast beef
~ **vanukas** caramel custard
ainosyltty brawn (US head
cheese)
aistettu fried, roasted
~ **muna** fried egg
aistetut perunat fried potatoes
aisti roast
aistinliemi gravy
aistos generic term for fried or
baked dishes
ala piece
~ **paisti** beef stew
alvattu cured, smoked
alvikinkku cured ham
annu generic term for sautéed
dishes
~ **kakku** kind of pancake
~ **pihvi** hamburger steak served
with fried onions
aprika sweet pepper

papu (pl **pavut**) bean
pariloitu grilled, barbecued
parsa asparagus
~ **kaali** broccoli
pasteija 1) paste 2) pastry, pie
pata (baked) casserole
~ **kukko** rye-flour pie with
vendace and bacon
~ **paisti** pot roast
patonki French bread
pehmeäksi keitetty muna soft-
boiled egg
pekoni bacon
~ **pannu** fried bacon, sausages,
potatoes and eggs
peltopyy partridge
persikka peach
persilja parsley
~ **voi** parsley butter
peruna potato
~ **lastut** crisps (US potato
chips)
~ **pannukakku** potato pancake
~ **muhennos** mashed potatoes
pihlajanmarja rowanberry
~ **jäädyke** rowanberry water-
ice
pihvi beefsteak
piimä sour milk
~ **juusto** fresh curd cheese
~ **piirakka** kind of cheese cake
piirakka pie
piiras (pl **piiraat**) small pie, pasty
pikkuleipä biscuit (US cookie)
pinaatti spinach
piparjuuri horse-radish
~ **liha** boiled beef with horse-
radish sauce
piparkakku gingerbread
pippuri pepper
~ **juusto** pepper cheese
~ **pihvi** pepper steak
porkkana carrot
~ **raaste** grated carrots

FINNISH

poron/kieli reindeer tongue
~**käristys** roast reindeer served in cream sauce
~**liha** reindeer meat
~**paisti** roast reindeer
~**seläke** saddle of reindeer
porsaan/kyljys pork chop
~**paisti** roast joint of pork
~**selkäpaisti** roast loin of pork
potka leg, shank
pulla bun
punainen viinimarja redcurrant
puna/juuri beetroot
~**kaali** red cabbage
puolikypsä medium (done)
puolukka lingonberry, kind of cranberry
~**puuro** lingonberry and semolina pudding
purjo leek
puuro porridge
pyttipannu kind of bubble and squeak; diced meat, potatoes and onions fried and served with a raw egg-yolk or a fried egg
pyy hazelhen
pähkinä nut
päivällinen dinner
päivän annos speciality of the day
pääruoka main course
päärynä pear
raaka raw
~**pihvi** steak tartare; raw, spiced minced beef
~**suolattu** cured in brine
raastettu grated
raavaanliha heifer meat
raejuusto cottage cheese
rahkapiirakka kind of cheese cake
ranskalaiset pavut French beans (US green beans)
ranskalaiset perunat chips (US French fries)

ranskanleipä white bread
raparperi rhubarb
rapu (pl **ravut**) freshwater crayfish
~**silakat** poached Baltic herrings, flavoured with tomato sauce and dill, served cold
reikäleipä ring-shaped rye bread
retiisi radish
riekko ptarmigan
rieska unleavened barley bread
riisi rice
~**puuro** rice pudding
riista game
rinta breast, brisket
rosolli herring salad with pickled beetroot, onions, hard-boiled eggs, capers and sour cream
rouhesämpylä whole-meal roll
ruijanpallas halibut
ruisleipä rye bread
ruohosipuli chive
ruoka (pl **ruoat**) food
~**laji** dish, course
~**lista** menu
rusina raisin
ruskea kastike gravy
ruskistettu sautéed
ruusukaali brussels sprout
saksanpähkinä walnut
salaatti salad
sammakonreidet frogs' legs
savu/kala smoked fish
~**kinkku** smoked ham
~**poro** smoked reindeer meat
~**silakat** smoked Baltic herrings
~**silli** smoked herring
savustettu smoked
sei, seiti black cod
seisova pöytä buffet with a large variety of hot and cold dishes, salads, cheeses and desserts
sekasalaatti mixed salad
seljanka salmon soup

selleri celery
setsuuri sweetened rye bread
sianliha pork
 ~**kastike** sliced pork in gravy
siansorkka (pl **siansorkat**) pigs'
 trotters (US pigs' feet)
sieni (pl **sienet**) mushroom
 ~**kastike** mushroom sauce
 ~**muhennos** creamed mushrooms
 ~**salaatti** salad of chopped
 mushrooms and onions with a
 cream sauce
siianmäti whitefish roe
siika whitefish
silakka Baltic herring
 ~**laatikko** baked casserole of
 sliced potatoes and Baltic herring
 ~**pihvi** breaded Baltic herring
 fillets stuffed with dill and
 parsley
 ~**rulla** salted and pickled Baltic herring
silavapannukakku pancake with
 diced bacon
silli herring
 ~**lautanen** plate of assorted
 herring
 ~**pöytä** buffet of a large
 variety of herring specialities
 ~**salaatti** herring salad with
 pickled beetroot, hard-boiled
 eggs, onions, apples, capers
 and topped with sour cream
 ~**tarjotin** assorted herring
 served on a tray
 ~**voileipä** open-faced sandwich with hard-boiled eggs and
 herring
simpukka mussel
sinappi mustard
 ~**silakat** Baltic herrings in
 mustard sauce

sipuli onion
 ~**pihvi** steak and fried onions
siskonmakkarakeitto vegetable
 soup with diced veal sausage
sitruuna lemon
smetana sour cream
sokeri sugar
 ~**herneet** sugar peas
 ~**kakku** sponge cake
sokeriton sugarless
sokeroitu sweetened
sorsa wild duck
sose mash, purée
stroganoff beef Stroganoff: thin
 sliced beef and mushrooms in a
 sour-cream sauce
suklaa chocolate
sulatejuusto processed cheese
suola salt
 ~**kurkku** pickled and salted
 gherkin
 ~**liha** cured beef, sliced and
 served cold
 ~**sienet** mushrooms preserved
 in brine
 ~**silli** salted herring
suolattu salted; preserved in
 brine
suomuurain (pl **suomuuraimet**)
 Arctic cloudberry
suutarinlohi sugar-salted, marinated Baltic herring
sveitsinleike cordon bleu:
 breaded veal scallop stuffed
 with ham and Swiss cheese
sämpylä roll
T-luupihvi T-bone steak
tahkojuusto kind of Swiss cheese
taimen trout
tarjoilupalkkio service charge
 ~ **ei sisälly hintaan** not included
 ~ **sisältyy hintaan** included
tartarpihvi steak tartare; raw,

spiced minced beef
taskurapu crab
tatti boletus mushroom
teeri black grouse
terveysruoka health food
tilli dill
  ~ **liha** boiled lamb or veal in
  dill sauce, flavoured with
  lemon juice or vinegar
  ~ **silli** poached herring
  seasoned with dill, white pepper and lemon juice
tomaatti tomato
tonnikala tunny (US tuna)
torttu tart, flan, cake
tumma leipä dark bread
tuore fresh
  ~ **suolattu lohi** fresh and
  slightly salted salmon
turska cod
täyte stuffing, filling
  ~ **kakku** layer cake
täytetty stuffed, filled
upotettu muna, uppomuna
  poached egg
uudet perunat spring potatoes
uuniperuna baked potato
uunissa paistettu baked
vadelma raspberry
valikoima assorted, mixed
valkoinen leipä white bread
valkokaali white cabbage
valkokastike white sauce
valkosipuli garlic
  ~ **perunat** baked sliced potatoes flavoured with butter
  and garlic
  '~ **voi** garlic butter
valkoturska whiting
vanilja vanilla
  ~ **kastike** vanilla sauce
vanukas pudding, custard
varhaisaamiainen breakfast
varras (pl **vartaat**) spit, skewer

vasikan/kateenkorva calf's sweetbread
  ~ **leike** veal cutlet
  ~ **liha** veal
  ~ **paisti** roast veal
vatkuli beef stew flavoured with
  bay leaves
velli gruel
venäläinen silli herring fillets with
  diced, pickled beetroot and cucumber, hard-boiled eggs and
  lettuce, served with sour cream
veri/ohukaiset blood pancakes
  ~ **makkara** blood sausage
  ~ **palttu** blood (black) pudding
vesimeloni watermelon
vihannes (pl **vihannekset**) vegetable
vihreä salaatti green salad
vihreät pavut French beans
  (US green beans)
viili processed sour milk
viilokki fricassée
viinietikka wine vinegar
  ~ **kastike** oil and vinegar dressing
viini/kukko chicken stewed in red
  wine
  ~ **lista** wine list
  ~ **marja** currant
  ~ **rypäle** grape
viipale slice
viipaloitu sliced
viiriäinen quail
vohveli wafer, waffle
voi butter
voileipä sandwich, usually open-
faced
  ~ **keksi** soda cracker
  ~ **pöytä** large buffet of cold
  and warm dishes; "smörgåsbord"
voipavut butter beans (US wax
beans)

voissa paistettu fried in butter
voisula melted butter
vorschmak minced lamb, herring fillets and fried onions cooked in broth, flavoured with catsup, mustard and marinated sprats, served with sour cream and baked potatoes
vuohenjuusto goat's milk cheese

vähän paistettu rare (US underdone)
välikyljys entrecôte, rib-eye steak
wienerleipä Danish pastry
wieninleike Wiener schnitzel; breaded veal scallop
yrttivoi herb butter
äyriäinen (pl **äyriäiset**) shellfish
öljy oil

Drink

A-olut beer with highest alcoholic content
akvaviitti spirits distilled from potatoes or grain, often flavoured with aromatic seeds and spices
aperitiivi aperitif
appelsiinilimonaati orangeade
Finlandia a Finnish vodka
gini gin
glögi mulled wine (Christmas speciality)
hedelmämehu fruit juice
Jaloviina blend of spirits and brandy
jäävesi iced water
kaakao cocoa
kahvi coffee
  ~ **kerman (ja sokerin) kera** with cream (and sugar)
kalja a type of very light (1% alcohol) beer, often home-made
kerma cream
keskiolut medium-strong beer
kivennäisvesi mineral water

konjakki cognac
Koskenkorva very strong *akvaviitti* made of grain
kuiva dry
  ~ **viini** dry wine
kuohuviini sparkling wine
Lakka Arctic cloudberry liqueur
Lapponia lingonberry (kind of cranberry) liqueur
likööri liqueur
limonaati lemonade
maito milk
  ~ **kahvi** coffee with milk
makea sweet
mehu squash (US fruit drink)
Mesimarja Arctic bramble liqueur
mineraalivesi mineral water
musta kahvi black coffee
olut beer
piimä junket
pilsneri lager; a mild, light beer
Polar cranberry liqueur
portviini port wine

FINNISH

punaviini red wine
rommi rum
roséviini rosé wine
samppanja champagne
siideri cider
sima beverage produced from cane and beet sugar, lemon, yeast, hops and water (May 1 speciality)
Suomuurain Arctic cloudberry liqueur
tee tea
~ **maidon kera** with milk
~ **sitruunan kera** with lemon
tonic-vesi tonic water

tumma olut porter
tuoremehu fresh fruit or vegetable juice
tynnyriolut draught (US draft) beer
vaalea olut lager
valkoviini white wine
vermutti vermouth
vesi water
viina brandy, spirits
viini wine
virvoitusjuoma lemonade, soft drink
viski whisky
väkijuomat spirits

French

Guide to pronunciation

Letter	Approximate pronunciation
Consonants	

b, c, d, f, k, l, m, n, p, s, t, v, x, z	are usually pronounced more or less as in English
ç	like **s** in so
ch	like **sh** in shut
g	before **e, i, y**, like **s** in leisure, otherwise as in go
gn	like **ni** in onion
h	always silent
j	like **s** in leisure
ll	either like **y** in yes or like **l** in least
qu	like **k** in kill
r	pronounced in the back of the mouth
w	like **v** in view or as in we

FRENCH

Vowels

a, à, â	something like **a** in c**a**r, but shorter
ai, ay	like **a** in l**a**te
aî, aient, ais, ait	like **e** in g**e**t
au	like **oa** in m**oa**t
é, er, et, ez	like **a** in l**a**te
è, ê	like **e** in g**e**t
e	followed by one consonant, or at the end of a one-syllable word, like **a** in **a**bout; followed by two consonants, like **e** in g**e**t
eau	see **au**
ei	like **e** in g**e**t
eu	like **ur** in f**ur**, but without any **r** sound
i	like **ee** in m**ee**t
o	like **oa** in m**oa**t or like **o** in n**o**t
ô	like **oa** in m**oa**t
oi	like **wha** in **wha**ck
ou, où	like **oo** in l**oo**t
u	pronounce **ee** as in s**ee**, but round your lips as if to pronounce **oo**
ui	like **wee** in b**e**tw**ee**n
y	like **ee** in m**ee**t

Nasal vowels

When the letter **n** or **m** follows a vowel, but is neither followed by a vowel nor by **n** or **m**, then the preceding vowel is pronounced nasally (through the nose as well as the mouth, similar to the Midwestern twang in America).

aim, ain	something like **ang** in r**ang**
am, an } em, en	something like **arn** in b**arn**
eim, ein } im, in	see **aim**
ien	something like **yan** in **yan**k

oin	something like **wang**
on	something like **orn** in **corn**-cob
un	see **aim**

Note

1) The letter **e** is generally not pronounced at the end of a word, but is used to indicate that the preceding consonants should be pronounced.

2) If there's no final **e**, then final consonants are generally not pronounced unless the next word begins with a vowel, in which case the consonant is "run-on" to the vowel at the beginning of the next word. (This is called liaison.) An example of this would be *sauce aux airelles* whereby the **x** of *aux* is pronounced as a **z** at the beginning of *airelles*.

Some useful expressions

Hungry

I'm hungry/I'm thirsty.	**J'ai faim/J'ai soif.**
Can you recommend a good restaurant?	**Pouvez-vous nous/me recommander un bon restaurant?**
Are there any good, cheap restaurants around here?	**Y a-t-il un restaurant bon marché dans les environs?**
I'd like to reserve a table for ... people.	**J'aimerais réserver une table pour ... personnes.**
We'll come at ... o'clock.	**Nous viendrons à ... heures.**

Asking

Good evening. I'd like a table for ... people.	**Bonsoir. J'aimerais une table pour ... personnes.**
Could we have a table...?	**Pouvons-nous avoir une table...?**
in the corner	**dans un angle**
by the window	**près de la fenêtre**
outside	**à l'extérieur**
on the terrace	**sur la terrasse**
May I please have the menu?	**Puis-je avoir la carte?**
What's this?	**Qu'est-ce que cela?**

Do you have…?	**Avez-vous…?**
a set menu	**un menu**
local dishes	**des spécialités locales**
a children's menu	**un menu pour enfant**
Waiter/Waitress!	**Garçon/Mademoiselle!**
What do you recommend?	**Que me recommandez-vous?**
Could I have (a/an)… please?	**Puis-je avoir…, s'il vous plaît?**
ashtray	**un cendrier**
another chair	**une chaise de plus**
finger bowl	**un rince-doigts**
fork	**une fourchette**
glass	**un verre**
knife	**un couteau**
napkin	**une serviette**
plate	**une assiette**
pepper mill	**un moulin à poivre**
serviette	**une serviette**
spoon	**une cuiller**
toothpick	**un cure-dent**

Ordering

I'd like a/an/some…	**J'aimerais…**
aperitif	**un apéritif**
appetizer	**une entrée**
beer	**une bière**
bread	**du pain**
butter	**du beurre**
cheese	**du fromage**
chips	**des pommes frites**
coffee	**un café**
dessert	**un dessert**
fish	**du poisson**
french fries	**des pommes frites**
fruit	**des fruits**
game	**du gibier**
ice-cream	**une glace**
lemon	**du citron**
lettuce	**de la laitue**

meat	**de la viande**
mineral water	**de l'eau minérale**
milk	**du lait**
mustard	**de la moutarde**
noodles	**des nouilles**
oil	**de l'huile**
olive oil	**de l'huile d'olive**
pepper	**du poivre**
potatoes	**des pommes de terre**
poultry	**de la volaille**
rice	**du riz**
rolls	**des petits pains**
saccharin	**de la saccharine**
salad	**de la salade**
salt	**du sel**
sandwich	**un sandwich**
seafood	**des fruits de mer**
seasoning	**des condiments**
soup	**de la soupe**
starter	**une entrée**
sugar	**du sucre**
tea	**du thé**
vegetables	**des légumes**
vinegar	**du vinaigre**
(iced) water	**de l'eau (glacée)**
wine	**du vin**

BON APPETIT!
ENJOY YOUR MEAL!

---

baked	**cuit au four**
baked in parchment	**en chemise**
boiled	**bouilli**
braised	**braisé**
cured	**salé**
fried	**frit**
grilled	**grillé**
marinated	**mariné**
poached	**poché**
roasted	**rôti**

FRENCH

FRENCH

sautéed	**sauté**
smoked	**fumé**
steamed	**cuit à la vapeur**
stewed	**à l'étouffée**
underdone (rare)	**saignant**
medium	**à point**
well-done	**bien cuit**

A VOTRE SANTÉ!
CHEERS!

---

glass	**un verre**
bottle	**une bouteille**
red	**rouge**
white	**blanc**
rosé	**rosé**
very dry	**très sec**
dry	**sec**
sweet	**doux**
light	**léger**
full-bodied	**moelleux**
sparkling	**mousseux**
neat (straight)	**sec**
on the rocks	**avec des glaçons**

The bill

I'd like to pay.	**L'addition, s'il vous plaît.**
We'd like to pay separately.	**Nous aimerions payer chacun notre part.**
You've made a mistake in this bill, I think.	**Je crois qu'il y a une erreur dans l'addition.**
What's this amount for?	**Que représente cette somme?**
Is service included?	**Est-ce que le service est compris?**
Is everything included?	**Est-ce que tout est compris?**
Do you accept traveller's cheques?	**Acceptez-vous les chèques de voyage?**

Thank you. This is for you.	**Merci. Voici pour vous.**
Keep the change.	**Gardez la monnaie.**
That was a very good meal.	**Le repas était délicieux.**
We enjoyed it, thank you.	**C'était très bon, merci.**

Complaints

That's not what I ordered. I asked for...	**Ce n'est pas ce que j'ai commandé. J'ai demandé...**
May I change this?	**Pouvez-vous me le changer?**
The meat is...	**La viande est...**
overdone	**trop cuite**
underdone	**pas assez cuite**
too rare	**trop saignante**
too tough	**trop dure**
This is too...	**C'est trop...**
bitter/salty/sweet	**amer/salé/sucré**
The food is cold.	**C'est froid.**
This isn't fresh.	**Ce n'est pas frais.**
What's taking you so long?	**Pourquoi cette attente?**
Where are our drinks?	**Quand donc viendront nos boissons?**
This isn't clean.	**Ce n'est pas propre.**
Would you ask the head waiter to come over?	**Je désire voir le maître d'hôtel.**

FRENCH

Numbers

1	**un, une**		11	**onze**
2	**deux**		12	**douze**
3	**trois**		13	**treize**
4	**quatre**		14	**quatorze**
5	**cinq**		15	**quinze**
6	**six**		16	**seize**
7	**sept**		17	**dix-sept**
8	**huit**		18	**dix-huit**
9	**neuf**		19	**dix-neuf**
10	**dix**		20	**vingt**

FRENCH

Food

à la, à l', au, aux in the manner of, as in, with

abats, abattis giblets, innards

abricot apricot

agneau lamb

aiglefin haddock

ail garlic

ailloli garlic mayonnaise

airelle a kind of cranberry

alouette sans tête slice of veal rolled and generally stuffed with minced meat, garlic and parsley

(à l')alsacienne usually garnished with sauerkraut, ham and sausages

amande almond

amuse-gueule appetizer

ananas pineapple

anchois anchovy

(à l')ancienne old style; usually with wine-flavoured cream sauce of mushrooms, onions or shallots

(à l')andalouse usually with green peppers, aubergines and tomatoes

andouille a kind of tripe sausage

andouillette smaller kind of tripe sausage

(à l')anglaise 1) usually boiled or steamed vegetables, especially potatoes 2) breaded and fried vegetables, meat, fish or fowl

anguille eel

~ **au vert** eel braised in a white sauce served with minced parsley and other greens

anis aniseed

artichaut (globe) artichoke

asperge asparagus

assiette plate

~ **anglaise** cold meat (US cold cuts)

~ **de charcuterie** assorted pork and other meat products

assorti assorted

aubergine aubergine (US eggplant)

ballottine (de volaille) boned fowl which is stuffed, rolled, cooked and served in gelatine

banane banana

bar bass

barbue brill

basilic basil

béarnaise sauce of egg-yolk, butter, vinegar, shallots, tarragon and white wine

bécasse woodcock

béchamel white sauce

beignet fritter generally filled with fruit, vegetables or meat

(à la) Bercy butter sauce of white wine and shallots

betterave beetroot

beurre butter

~ **blanc** white butter sauce of shallots, vinegar and white wine

~ **maître d'hôtel** butter with chopped parsley and lemon juice

~ **noir** browned butter sauce of vinegar and parsley

bifteck beef steak

(à la) bigarade brown sauce generally with oranges, sugar and vinegar

biscotte rusk (US zwieback)

biscuit biscuit (US cookie)

bisque cream soup of lobster or crayfish (US chowder)

blanc de volaille boned breast of fowl

blanchaille whitebait

blanquette de veau veal stew in white sauce

(au) bleu 1) of fish (usually trout), boiled very fresh 2) of cheese, blue-veined 3) of meat, very underdone (US rare)

bœuf beef

~ **bourguignon** chunks of beef stewed in red wine with onions, bacon and mushrooms

~ **en daube** larded chunks of beef marinated in red wine with vegetables and stewed

~ **miro(n)ton** cold boiled beef or beef stew with onion sauce

~ **mode** larded chunks of beef braised in red wine with carrots and onions

~ **salé** corned beef

bolet boletus mushroom

bombe glacée moulded ice-cream dessert

(à la) bordelaise red wine sauce with shallots, beef marrow and boletus mushrooms

bouchée à la reine vol-au-vent; puff-pastry shell filled with meat, sweetbreads or seafood and sometimes mushrooms

boudin black pudding (US blood sausage)

bouillabaisse assorted fish and shellfish stewed in white wine, garlic, saffron and olive oil

bouilli 1) boiled 2) boiled beef

bouillon bouillon, broth, stock

(à la) bourguignonne button mushrooms, pearl onions or shallots braised in rich red wine

braisé braised

brandade (de morue) prepared cod with cream, oil and garlic

brie white, mellow cheese

brioche small roll or cake

(à la) broche (on a) spit

brochet pike

(en) brochette (cooked on a) skewer

cabillaud fresh cod

café glacé coffee-flavoured ice-cream dessert

caille quail

camembert soft cheese with pungent flavour

canard (caneton) duck (duckling)

~ **à l'orange** roast duck braised with oranges and orange liqueur

cannelle cinnamon

cantal smooth, firm cheese not unlike Cheddar

câpre caper

FRENCH

carbonnade charcoal-grilled meat
~ **flamande** beef slices, onions and herbs braised in beer

cardon cardoon (vegetable)

carotte carrot

carottes Vichy steamed carrots

carpe carp

carré loin, rack
~ **de l'Est** usually square-shaped cheese of pungent flavour

carrelet plaice

carte des vins wine list

cassis blackcurrant

cassoulet toulousain butter-bean stew of goose or with mutton, pork and sometimes sausage

céleri celery (usually celery root)
~ **en branche** branch celery
~-**rave** celeriac, celery root

cèpe boletus mushroom

cerfeuil chervil

cerise cherry

cervelle brains

champignon mushroom
~ **de Paris** button mushroom

chanterelle chanterelle mushroom

charbonnade charcoal-grilled meat

charcuterie various kinds of cold pork products

charlotte fruit dessert (usually apples) made in a deep, round mould

chasse venison

chasseur hunter's style; sauce of mushrooms, tomatoes, wine and garlic herbs

chateaubriand thick slice of beef taken from the fillet

chaud warm

chaudrée fish and seafood stew, often with garlic, herbs, onions and white wine

chausson aux pommes apple dumpling (US turnover)

chevreuil deer

chicorée endive (US chicory)

chou cabbage
~ **de Bruxelles** brussels sprouts
~ **à la crème** cream puff
~-**fleur** cauliflower
~ **rouge** red cabbage

choucroute sauerkraut
~ **garnie** usually with ham, bacon and sausage

ciboulette chive

citron lemon

civet de lapin (lièvre) jugged rabbit (hare)

clafoutis fruit baked in pancake batter, brandy often added

clémentine pipless (US seedless) tangerine

cochon de lait suck(l)ing pig

(en) cocotte casserole

cœur heart
~ **d'artichaut** artichoke heart

(à la) Colbert dipped in egg batter and breadcrumbs, fried

colin hake

concombre cucumber

confit d'oie pieces of goose preserved in its own fat

confiture jam

consommation general word for drinks

consommé clear soup served hot or cold
~ **Célestine** with chicken and noodles
~ **aux cheveux d'ange** with thin noodles
~ **Colbert** with poached eggs, spring vegetables
~ **julienne** with shredded vegetables
~ **madrilène** cold and fla-

voured with tomatoes
~ **princesse** with diced chicken and asparagus tips
~ **aux vermicelles** with thin noodles
contre-filet sirloin
coq au vin chicken stewed in red wine with mushrooms, bacon, onions and herbs
coquelet cockerel
coquillage shellfish
coquille Saint-Jacques scallop gratinéed in its shell
corbeille de fruits basket of assorted fruit
cornichon small gherkin (US pickle)
côte chop or rib
~ **de bœuf** rib of beef
~ **de veau** veal chop
côtelette cutlet, chop
~ **d'agneau** lamb chop
~ **de porc** pork chop
coupe a metal or glass dish usually for individual desserts
~ **glacée** ice-cream dessert
courgette vegetable marrow (US zucchini)
couvert cover charge
~, **vin et service compris** price includes wine, service and cover charges
crabe crab
crème 1) a dessert with cream or a creamy dessert
~ **anglaise** custard
~ **caramel** caramel custard
~ **Chantilly** whipped cream
~ **glacée** ice-cream
crème 2) a creamy soup
crêpe large, paper-thin pancake
~ **Suzette** pancake with orange sauce, flamed with brandy and often orange liqueur

cresson (water)cress
crevette shrimp
croissant crescent-shaped flaky roll (usually served for breakfast)
croque-monsieur grilled or baked ham-and-cheese sandwich
croustade pie, pastry shell filled with fish, seafood, meat or vegetables
(en) croûte (in a) pastry crust
croûton small piece of bread, toasted or fried
cru raw
crudités raw vegetables usually served sliced, grated or diced as an hors d'oeuvre
crustacé shellfish
cuisse leg or thigh
cuisses de grenouilles frogs' legs
cuit cooked
bien ~ well-done
cumin caraway, cumin
darne thick fillet of fish, usually of salmon
datte date
daurade gilt-head
déjeuner lunch
délice often used to describe a dessert speciality of the chef
demi half
~-**sel** soft cream cheese, slightly salty
demoiselle de Cherbourg small rock lobster
(à la) dieppoise garnish of mussels and shrimp served in white-wine sauce
dinde, dindon turkey
dindonneau young turkey
dîner dinner
diplomate moulded custard dessert with crystallized fruit and lined with sponge fingers

FRENCH

steeped in liqueur

dodine de canard boned duck, rolled, stuffed, sometimes served cold in gelatine

(à la) du Barry garnish of cauliflower and cheese sauce, gratinéed

(aux) duxelles with minced mushrooms sautéed with butter, white wine and herbs

échalote shallot

écrevisse (freshwater) crayfish
  ~ **à la nage** simmered in white wine, aromatic vegetables and herbs

églefin haddock

émincé slices of cooked meat in gravy or thick cream sauce

endive chicory (US endive)
  ~ **à la bruxelloise** steamed chicory rolled in a slice of ham

entrecôte rib-eye steak

entrée dish served between the hors d'oeuvre or soup and the main course; the first course in a smaller dinner (US starter)

entremets small dish served before cheese; today it often means dessert

épaule shoulder

éperlan smelt

épice spice

épicé hot, peppered

épinard spinach

escalope de veau veal scallop, thin slice of veal

escalope viennoise wiener schnitzel; breaded veal cutlet

escargot snail

estouffade braised or steamed in tightly sealed vessel with minimum of cooking liquid

estragon tarragon

étuvé steamed, stewed with minimum of cooking liquid

faisan pheasant

farci stuffed

fenouil fennel

féra dace (fish)

fève broad bean

filet meat or fish fillet
  ~ **de bœuf** fillet of beef (US tenderloin)
  ~ **mignon** small round veal or pork fillet
  ~ **de sole** fillet of sole

(à la) financière rich sauce of pike dumplings, truffles, mushrooms, Madeira wine, sometimes with olives and crayfish

(aux) fines herbes with herbs

(à la) flamande Flemish style; usually a garnish of braised potatoes, carrots, cabbage, turnips, bacon and sausage (sometimes simmered in beer)

flambé dish flamed usually with brandy

flétan halibut

foie liver
  ~ **gras** goose or duck liver

fond d'artichaut artichocke heart (US bottom)

fondue (au fromage) melted-cheese mixture in a pot into which pieces of bread are dipped

fondue bourguignonne bite-size pieces of meat dipped into boiling oil at the table and eaten with a variety of sauces

fondue chinoise paper-thin slices of beef dipped into boiling bouillon and eaten with a variety of sauces

(à la) forestière forester's style; generally sautéed in butter with morel mushrooms, potatoes and bacon

(au) four baked

frais, fraîche fresh

fraise strawberry

~ **des bois** wild

framboise raspberry

frappé chilled, iced

friand patty with meat filling

fricandeau braised, larded veal

fricassée browned pieces of meat braised with seasonings and vegetables and served in a thick sauce

frit fried

frites chips (US french fries)

friture (de poisson) fried fish

fromage cheese

~ **frais** fresh curd cheese

~ **de tête** brawn (US head-cheese)

fruit confit candied fruit

fruits de mer mussels, oysters, clams

fumé smoked

galette flat, plain cake

garbure thick cabbage soup made of salted pork, spices and *confit d'oie*

garni garnished

(avec) garniture (with) vegetables

gâteau cake, flan, tart

gaufre waffle

gaufrette small, crisp, sweet wafer

(en) gelée jellied

gélinotte hazel-hen, hazel-grouse (US prairie chicken)

gibelotte de lapin rabbit stew in wine sauce

gibier game

~ **de saison** game in season

gigot d'agneau leg of lamb

girolle chanterelle mushroom

glace ice-cream

~ **(à la) napolitaine** ice-cream

layers of different flavours

glacé iced, glazed

goujon gudgeon

gras-double tripe simmered in wine and onions

(au) gratin browned with breadcrumbs or cheese

gratin dauphinois sliced potatoes gratinéed in the oven with eggs, cream and cheese

gratin de fruits de mer shellfish in heavy cream sauce and gratinéed

grillade grilled meat

grillé grilled

grive thrush

groseille à maquereau gooseberry

groseille rouge redcurrant

gruyère a hard cheese rich in flavour

haché minced, hashed

hachis mince, hash

hareng herring

haricot bean

~ **de mouton** stew of mutton with beans and potatoes

~ **vert** French bean (US green bean)

Henri IV artichoke hearts garnished with béarnaise sauce

hollandaise sauce of egg-yolks, butter and lemon juice or vinegar

homard lobster

~ **à l'américaine** (or **à l'armoricaine**) lobster flamed in brandy, simmered in white wine with garlic, tomatoes and herbs

~ **cardinal** flamed in brandy, diced, served in its shell with truffles and chopped mushrooms and gratinéed

~ **Newburg** cut into sections, cooked in brandy and fish stock

~ **Thermidor** simmered in white wine, sautéed in butter with mushrooms, herbs, spices, mustard, flamed in brandy and gratinéed with cheese

huile oil

huître oyster
~ **belon** flat, pinkish oyster
~ **de claire** similar to bluepoint oyster
~ **portugaise** small, fat oyster

jambon ham
~ **de Bayonne** raw, with a slightly salty flavour
~ **cru** raw, cured
~ **à l'os** baked ham

jardinière cooked assorted vegetables

jarret shank, shin

julienne vegetables cut into fine strips

jus gravy, juice

lamproie lamprey

langouste spiny lobster

langoustine Norway lobster, prawn, crawfish

langue tongue

lapin rabbit

lard bacon

légume vegetable

lentille lentil

levraut young hare, leveret

lièvre hare

limande dab

livarot small, round cheese from Normandy

longe de veau loin of veal

(à la) lorraine usually braised in red wine with red cabbage

loup (de mer) (sea) bass

(à la) lyonnaise generally sautéed with onions

macédoine mixed, diced vegetables or fruit

(au) madère with Madeira wine

maigre lean

maïs maize (US corn)

maître d'hôtel sautéed in butter with chopped parsley and lemon juice

maquereau mackerel

marcassin young boar

marchand de vin red wine sauce seasoned with shallots

mariné marinated

marinière sailor's style; garnish of mussels with other seafood simmered in white wine and spices

marjolaine marjoram

maroilles strong, semi-hard cheese from Picardy

marron chestnut

matelote freshwater-fish stew (especially of eel) with wine, onions, mushrooms

médaillon small, round cut of meat

menthe mint

menu in France, generally means *menu à prix fixe*, set meal at a fixed price

merguez very spicy sausage

merlan whiting

merluche dried hake

meunière floured and sautéed in butter with lemon juice and chopped parsley

miel honey

mijoté simmered

millefeuille flaky pastry with cream filling (US napoleon)

(à la) Mirabeau with anchovies, olives, tarragon

mirabelle small yellow plum

(à la) mode in the style (of); often means made according to a local recipe

moelle marrow (bone)

morille morel mushroom

Mornay *béchamel* sauce with cheese

moule mussel

moules marinière mussels simmered in white wine with shallots, thyme and parsley

mousse 1) any frothy cream dish 2) chopped or pounded meat or fish with eggs and cream

mousseline 1) frothy mixture containing cream, usually whipped 2) variation of hollandaise sauce with whipped cream

moutarde mustard

mouton mutton

munster soft cheese with a pungent flavour

mûre mulberry or blackberry

myrtille bilberry (US blueberry)

nature/au naturel plain, without dressing, sauce or stuffing

navarin mutton stew with turnips

navet turnip

(à la/en) neige snow-like; i.e. with beaten egg-whites

(à la) niçoise Riviera style; usually with garlic, anchovies, olives, onions, tomatoes

(à la) nivernaise a garnish of carrots, onions, potatoes

noisette 1) hazelnut 2) boneless round piece of meat usually taken from loin or rib

noix walnut

~ **de coco** coconut

~ **(de) muscade** nutmeg

~ **de veau** pope's eye of veal

(à la) normande usually cooked with gudgeon, shrimps, mushrooms, cream and sometimes truffles

nouilles noodles

œuf egg

~ **brouillé** scrambled

~ **à la coque** soft-boiled

~ **dur** hard-boiled

~ **farci** stuffed

~ **en gelée** lightly poached and served in gelatine

~ **au jambon** ham and eggs

~ **au/sur le plat** fried

~ **poché** poached

~ **Rossini** with truffles and Madeira wine

oie goose

oignon onion

omble-chevalier freshwater fish of the char family

omelette omelet

~ **norvégienne** ice-cream dessert covered with beaten egg-whites, quickly browned in oven and served flaming (US baked Alaska)

ortolan small game bird like a finch

os bone

~ **à moelle** marrow bone

oseille sorrel

oursin sea urchin

pain bread

palourde clam

pamplemousse grapefruit

panaché mixed; two or more kinds of something

pané breaded, rolled in breadcrumbs

(en) papillote encased in greased paper and baked

parfait ice-cream dessert

Parmentier containing potatoes

pastèque watermelon

pâté 1) a moulded pastry case which holds meat or fish 2) a thickish paste often of liver (contained in an earthenware dish)

FRENCH

~ **ardennais** a purée of pork and seasonings encased in a loaf of bread, served in slices

~ **de campagne** strongly flavoured with a variety of meat

~ **en croûte** in a pastry crust

~ **de foie gras** goose (or duck) liver paste

pâtes noodles, macaroni, spaghetti

paupiette (de veau) veal bird, thin slice of veal rolled around stuffing

(à la) paysanne country style; usually containing various vegetables

pêche peach

perche perch

perdreau young partridge

perdrix partridge

(à la) périgourdine preparation with truffles

persil parsley

petit small

~ **déjeuner** breakfast

~ **four** small, fancy cake (US fancy cookie)

~ **pain** roll

~ **pois** green pea

~ **salé (au chou)** salt pork (with cabbage)

~-**suisse** a mild-flavoured, double-cream cheese

pied de porc pig's trotter (US pig's foot)

pigeonneau squab

piment pimento

pintade guinea hen

piperade omelet with green peppers, garlic, tomatoes, ham

piquant sharp-tasting, spicy (e.g. of a sauce)

pissaladière onion and anchovy tart with black olives

plat plate

~ **du jour** speciality of the day

~ **principal** main dish

plateau de fromages cheese board

plie plaice

poché poached

(à la) poêle fried

(à) point medium

pointe d'asperge asparagus tip

poire pear

~ **à la Condé** served hot on a bed of vanilla-flavoured rice

~ **Belle Hélène** with vanilla ice-cream and chocolate sauce

poireau leek

pois pea

~ **chiche** chick pea

poisson fish

~ **d'eau douce** freshwater

~ **de mer** saltwater

poitrine breast, brisket

(au) poivre (with) pepper

poivron sweet pepper

pomme apple

pommes (de terre) potatoes

~ **allumettes** matchsticks

~ **chips** crisps (US potato chips)

~ **dauphine** mashed in butter and egg-yolks, mixed in seasoned flour and deep-fried

~ **duchesse** mashed with butter and egg-yolks

~ **en robe des champs** in their jackets

~ **frites** chips (US french fries)

~ **mousseline** mashed

~ **nature** boiled, steamed

~ **nouvelles** new

~ **vapeur** steamed, boiled

pont-l'évêque soft cheese, strong and pungent in flavour

porc pork

port-salut soft cheese, yellow in colour, mild in taste

potage soup
  ~ **bonne femme** potato, leek, mushroom, onion, rice and sometimes bacon
  ~ **cancalais** fish consommé (often with oysters or other seafood)
  ~ **Condé** mashed red beans
  ~ **Crécy** carrots
  ~ **cultivateur** mixed vegetables and bacon or pork
  ~ **du Barry** cream of cauliflower
  ~ **julienne** vegetables
  ~ **Longchamp** peas, sorrel and chervil
  ~ **Saint-Germain** split-pea, leek and onion
  ~ **soissonnais** haricot bean
pot-au-feu 1) stockpot of beef, potatoes and aromatic vegetables 2) stew
potée boiled pork or beef with vegetables, especially cabbage
potiron pumpkin
poularde fat pullet
  ~ **de Bresse** grain-fed; reputedly the finest available
  ~ **demi-deuil** with truffles inserted under the skin and simmered in broth
poule hen
  ~ **au pot** stewed with vegetables
  ~ **au riz** stewed in bouillon and served with rice
poulet chicken
  ~ **Marengo** sautéed in olive oil, cooked with white wine, tomatoes, garlic, shallots and mushrooms
pourboire tip (but *service* is the percentage added to the bill)
praire clam

pré-salé lamb pastured in the salt meadows on the Atlantic seashore
(à la) printanière with spring vegetables
prix price
  ~ **fixe** at a fixed price
profiterole au chocolat puff pastry filled with whipped cream or custard and covered with hot chocolate
(à la) provençale often with garlic, onions, herbs, olives, oil and tomatoes
prune plum
pruneau (blue) plum
  ~ **sec** prune
pudding blancmange, custard
puits d'amour pastry shell filled with liqueur-flavoured custard
purée pulped and strained fruit or vegetables
  ~ **de pommes de terre** mashed potatoes
quenelle light dumpling made of fish, fowl or meat
queue tail
quiche flan, open tart with meat or vegetable filling, eggs and cream
  ~ **lorraine** tart with cheese, bacon, eggs and cream
râble de lièvre saddle of hare
raclette hot, melted cheese scraped from a block of cheese; accompanied with boiled potatoes and gherkins
radis radish
(en) ragoût stew(ed)
raie skate, ray
raisin grape
  ~ **sec** raisin, sultana
ramequin small cheese tart
rascasse a Mediterranean fish, an

FRENCH

essential ingredient of *bouilla-baisse*

ratatouille Mediterranean stew of tomatoes, peppers, onions, garlic and aubergines, served hot or cold

ravigote vinegar sauce with chopped hard-boiled eggs, capers and herbs

reblochon soft, mild cheese, pale cream colour (Savoy)

(à la) reine with mince meat or fowl

reine-claude greengage

repas meal

rhubarbe rhubarb

(à la) Richelieu garnish of tomatoes, peas, bacon and potatoes

rillettes usually minced pork (sometimes goose or duck) baked in its own fat

ris de veau sweetbread

rissole fritter, pasty

riz rice

~ **pilaf** rice boiled in a bouillon, sometimes with onions

rognon kidney

romarin rosemary

roquefort blue-veined cheese made from ewe's milk; strong, salty with piquant flavour

rosbif roast beef

rôti roast(ed)

rouelle de veau shank of veal (usually a round cut)

roulade 1) a rolled slice of meat or fish with stuffing 2) dessert with cream or jam stuffing (Swiss roll)

sabayon creamy dessert of egg-yolks, sugar and white wine flavoured with a citrus fruit, served warm

safran saffron

saignant underdone (US rare)

saint-pierre John Dory (fish)

salade salad

~ **chiffonnade** shredded lettuce and sorrel in melted butter, served with a dressing

~ **de fruits** fruit salad (US fruit cocktail)

~ **niçoise** lettuce, tomatoes, green beans, hard-boiled eggs, tunny, olives, green pepper, potatoes and anchovies

~ **russe** cooked vegetables in mayonnaise

~ **verte** green

salé salted

salmis game or fowl partially roasted, then simmered in wine and vegetable *purée*

salpicon garnish or stuffing of one or various elements held together by sauce

salsifis salsify

sandre pike perch

sanglier wild boar

sarcelle teal, small freshwater duck

sauce sauce

~ **béarnaise** vinegar, egg-yolks, butter, shallots and tarragon

~ **béchamel** white sauce

~ **au beurre blanc** butter, shallots, vinegar or lemon juice

~ **au beurre noir** browned butter

~ **bordelaise** brown sauce with boletus mushrooms, red wine, shallots and beef marrow

~ **bourguignonne** red wine sauce with herbs, onions and spices (sometimes tarragon)

~ **café de Paris** cream, mustard and herbs

~ **chasseur** brown sauce with

wine, mushrooms, onions, shallots and herbs

~ **diable** hot, spicy sauce with white wine, herbs, vinegar and cayenne pepper

~ **financière** cream, Madeira wine, herbs, spices, mushrooms, truffles and olives

~ **hollandaise** butter, egg-yolks and vinegar or lemon juice

~ **lyonnaise** onions, white wine and butter

~ **madère** brown sauce with Madeira wine base

~ **Mornay** *béchamel* sauce with cheese

~ **ravigote** vinegar sauce with chopped hardboiled eggs, capers and herbs; served cold

~ **rémoulade** mayonnaise enriched with mustard and herbs

~ **suprême** chicken-stock base, thick and bland, served with fowl

~ **tartare** mayonnaise base with gherkins, chives, capers and olives

~ **vinaigrette** oil, vinegar and herbs (sometimes mustard)

saucisse sausage

~ **de Francfort** frankfurter

saucisson a large sausage

saumon salmon

sauté lightly browned in hot butter, oil or fat, sautéed

savarin sponge cake steeped in rum and usually topped with cream

sel salt

selle saddle

selon grosseur (or **grandeur**) price according to size, e.g. of a lobster, often abbreviated **s.g.**

service (non) compris service (not)

included

sorbet water ice (US sherbet)

soufflé à la reine soufflé with finely chopped poultry or meat

soufflé Rothschild vanilla-flavoured soufflé with candied fruit

soupe soup

~ **au pistou** vegetables, noodles, garlic, basil and cheese

~ **à l'oignon** onion

~ **à l'oignon gratinée** onion soup topped with toast and grated cheese; gratinéed

spécialité (du chef) (chef's) speciality

steak steak

~ **haché** hamburger

~ **au poivre** broiled with crushed peppercorns (often flamed in brandy)

~ **tartare** minced beef, eaten raw, with sauce of egg-yolks, mustard, capers, onions, oil and parsley

sucre sugar

suprême de volaille boned chicken breast with creamy sauce

sur commande to your special order

(en) sus in addition, additional charge

tarte open(-faced) flan, tart

~ **Tatin** upside-down tart of caramelized apples

tartelette small tart

tendrons de veau breast of veal

(en) terrine a preparation of meat, fish, fowl or game baked in an earthenware dish called a *terrine*, served cold

tête head

thon tunny (US tuna)

(en) timbale meat, fish, seafood,

fruit or vegetables cooked in a pastry case or mould

tomate tomato

tomme a mild soft cheese

topinambour Jerusalem artichoke

tortue turtle

tournedos round cut of prime beef
  ~ **Rossini** garnished with foie gras and truffles, served with Madeira wine sauce

tout compris all-inclusive (price of a meal)

tranche slice
  ~ **napolitaine** cassata; slice of layered ice-cream and crystallized fruit

tripes tripe
  ~ **à la mode de Caen** baked with calf's trotters (US calf's feet), vegetables, apple brandy or cider

truffe truffle

truite trout

vacherin a mellow cheese
  ~ **glacé** an ice-cream dessert with meringue

vanille vanilla

(à la) vapeur steamed

varié assorted

veau veal

velouté a creamy soup (of vegetables or poultry), thickened with butter and flour

vert-pré a garnish of cress

viande meat
  ~ **séchée** dried beef served as hors d'oeuvre in paper-thin slices

viandes froides various cold slices of meat and ham (US cold cuts)

vinaigre vinegar

vinaigrette salad sauce of vinegar, oil, herbs and mustard

volaille fowl

vol-au-vent puff-pastry shell filled with meat, sweetbreads or fish and sometimes mushrooms

waterzooi de poulet chicken poached in white wine and shredded vegetables, cream and egg-yolks

yaourt yoghurt

Drink

Alsace (93 communes situated on the River Rhine) produces virtually only dry white wine, notably *Gewurztraminer, Riesling, Sylvaner, Traminer;* the terms *grand vin* and *grand cru* are sometimes employed to indicate a wine of exceptional quality

Amer Picon an aperitif with wine and brandy base and quinine flavouring

Anjou a region of the Loire district producing fine rosé and white wine

apéritif often bittersweet, some aperitifs have a wine and brandy base with herbs and bitters (like *Amer Picon, Byrrh, Dubonnet*), others, called *pastis,* have an aniseed base (like *Pernod* or *Ricard*); an aperitif may also be simply vermouth (like *Noilly Prat*) or a liqueur drink like *blanc-cassis*

appellation d'origine contrôlée (A.O.C.) officially recognized wines of which there are over 250 in France; standards of quality are rigidly checked by government inspectors

armagnac a wine-distilled brandy from the Armagnac region, west of Toulouse

Beaujolais Burgundy's most southerly and extensive vineyards which produce mainly red wine, e.g., *Brouilly, Chénas, Chiroubles, Côte de Brouilly, Fleurie, Juliénas, Morgon, Moulin-à-Vent*

Belgique Belgium; though the Romans introduced wine-making to Belgium, the kingdom today only incidentally produces wine, primarily white, sometimes rosé and sparkling wine

bénédictine forest-green liqueur; brandy base, herbs and orange peel, reputedly secret formula

Berry a region of the Loire district producing red, white and rosé wine; e.g., *Châteaumeillant, Menetou-Salon, Quincy, Reuilly, Sancerre, Sauvignon*

bière beer
~ **blonde** light
~ **(en) bouteille** bottled
~ **brune** dark
~ **pression** draught (US draft)
~ **des Trappistes** malt beer brewed by Trappist monks

blanc-cassis white wine mixed with blackcurrant liqueur

Blayais a region of Bordeaux producing mainly red and white wine

boisson drink

Bordeaux divided into several regions: Blayais, Bourgeais, Entre-Deux-Mers, Fronsac, Graves, Médoc, Pomerol, St-Emilion, Sauternais; among the officially recognized wines are 34 reds, 23 whites and two rosés divided into three categories: general (e.g., *Bordeaux* or *Bordeaux supérieur*), regional (e.g., *Entre-Deux-Mers, Graves, Médoc*) and communal (e.g., *Margaux, Pauillac, Sauternes*); Bordeaux red wine is known as claret in America and Britain

Bourgeais a region of Bordeaux producing red and white table wine

Bourgogne Burgundy, divided into five regions: Beaujolais, Chablis, Côte Chalonnaise, Côte d'Or (which comprises the Côte de Beaune and the Côte de Nuits) and Mâconnais; Burgundy counts the largest number of officially recognized wines of France's wine-growing districts; there are four categories of wine: generic or regional (e.g., *Bourgogne* red, white or rosé), subregional (e.g., *Beaujolais, Beaujolais supérieur, Beaujolais-Villages, Côte de Beaune-Villages, Mâcon, Mâcon supérieur, Mâcon-Villages*), communal (e.g., *Beaune, Chablis, Fleurie, Meursault, Nuits-St-Georges, Volnay*) and vineyard *(climat)* (e.g., *Chambertin, Clos de Vougeot, Musigny*)

FRENCH

brut extra dry, refers to *Champagne*

Byrrh an aperitif with wine base and quinine, fortified with brandy

cacao cocoa

café coffee

~ **complet** with bread, roll, butter and jam; the Continental breakfast

~ **crème** with cream

~ **espresso** espresso

~ **filtre** percolated or dripped through a filter

~ **frappé** iced

~ **au lait** white (with milk)

~ **liégeois** cold with ice-cream, topped with whipped cream

~ **nature, noir** simple, black

~ **sans caféine** caffeine-free

calvados an apple brandy from Normandy

cassis blackcurrant liqueur

Chablis a region of Burgundy noted for its white wine

chambrer to bring wine gently to room *(chambre)* temperature

Champagne district divided into three large regions: Côte des Blancs, Montagne de Reims and Vallée de la Marne with some 200 kilometres (120 miles) of underground caves where the wine ferments; there are ordinary red, white and rosé wines but the production is overwhelmingly centered upon the sparkling white and rosé (usually referred to in English as pink Champagne) for which the region is universally known; vineyards are of little importance in classifying wines from Champagne since, according

to tradition, certain varieties of Champagne are produced by blending wine from different vineyards in proportions which are carefully-guarded secrets; sparkling Champagne is sold according to the amount of sugar added: *brut* (extra dry) contains up to 1.5 per cent sugar additive, *extra-sec* (very dry), 1.5–2.5 per cent, *sec* (dry), 2.5–5 per cent, *demi-sec* (slightly sweet), 5–8 per cent and *doux* (sweet), 8–15 per cent

Chartreuse a yellow or green liqueur of herbs and spices produced by monks of Grande Chartreuse in the French Alps

château castle; term employed traditionally in the district of Bordeaux to indicate a wine of exceptional quality; synonyms: *clos, domaine*

chocolat chocolate

cidre cider

citron pressé freshly squeezed lemon juice

citronnade lemon squash (US lemon drink)

claret see *Bordeaux*

clos vineyard; generally indicates a wine of exceptional quality

cognac cognac; the famed wine-distilled brandy from the Charente and Charente-Maritime regions

Cointreau orange liqueur

Corse Corsica; this Mediterranean island, a French department, produces fine wine, particularly from the hilly areas and Cape Corsica; red, white and rosé wine is characterized by a rich, full-bodied taste; the best wine, grown near Bastia, is the rosé *Patrimonio*

Côte de Beaune the southern half of Burgundy's celebrated Côte d'Or producing chiefly red wine; e.g., the prestigious *Aloxe-Corton* as well as *Beaune, Blagny, Chassagne-Montrachet, Meursault, Pernand-Vergelesses, Puligny-Montrachet, Santenay, Savigny-lès-Beaune, Volnay*

Côte de Nuits a region of Burgundy especially noted for its red wine, e.g., *Chambolle-Musigny, Fixin, Gevrey-Chambertin, Morey-St-Denis, Nuits-St-Georges, Vosne-Romanée*

Côte d'Or a famed region of Burgundy composed of the Côte de Beaune and de Nuits which is noted for its red and white wine

Côtes du Rhône extend from Vienne to Avignon along the banks of the River Rhone between the Burgundy and Provence wine districts; over a hundred communes offer a wide diversity in white, red and rosé wine of varying character; divided into a northern and southern region with notable wine: *Château-Grillet, Château-neuf-du-Pape, Condrieu, Cornas, Côte-Rôtie, Crozes-Hermitage, Hermitage, Lirac, St-Joseph, St-Péray, Tavel*

crème 1) cream   2) sweetened liqueur like *crème de menthe, crème de cacao*

cru growth 1) refers to a particular vineyard and its wine 2) a system of grading wine; *premier cru, grand cru, cru classé*

curaçao originally from the name of the island of the Dutch Antilles, now applied to liqueur made from orange peel

cuvée a blend of wine from various vineyards, especially, according to tradition, in the making of Champagne

domaine estate; used on a wine label it indicates a wine of exceptional quality

eau water

  ~ **gazeuse** fizzy (US carbonated)

  ~ **minérale** mineral

Entre-Deux-Mers a vast Bordeaux region called "between two seas"—actually it's between two rivers—which produces white wine

extra-sec very dry (of Champagne)

framboise raspberry liqueur or brandy

frappé 1) iced 2) milk shake

Fronsac a Bordeaux region producing chiefly red wine

Gueuzelambic a strong Flemish bitter beer brewed from wheat and barley

grand cru, grand vin indicates a wine of exceptional quality

Grand Marnier an orange liqueur

Graves a Bordeaux region especially noted for its white wine but also its red

Jura a six-kilometre- (four-mile-) wide strip which runs 80 kilometres (50 miles) parallel to the western Swiss border and Burgundy; offers white, red, rosé, golden and sparkling wine; there are four formally recognized wines: *Arbois, Château-*

Chalon, Côtes du Jura and *l'Etoile*

kirsch spirit distilled from cherries

Kriekenlambic a strong Brussels bitter beer flavoured with morello cherries

lait milk

~ **écrémé** skimmed

Languedoc district, formerly a French province, to the southwest of the Rhone delta; its ordinary table wine is often referred to as *vin du Midi* but other officially recognized wines, mostly white, are produced, including *Blanquette de Limoux* (sparkling), *Clairette du Languedoc, Fitou* and the *Muscats* from Frontignan, Lunel, Mireval and St-Jean-de-Minervois

limonade 1) lemonade   2) soft drink

Loire a district of 200,000 hectares (80,000 acres) sprawled over the vicinity of France's longest river, the Loire; produces much fine red, white and rosé wine in four regions: Anjou (e.g., *Coteaux-de-l'Aubance, Coteaux-du-Layon, Coteaux-de-la-Loire, Saumur*), Berry and Nivernais *(Menetou-Salon, Pouilly-sur-Loire, Quincy, Reuilly, Sancerre)*, Nantais *(Muscadet)* and Touraine *(Bourgueil, Chinon, Montlouis, Vouvray)*

Lorraine a flourishing and renowned wine district up to the 18th century, today it is of minor importance; good red, white and rosé wine continue to be produced (e.g., *Vins de la Moselle, Côtes-de-Toul*)

Mâcon a region of Burgundy producing basically red wine

marc spirit distilled from grape residue

Médoc a Bordeaux region producing highly reputed red wine including *Listrac, Margaux, Moulis, Pauillac, St-Estèphe, St-Julien*

mirabelle a brandy made from small yellow plums, particularly produced in the Alsace-Lorraine area

Muscadet a white wine from the Nantes area (Loire)

muscat 1) a type of grape 2) name given to dessert wine; especially renowned is the muscat from Frontignan (Languedoc)

Nantais a region of the Loire chiefly renowned for its *Muscadet* white wine but offers other wine, e.g., *Coteaux d'Ancenis, Gros-Plant*

Neuchâtel a Swiss region producing primarily white wine (e.g., *Auvernier, Cormondrèche, Cortaillod, Hauterive*)

Noilly Prat a French vermouth

orange pressée freshly squeezed orange juice

pastis aniseed-flavoured aperitif

Pernod an aniseed-flavoured aperitif

pétillant slightly sparkling

Pomerol a Bordeaux region producing red wine (e.g., *Château Pétrus, Lalande-de-Pomerol, Néac*)

Provence France's most ancient wine-producing district; it traces its history back over two-and-a-half milleniums when Greek colonists planted the first vineyards on the Mediterranean coast of Gaul; red, white and rosé wine is produced, e.g., *Bandol, Bellet, Cassis, Coteaux-d'Aix-en-Provence, Coteaux-des-Baux, Coteaux-de-Pierrevert, Côtes-de-Provence, Palette*

quetsche spirit distilled from plums

rancio dessert wine, especially from Roussillon, which is aged in oak casks under the Midi sun

Ricard an aniseed-flavoured aperitif

Roussillon district which was a French province with Perpignan as its capital; its wine is similar in character to that of the Languedoc to the immediate north; good red, white and rosé table wine, e.g., *Corbières du Roussillon* and *Roussillon Dels Aspres;* this region produces three quarters of France's naturally sweet wine, usually referred to as *rancio*, which is aged in oak casks under the Midi sun; notable examples among them are *Banyuls, Côtes-d'Agly, Côtes-du-Haut-Roussillon; Grand-Roussillon, Muscat de Rivesaltes, Rivesaltes*

St-Emilion a Bordeaux region producing red wine including *Lussac, Montagne, Parsac, Puisseguin, St-Georges*

St-Raphaël a quinine-flavoured aperitif

Sauternais a Bordeaux region noted for its white wine *(Sauternes)*, notably the prestigious *Château d'Yquem*

Savoie Savoy; the Alpine district

producing primarily dry, light and often slightly acid white wine (e.g., *Crépy, Seyssel*) but also good red, rosé and sparkling wine which is chiefly produced around Chambéry

Sud-Ouest a district in southwestern France producing quite varying types of wine, mostly white but some red and even rosé; the district includes the former province of Aquitaine, Béarn, Basque Country and Languedoc; wines of particular note are *Bergerac, Côtes-de-Duras, Gaillac, Jurançon, Madiran, Monbazillac, Montravel*

Suisse Switzerland; two-thirds of the nation's wine production consists of white wine; some 230 different vineyards are scattered over a dozen of Switzerland's 23 cantons though only four have a special significance: Neuchâtel, Tessin, Valais and Vaud

Suze an aperitif based on gentian

thé tea

Touraine for 14 centuries a celebrated wine district of the Loire producing red, white and rosé wine (e.g., *Bourgueil, Chinon, Montlouis, St-Nicolas-de-Bourgueil, Vouvray*)

Triple Sec an orange liqueur

Valais sometimes referred to as the California of Switzerland, this Swiss region produces nearly a quarter of the nation's wine; the region in the Rhone Valley is noted for providing Switzerland's best red wine (e.g., *Dôle*) and much of its finest white wine (e.g., *Arvine,*

FRENCH

Ermitage, Fendant, Johannisberg, Malvoisie)

Vaud a Swiss region producing primarily white wine (e.g., *Aigle, Dézaley, Mont-sur-Rolle, Lavaux, Yvorne*)

V.D.Q.S. (vin délimité de qualité supérieure) regional wine of exceptional quality, produced according to carefully defined specifications and checked by government inspectors

Vieille Cure a wine-distilled liqueur

vin wine

~ **blanc** white

~ **chambré** wine at room temperature

~ **doux** sweet, dessert

~ **gris** pinkish

~ **mousseux** sparkling

~ **ordinaire** table

~ **du pays** local

~ **rosé** rosé (pink in reference to Champagne)

~ **rouge** red

~ **sec** dry

V.S.O.P. (very special old pale) in reference to cognac, indicates that it has been aged at least 5 years

(vin de) xérès sherry

German

Guide to pronunciation

Letter	Approximate pronunciation
Consonants	
f, h, k, l, m, n, p, t, x	normally pronounced as in English
b	1) at the end of a word or between a vowel and a consonant, like **p** in up 2) elsewhere as in English
c	1) before **e, i, ö** and **ä,** like **ts** in hits 2) elsewhere like **c** in cat
ch	like **ch** in Scottish loch
d	1) at the end of a word or between a vowel and a consonant, like **t** in eat 2) elsewhere, like **d** in do
g	always hard as in go, but at the end of a word, more like **ck** in tack
j	like **y** in yes
qu	like **k** followed by **v** in vat

r	generally rolled in the back of the mouth
s	1) before or between vowels, like **z** in **z**oo 2) before **p** and **t** at the beginning of a syllable, like **sh** in **sh**ut 3) elsewhere, like **s** in **s**it
ß	always like **s** in **s**it
sch	like **sh** in **sh**ut
tsch	like **ch** in **ch**ip
tz	like **ts** in hi**ts**
v	like **f** in **f**or
w	like **v** in **v**ice
z	like **ts** in hi**ts**

Vowels

In German, vowels are generally long when followed by **h** or by one consonant and short when followed by two or more consonants.

a	1) short, like **u** in c**u**t 2) long, like **a** in c**a**r
ä	1) short, like **e** in l**e**t 2) long, like **ai** in h**ai**r
e	1) short, like **e** in l**e**t 2) long, like **a** in l**a**te 3) in unstressed syllables, it's generally pronounced like **a** in **a**bout
i	1) short, like **i** in h**i**t 2) long, like **ee** in m**ee**t
ie	like **ee** in b**ee**
o	1) short, like **o** in g**o**t 2) long, like **o** in n**o**te
ö	like **ur** in f**ur** (long or short)
u	like **oo** in m**oo**n (long or short)
ü	like French **u** in **u**ne; no English equivalent. Round your lips and try to say **ea** as in m**ea**n (long or short)
y	like German **ü**

Diphthongs

ai, ay, ei, ey	like **igh** in h**igh**
au	like **ow** in n**ow**
äu, eu	like **oy** in b**oy**

Some useful expressions

Hungry

I'm hungry/I'm thirsty.	**Ich habe Hunger/Ich habe Durst.**
Can you recommend a good restaurant?	**Können Sie mir ein gutes Restaurant empfehlen?**
Are there any good, cheap restaurants around here?	**Gibt es gute und preiswerte Restaurants in der Nähe?**
I'd like to reserve a table for ... people.	**Ich möchte einen Tisch für ... Personen reservieren lassen.**
We'll come at ... o'clock.	**Wir kommen um ... Uhr.**

Asking

Good evening. I'd like a table for ... people.	**Guten Abend. Ich hätte gern einen Tisch für ... Personen.**
Could we have a table...?	**Können wir einen Tisch... haben?**
in the corner	**in der Ecke**
by the window	**am Fenster**
outside	**im Freien**
on the terrace	**auf der Terrasse**
May I please have the menu?	**Kann ich bitte die Speisekarte haben?**
What's this?	**Was ist das?**
Do you have...?	**Haben Sie ...?**
a set menu	**ein Tagesgedeck**
local dishes	**Spezialitäten**
a children's menu	**ein Menü für Kinder**
Waiter/Waitress!	**Herr Ober/Fräulein!**
What do you recommend?	**Was empfehlen Sie mir?**
Could I have (a/an)... please?	**Könnte ich bitte... haben?**
ashtray	**einen Aschenbecher**
another chair	**noch einen Stuhl**
finger bowl	**eine Fingerschale**

GERMAN

fork	eine Gabel
glass	ein Glas
knife	ein Messer
napkin	eine Serviette
pepper mill	eine Pfeffermühle
plate	einen Teller
serviette	eine Serviette
spoon	einen Löffel
toothpick	einen Zahnstocher

Ordering

I'd like a/an/some...	Ich hätte gern...
aperitif	einen Aperitif
appetizer	eine Vorspeise
beer	ein Bier
bread	etwas Brot
butter	etwas Butter
cheese	etwas Käse
chips	Pommes frites
coffee	einen Kaffee
dessert	einen Nachtisch
fish	ein Fischgericht
french fries	Pommes frites
fruit	etwas Obst
game	Wild
ice-cream	ein Eis/(Switzerland: eine Glace)
lemon	etwas Zitrone
lettuce	Kopfsalat
meat	Fleisch
mineral water	ein Mineralwasser
milk	Milch
mustard	etwas Senf
noodles	Nudeln
oil	etwas Öl
olive oil	etwas Olivenöl
pepper	etwas Pfeffer
potatoes	Kartoffeln
poultry	Geflügel
rice	Reis
rolls	einige Brötchen

GERMAN

saccharin	Süßstoff
salad	Salat
salt	etwas Salz
sandwich	ein Sandwich
seafood	Meeresfrüchte
seasoning	etwas Würze
soup	eine Suppe
starter	eine Vorspeise
sugar	etwas Zucker
tea	einen Tee
vegetables	Gemüse
vinegar	etwas Essig
(iced) water	(Eis-)Wasser
wine	(einen) Wein

**GUTEN APPETIT!/
MAHLZEIT!**
ENJOY YOUR MEAL!

---

baked	gebacken
baked in parchment	in Pergamentpapier gebacken
boiled	gekocht
braised	gedünstet
cured	gepökelt
fried	(in der Pfanne) gebraten
grilled	gegrillt
marinated	mariniert
poached	pochiert
roasted	(im Ofen) gebraten
sautéed	geschwenkt
smoked	geräuchert
steamed	gedämpft
stewed	geschmort
underdone (rare)	blutig
medium	mittel
well-done	gut durchgebraten

ZUM WOHL!/PROST!
CHEERS!

GERMAN

glass	ein Glas
bottle	eine Flasche
red	rot
white	weiß
rosé	rosé
very dry	sehr trocken
dry	trocken
sweet	süß
light	leicht
full-bodied	vollmundig
sparkling	moussierend
neat (straight)	pur
on the rocks	mit Eis

The bill

I'd like to pay.	Ich möchte gern zahlen.
We'd like to pay separately.	Wir möchten getrennt bezahlen.
You've made a mistake in this bill, I think.	Ich glaube, Sie haben sich verrechnet.
What's this amount for?	Wofür ist dieser Betrag?
Is service included?	Ist Bedienung inbegriffen?
Is everything included?	Ist alles inbegriffen?
Do you accept traveller's cheques?	Kann ich mit Reiseschecks bezahlen?
Thank you. This is for you.	Danke, das ist für Sie.
Keep the change.	Behalten Sie das Wechselgeld.
That was a very good meal.	Das Essen war sehr gut.
We enjoyed it, thank you.	Danke, es hat gut geschmeckt.

Complaints

That's not what I ordered. I asked for...	Das habe ich nicht bestellt. Ich wollte...
May I change this?	Können Sie mir dafür etwas anderes bringen?

The meat is…	Das Fleisch ist…
overdone	zu stark gebraten
underdone	zu roh
too tough	zu zäh
This is too…	Das ist zu…
bitter/salty/sweet	bitter/salzig/süß
The food is cold.	Das Essen ist kalt.
This isn't fresh.	Das ist nicht frisch.
What's taking you so long?	Weshalb dauert es so lange?
Where are our drinks?	Wo bleiben unsere Getränke?
This isn't clean.	Das ist nicht sauber.
Would you ask the head waiter to come over?	Würden Sie den Oberkellner zu uns bitten?

Numbers

1	eins, ein, eine	11	elf
2	zwei	12	zwölf
3	drei	13	dreizehn
4	vier	14	vierzehn
5	fünf	15	fünfzehn
6	sechs	16	sechzehn
7	sieben	17	siebzehn
8	acht	18	achtzehn
9	neun	19	neunzehn
10	zehn	20	zwanzig

GERMAN

Food

Aal eel

Abendbrot, Abendessen evening meal, supper

Allgäuer Bergkäse hard cheese from Bavaria resembling *Emmentaler*

Allgäuer Rahmkäse a mild and creamy Bavarian cheese

Altenburger a mild, soft goat's milk cheese

Ananas pineapple

Anis aniseed

~**brot** aniseed-flavoured cake or biscuit

Apfel apple

Apfelsine orange

Appenzeller (Käse) slightly bitter, fully flavoured cheese

Appetithäppchen, Appetitschnittchen appetizer, canapé

Aprikose apricot

Artischocke artichoke

Artischockenboden artichoke bottom

Aubergine aubergine (US eggplant)

Auflauf 1) soufflé 2) a meat, fish, fowl, fruit or vegetable dish which is oven-browned

Aufschnitt cold meat (US cold cuts)

Auster oyster

Backforelle baked trout

Backhähnchen, Backhendl, Backhuhn fried chicken

Backobst dried fruit

Backpflaume prune

Backsteinkäse strong cheese from Bavaria resembling *Limburger*

Banane banana

Barsch perch

Bauernbrot rye or wholemeal bread

Bauernfrühstück breakfast usually consisting of eggs, bacon and potatoes

Bauernomelett diced bacon and onion omelet

Bauernschmaus sauerkraut garnished with bacon, smoked pork, sausages and dumplings or potatoes

Bauernsuppe a thick soup of sliced frankfurters and cabbage

Baumnuß walnut

Bayerische Leberknödel veal-liver dumplings, served with sauerkraut

Bedienung (nicht) (e)inbegriffen service (not) included

Beere berry

Beilage side dish, sometimes a garnish

belegtes Brot/Brötchen roll with any of a variety of garnishes

Berliner (Pfannkuchen) jam-filled doughnut (US jelly donut)

Berliner Luft dessert made of eggs and lemon, served with raspberry juice

Berner Platte a mound of sauerkraut or French beans liberally garnished with smoked pork chops, boiled bacon and beef, sausages, tongue, ham and boiled potatoes

Beuschel heart, kidney and liver of calf or lamb in a slightly sour sauce

Bienenstich cake with honey and almonds

Bierrettich black radish, generally cut, salted and served with beer

Biersuppe a sweet, spicy soup made on beer

Birchermus, Birchermüsli uncooked oats with raw, shredded fruit, chopped nuts in milk or yoghurt

Birne pear

Bischofsbrot fruit-nut cake

Biskuitrolle Swiss roll; jelly and butter-cream roll

Bismarckhering pickled herring, seasoned with onions

blau word to designate fish freshly poached

Blaubeere bilberry (US blueberry)

Blaukraut red cabbage

Blumenkohl cauliflower

Blutwurst black pudding (US blood sausage)

Bockwurst boiled sausage

Bohne bean

Bouillon broth, consommé

Brachse, Brasse bream

Bratapfel baked apple

Braten roast, joint
~ **soße** gravy

Bratfisch fried fish

Brathähnchen, Brathendl, Brathuhn roast chicken

Bratkartoffel fried potato

Bratwurst fried sausage

Braunschweiger Kuchen rich cake with fruit and almonds

Brei porridge, mash, purée

Brezel salted, knot-shaped roll (US pretzel)

Bries, Brieschen, Briesel sweetbread

Brombeere blackberry

Brot bread
~ **suppe** broth with stale bread

Brötchen roll

Brühe broth, consommé

Brunnenkresse watercress

Brüsseler Endivie chicory (US endive)

Brust breast
~ **stück** brisket

Bückling bloater

Bulette meat- or fishball

Bündnerfleisch cured, dried beef served in very thin slices

Butt(e) brill

Champignon button mushroom

Chicorée chicory (US endive)

Cornichon small gherkin (US pickle)

Dampfnudel steamed sweet dumpling, served warm with vanilla sauce

Dattel date

deutsches Beefsteak hamburger, sometimes topped with a fried egg

doppeltes Lendenstück a thick fil-

GERMAN

let of beef (US tenderloin)

Dörrobst dried fruit

Dorsch cod

Dotterkäse cheese made from skimmed milk and egg-yolk

durchgebraten well-done

Egli perch

Ei egg

   ~ **dotter,** ~ **gelb** egg-yolk

   ~ **schnee** beaten egg-white

   ~ **weiß** egg-white

Eierauflauf egg soufflé

Eierkuchen pancake

Eierschwamm(erl) chanterelle mushroom

eingemacht preserved (of fruit or vegetables)

Eintopf stew, usually of meat and vegetables

Eis ice, ice-cream

   ~ **bombe** ice-cream dessert

   ~ **krem** ice-cream

Eisbein mit Sauerkraut pickled pig's knuckle with sauerkraut

Emmentaler (Käse) a semi-hard, robust Swiss cheese with holes

Endivie endive (US chicory)

Ente duck

Erbse pea

Erdbeere strawberry

Erdnuß peanut

errötende Jungfrau raspberries with cream

Essig vinegar

   ~ **gurke** gherkin (US pickle)

Eßkastanie chestnut

Extraaufschlag extra charge, supplementary charge

Fadennudel thin noodle, vermicelli

falscher Hase a meat loaf of beef and pork

Fasan pheasant

Faschiertes minced meat

faschiertes Laibchen meatball

Feige fig

Felchen variety of lake trout

Fenchel fennel

fester Preis, zu festem Preis fixed price

Filet fillet

   ~ **Stroganoff** thin slices of beef cooked in a sauce of sour cream, mustard and onions

Fisch fish

   ~ **klößchen** fishball

   ~ **schüssel** casserole of fish and diced bacon

Fladen pancake

Flädle, Flädli thin strips of pancake added to soup

flambiert flambé (food set aflame with brandy)

Flammeri a pudding made of rice or semolina and served with stewed fruit or vanilla custard

Fleisch meat

   ~ **käse** seasoned meat loaf made of beef and other minced meats

   ~ **kloß** meat dumpling

   ~ **roulade,** ~ **vogel** slice of meat rolled around a stuffing and braised; veal bird

Flunder flounder

Forelle trout

Frankfurter (Würstchen) frankfurter (sausage)

Frikadelle a meat, fowl or fish dumpling

Frikassee fricassée, stew

frisch fresh

Frischling young wild boar

Froschschenkel frogs' legs

Frucht fruit

Frühlingssuppe soup with diced spring vegetables

Frühstück breakfast

Frühstückskäse a strong cheese with a smooth texture

Frühstücksspeck smoked bacon

Füllung stuffing, filling, forcemeat

Fürst-Pückler-Eis(bombe) chocolate, vanilla and strawberry ice-cream dessert

Gabelfrühstück brunch

Gans goose

Gänseklein goose giblets

Garnele shrimp

Garnitur garnish

Gebäck pastry

gebacken baked

gebraten roasted, fried

gedämpft steamed

Gedeck meal at a set price

gedünstet braised, steamed

Geflügel fowl

~ **klein** giblets

Gefrorenes ice-cream

gefüllt stuffed

gegrillt grilled

gehackt minced or chopped

Gehacktes minced meat

gekocht cooked, boiled

Gelee 1) aspic 2) jelly 3) jam

gemischt mixed

Gemüse vegetable

gepökelt pickled

geräuchert smoked

Gericht dish

geröstet roasted

Gerste barley

gesalzen salted

geschmort stewed, braised

Geschnetzeltes meat cut into thin, small slices

Geselchtes cured and smoked pork

gesotten simmered, boiled

gespickt larded

gesülzt jellied, in aspic

Gewürz spice

~ **gurke** gherkin (US pickle)

~ **kuchen** spice cake

~ **nelke** clove

gewürzt spiced, hot

Gipfel crescent-shaped roll

Gittertorte almond cake or tart with a raspberry topping

Gitzi kid

Glace ice-cream

Glattbutt brill

Gnagi cured pig's knuckle

Götterspeise fruit jelly dessert (US Jell-O)

Granat prawn

~ **apfel** pomegranate

gratiniert oven-browned, gratinéed

Graubrot brown bread (US black bread)

Graupensuppe barley soup

Greyerzer (Käse) Gruyère, a cheese rich in flavour, smooth in texture

Griebenwurst a larded frying sausage

Grieß semolina

grilliert grilled

Gröstl grated, fried potatoes with pieces of meat

Gründling gudgeon

grüne Bohne French bean (US green bean)

Grünkohl kale

Gugelhopf, Gugelhupf a moulded cake with a hole in the centre; usually with almonds and raisins

Güggeli spring chicken

Gulasch goulash

Gurke cucumber, gherkin

Hachse knuckle, shank

Hackbraten meat loaf of beef and pork

Hackfleisch minced meat

Haferbrei oatmeal, porridge
Haferflocken rolled oats
Hähnchen spring chicken
halb half
~ **gar** rare (US underdone)
Hamme ham
Hammel(fleisch) mutton
Handkäse cheese made from sour milk, with a pungent aroma
Haschee hash
Hase hare
Hasenpfeffer jugged hare
Haselnuß hazelnut
Hauptgericht main course
hausgemacht, von Haus home-made
Hausmannskost plain food
Haxe knuckle, shank
Hecht pike
Hefekranz ring-shaped cake
Heidelbeere bilberry (US blueberry)
Heilbutt halibut
heiß very warm (hot)
Hering herring
~ **Hausfrauenart** herring fillets with onions in sour cream
Heringskartoffeln a casserole of layers of herring and potatoes
Heringskönig John Dory (fish)
Herz heart
Himbeere raspberry
Himmel und Erde slices of black pudding served with mashed potatoes and apple sauce
Hirn brains
Hirsch stag (venison)
Hirse millet
hohe Rippe roast ribs of beef
Holsteiner Schnitzel breaded veal cutlet served with vegetables and topped with a fried egg
Honig honey
Hörnchen crescent-shaped roll

Huhn chicken
Hühnchen chicken
Hühnerklein chicken giblets
Hummer lobster
Husarenfleisch braised beef, veal and pork fillets, with sweet peppers, onions and sour cream
Hutzelbrot bread made of prunes and other dried fruit
Imbiß snack
Ingwer ginger
italienischer Salat finely sliced veal, salami, tomatoes, anchovies, cucumber and celery in mayonnaise
(nach) Jägerart sautéed with mushrooms and sometimes onions
Jakobsmuschel scallop
Johannisbeere redcurrant
jung young, spring
Jungfernbraten roast pork with bacon
Kabeljau cod
Kaisergranat Norway lobster, Dublin Bay prawn
Kaiserschmarren delicious, fluffy pancakes with raisins served with a compote or chocolate sauce
Kalb(fleisch) veal
Kalbsbries veal sweetbread
Kalbskopf calf's head
Kalbsmilch veal sweetbread
Kalbsnierenbraten roast veal stuffed with kidneys
Kaldaunen tripe
kalt cold
Kaltschale chilled fruit soup
Kammuschel scallop
kandierte Frucht crystallized fruit (US candied fruit)
Kaninchen rabbit
Kapaun capon

Kaper caper
Karamelkrem caramel custard
Karfiol cauliflower
Karotte carrot
Karpfen carp
Kartoffel potato
  ~ **puffer** potato fritter
Käse cheese
  ~ **platte** cheese board
  ~ **stange** cheese straw, cheese stick
Kasseler Rippenspeer smoked pork chops, often served with sauerkraut
Kastanie chestnut
Katenrauchschinken country-style smoked ham
Katenwurst country-style smoked sausage
Katzenjammer cold slices of beef in mayonnaise with cucumbers or gherkins
Kaviar caviar
Keks biscuit (US cookie)
Kerbel chervil
Kesselfleisch boiled pork served with vegetables
Keule leg, haunch
Kieler Sprotte smoked sprat
Kipfel crescent-shaped roll
Kirsche cherry
Kitz kid
Kliesche dab
Klops meatball
Kloß dumpling
Klößchen small dumpling
Kluftsteak rumpsteak
Knackwurst a lightly garlic-flavoured sausage, generally boiled
Knoblauch garlic
Knochen bone
  ~ **schinken** cured ham
Knödel dumpling

Knöpfli thick noodle
Kohl cabbage
  ~ **rabi**, ~ **rübe** turnip
  ~ **roulade** cabbage leaves stuffed with minced meat
Kompott stewed fruit, compote
Konfitüre jam
Königinpastetchen vol-au-vent; puff-pastry shell filled with diced chicken and mushrooms
Königinsuppe creamy chicken soup with pieces of chicken breast
Königsberger Klops cooked meatball in white caper sauce
Kopfsalat green salad, lettuce
Korinthe currant
Kotelett chop, cutlet
Krabbe crab
Kraftbrühe broth, consommé
Krainer spiced pork sausage
Kranzkuchen ring-shaped cake
Krapfen 1) fritter 2) jam-filled doughnut (US jelly donut)
Krauskohl kale
Kraut cabbage
Kräutersoße herb dressing
Krautsalat coleslaw
Krautstiel white beet, Swiss chard
Krautwickel stuffed cabbage
Krebs freshwater crayfish
Krem cream, custard
  ~ **schnitte** custard slice (US napoleon)
Kren horse-radish
  ~ **fleisch** pork stew with vegetables and horse-radish
Kresse cress
Krustentier shellfish
Kuchen cake
Kukuruz maize (US corn)
Kümmel caraway
Kürbis pumpkin
Kuttelfleck, Kutteln tripe

GERMAN

Labskaus thick stew of minced, marinated meat with mashed potatoes

Lachs salmon

~**forelle** salmon trout

Lamm(fleisch) lamb

Languste spiny lobster, crawfish

Lattich lettuce

Lauch leek

Leber liver

~**käse** seasoned meat loaf made of minced liver, pork and bacon

Lebkuchen gingerbread

Leckerli honey-flavoured ginger biscuit

legiert thickened, usually with egg-yolk (refers to sauces or soups)

Leipziger Allerlei spring carrots, peas and asparagus (sometimes with mushrooms)

Lende loin

Lendenbraten roast tenderloin

Lendenstück fillet of beef (US tenderloin)

Limburger (Käse) a semi-soft, strong-smelling whole-milk cheese

Linse lentil

Linzer Torte almond cake or tart with a raspberry-jam topping

Löwenzahn young dandelion green, usually prepared as salad

Lunge light (lung of an animal)

Mahlzeit meal

Mainauer (Käse) semi-hard, full-cream round cheese with a red rind and yellow interior

Mainzer Rippchen pork chop

Mais maize (US corn)

Makrele mackerel

Makrone macaroon

Mandarine mandarin

Mandel almond

Mangold white beet, Swiss chard

Marille apricot

mariniert marinated, pickled

Mark (bone) marrow

Marmelade jam

Marone chestnut

Mastente fattened duckling

Masthühnchen broiler, spring chicken

Matjeshering slightly salted young herring

Matrosenbrot a sandwich with chopped, hard-boiled eggs, anchovies and seasoning

Maulbeere mulberry

Maultasche a kind of ravioli filled with meat, vegetables and seasoning

Meerrettich horse-radish

Mehlnockerl small dumpling

Mehlsuppe brown-flour soup

Melone melon

Menü meal at a set price

Meringe(l) meringue

Mettwurst spiced and smoked pork sausage, usually for spreading on bread

Miesmuschel mussel

Milke sweetbread

Mirabelle small yellow plum

Mittagessen midday meal, lunch

Mohn poppy

Möhre, Mohrrübe carrot

Mondseer (Käse) whole-milk yellow cheese with a moist texture

Morchel morel mushroom

Morgenessen breakfast

Morgenrötesuppe thick soup of meat, tapioca, tomatoes and chicken stock

Mostrich mustard

Mus stewed fruit, purée, mash

Muschel mussel

Muskat(nuß) nutmeg

Nachspeise, Nachtisch dessert, sweet

naturell plain

Nelke clove

Nidel, Nidle cream

Niere kidney

Nierenstück loin

Nockerl small dumpling

Nudel noodle

Nürnberger Bratwurst frying sausage made of veal and pork

Nuß 1) nut 2) approx. rumpsteak

Obst fruit

  ~ **salat** fruit salad

Ochs(enfleisch) beef

Ochsenauge fried egg (US sunny side up)

Ochsenmaulsalat ox muzzle salad

Ochsenschwanz oxtail

Ohr ear

Öl oil

Omelett(e) omelet

Palatschinken pancake usually filled with jam or cheese, sometimes served with a hot chocolate and nut topping

Pampelmuse grapefruit

paniert breaded

Paprikaschote sweet pepper

Paradeis(er), Paradiesapfel tomato

Pastetchen filled puff-pastry case

Pastete pastry, pie

Patisserie pastry

Pellkartoffel potato boiled in its jacket

Perlgraupe pearl barley

Petersilie parsley

Pfahlmuschel mussel

Pfannkuchen pancake

Pfeffer pepper

  ~ **kuchen** very spicy gingerbread

  ~ **nuß** ginger(bread)-nut

  ~ **schote** hot pepper

Pfifferling chanterelle mushroom

Pfirsich peach

  ~ **Melba** peach-halves poached in syrup, served over vanilla ice-cream, topped with raspberry sauce and whipped cream

Pflaume plum

Pichelsteiner (Fleisch) meat and vegetable stew

pikant spiced, highly seasoned

Pilz mushroom

Platte platter

Plätzchen biscuit (US cookie)

Plätzli scallop, cutlet

pochiert poached

Pökelfleisch marinated meat

Pomeranzensoße sauce of bitter oranges, wine and brandy, usually served with duck

Pommes frites chips (US french fries)

Porree leek

Poulet chicken

Praline praline; chocolate with a sweet filling

Preiselbeere cranberry

Preßkopf brawn (US headcheese)

Printe honey-flavoured biscuit (US cookie)

Pudding custard, pudding

Püree mash, purée

Puter turkey

Quargel a small, round cheese, slightly acid and salty

Quark(käse) fresh white cheese

Quitte quince

Radieschen radish

Ragout stew

Rahm cream

Rande beetroot

Räucheraal smoked eel

GERMAN

Räucherhering smoked herring
Räucherlachs smoked salmon
Räucherspeck smoked bacon
Rebhuhn partridge
Rechnung bill (US check)
Regensburger a highly spiced and smoked sausage
Reh deer, venison
  ~**pfeffer** jugged venison, fried and braised in its marinade, served with sour cream
Reibekuchen potato pancake
Reibkäse grated cheese
Reis rice
  ~**fleisch** veal braised with rice, tomatoes and other vegetables
Rettich black radish
Rhabarber rhubarb
Ribisel redcurrant
Rinderbrust brisket of beef
Rind(fleisch) beef
Rippe rib
Rippchen, Rippenspeer, Rippenstück, Rippli chop (usually smoked pork)
Rochen skate, ray
Rogen roe (generally cod's roe)
Roggenbrot rye bread
roh raw
Rohkost uncooked vegetables, vegetarian food
Rohschinken cured ham
Rollmops soused herring fillet rolled around chopped onions or gherkins
Rosenkohl brussels sprout
Rosine raisin
Rosmarin rosemary
Rostbraten rumpsteak
Rösti grated, fried (US hashed-brown) potatoes
Röstkartoffel roast potato
rote Beete/Rübe beetroot
rote Grütze fruit jelly served with cream

Rotkohl, Rotkraut red cabbage
Rotzunge lemon sole
Roulade beef olives; usually thin slices of beef, stuffed, rolled and braised
Rücken chine, saddle
Rüebli carrot
Rührei scrambled egg
russische Eier Russian eggs; egg halves topped with caviar served with remoulade sauce
Sachertorte rich chocolate layer cake with jam filling
Safran saffron
Saft juice
Sahne cream
Saibling char
Saitenwurst a variety of frankfurter or wiener sausage
Salat salad
Salbei sage
Salm salmon
Salz salt
  ~**fleisch** salted meat
  ~**gurke** pickled cucumber
  ~**kartoffel** boiled potato
Salzburger Nockerl dumpling made of beaten egg-yolks, egg whites, sugar and flour, fried in butter
Sandmuschel clam
Sardelle anchovy
Sardellenring rolled anchovy
Sardine sardine, pilchard
Sattel chine, saddle
Saubohne broad bean
sauer sour
Sauerampfer sorrel
Sauerbraten pot roast marinated with herbs
Schalentier shellfish
Schalotte shallot
Schaschlik chunks of meat, sliced

GERMAN

of kidneys and bacon, grilled then braised in a spicy sauce of tomatoes, onions and bacon

Schaumrolle puff-pastry rolls filled with whipped cream or custard

Scheibe slice

Schellfisch haddock

Schildkrötensuppe turtle soup

Schillerlocke pastry cornet with vanilla cream filling

Schinken ham

~ **brot** ham sandwich, usually open(-faced)

Schlachtplatte cold meat, liver sausage and sauerkraut

Schlagobers, Schlagrahm, Schlag-sahne whipped cream

Schlegel leg, haunch

Schleie tench

Schmelzkäse a soft and pungent cheese, usually for spreading on bread

Schmorbraten pot roast

Schmorfleisch meat stew

Schnecke 1) cinnamon roll 2) snail

Schnepfe snipe

Schnittbohne sliced French bean

Schnitte slice, cut

Schnittlauch chive

Schnitzel cutlet

Schokolade chocolate

Scholle plaice

Schulter shoulder

Schwamm(erl) mushroom

schwarze Johannisbeere/Ribisel blackcurrant

Schwarzwälder Kirschtorte a chocolate layer cake filled with cream and cherries, flavoured with *Kirsch*

Schwarzwälder Schinken a variety of smoked ham from the Black Forest

Schwarzwurzel salsify

Schwein(efleisch) pork

Seezunge sole

Selchfleisch smoked pork

Sellerie celery

Semmel roll

~ **brösel** breadcrumbs

~ **knödel** dumpling made of diced white bread

Senf mustard

Siedfleisch boiled meat

Soße sauce, gravy

Spanferkel suck(l)ing pig

spanische Soße a brown sauce with herbs

Spargel asparagus

Spätzle, Spätzli thick noodle

Speck bacon

~ **knödel** dumpling made with bacon, eggs and white bread

Speise food

~ **eis** ice-cream

~ **karte** menu, bill of fare

Spekulatius spiced biscuit (US cookie)

Spezialität speciality

~ **des Hauses** chef's speciality

~ **des Tages** day's speciality

Spiegelei fried egg (US sunny side up)

(am) Spieß (on the) spit

Spinat spinach

Sprossenkohl brussels sprout

Sprotte sprat

Stachelbeere gooseberry

Steckrübe turnip

Steinbuscher (Käse) semi-hard creamy cheese; strong and slightly bitter

Steinbutt turbot

Steingarnele prawn

Steinpilz boletus mushroom

Stelze knuckle of pork

GERMAN

GERMAN

Stierenauge fried egg (US sunny side up)

Stock mashed potatoes
~**fisch** stockfish, dried cod

Stollen loaf cake with raisins, almonds, nuts and candied lemon peel

Stoßsuppe caraway soup

Stotzen leg, haunch

Strammer Max slice of bread or sandwich with spiced minced pork (sometimes sausage or ham) served with fried eggs and onions

Streichkäse any soft cheese spread, with different flavours

Streuselkuchen coffee cake with a topping made of butter, sugar, flour and cinnamon

Strudel paper-thin layers of pastry filled with apple slices, nuts, raisins and jam or honey

Stück piece, slice

Sülze 1) jellied, in aspic 2) brawn (US headcheese)

Suppe soup

süß sweet
~**sauer** sweet-and-sour (of sauces)

Süßigkeit sweet (US candy)

Süßspeise dessert, pudding

Tagesgericht day's special

Tagessuppe day's soup

Tascherl pastry turnover with meat, cheese or jam filling

Tatar raw, spiced minced beef

Tatarenbrot open(-faced) sandwich with *Tatar*

Taube pigeon (US squab)

Teigwaren macaroni, noodles, spaghetti

Teller plate, dish
~**gericht** one-course meal

Thunfisch tunny (US tuna)

Thymian thyme

Tilsiter (Käse) semi-hard cheese, mildly pungent

Tomate tomato

Topfen fresh white cheese
~**strudel** flaky pastry filled with creamed, vanilla-flavoured white cheese, rolled and baked

Topfkuchen moulded cake with raisins

Törtchen small tart or cake

Torte layer cake, usually rich

Traube grape

Trüffel truffle

Truthahn turkey

Tunke sauce, gravy

Türkenkorn maize (US corn)

Vanille vanilla

verlorenes Ei poached egg

Voressen meat stew

Vorspeise starter, first course

Wacholderbeere juniper berry

Wachtel quail

Waffel waffle

Walnuß walnut

Wassermelone watermelon

Weinbeere, Weintraube grape

Weinkarte wine list

Weinkraut white cabbage, often braised with apples and simmered in wine

weiße Bohne haricot bean (US navy bean)

Weißbrot white bread

Weißkäse fresh white cheese

Weißkohl, Weißkraut white cabbage

Weißwurst sausage made of veal and bacon, flavoured with parsley, onion and lemon peel

Weizen wheat

Welschkorn maize (US corn)

Westfälischer Schinken a well-known variety of cured and smoked ham

Wiener Schnitzel breaded veal cutlet

Wiener Würstchen, Wienerli wiener, frankfurter (sausage)

Wild(bret) game, venison

Wildente wild duck

Wildschwein wild boar

Wilstermarschkäse semi-hard cheese, similar to *Tilsiter*

Windbeutel cream puff

Wirsing(kohl) savoy cabbage

Wittling whiting

Wurst sausage

Würstchen small sausage

würzig spiced

Zander pike-perch

Zervelat(wurst) a seasoned and smoked sausage made of pork, beef and bacon

Zichorie chicory (US endive)

Ziege goat

Zimt cinnamon

Zitrone lemon

Zucker sugar

Zunge tongue

Zutat (added) ingredient

Zwetsch(g)e plum

Zwiebel onion
   ~**fleisch** beef sautéed with onions
   ~**wurst** liver and onion sausage

Zwischenrippenstück approx. rib-eye steak, entrecôte

GERMAN

Drink

Abfüllung bottled, from wine brought directly from the grower

Abzug wine bottled on the estate or at the vineyard where the grapes were grown, e.g., *Schloßabzug, Kellerabzug*

Ahr the region, named after its tributary of the Rhine, has the continent's northernmost vineyards; the red wine—pale, delicious with a fine aroma—is the best in Germany, which produces little red wine; try it around the towns of Ahrweiler, Neuenahr and Walporzheim

Apfelmost apple cider

Apfelsaft apple juice

Apfelwein apple cider with a high alcoholic content

Aprikosenlikör apricot liqueur

Auslese wine produced from choice grapes

Baden this wine-producing region is situated in the southwestern part of Germany with Switzerland to the south and Alsace, France, to the west; vineyards are especially found on the outskirts of the Black Forest facing the valley of the Rhine; some examples of the wine are *Kaiserstuhl*, produced at the foot of a one-time volcano to the west of Freiburg, *Markgräfler*, *Mauerwein* and *Seewein* from the Lake of Constance

Beerenauslese wine produced

from choice, very mature grapes resulting in a dessert wine

Bier beer
dunkles ~ dark
helles ~ light, lager

Bock(bier) a beer with a high malt content

Branntwein brandy, spirits

Brauner coffee with milk
kleiner ~ small cup of coffee with milk

Danziger Goldwasser a caraway seed-flavoured liqueur flecked with tiny golden leaves

Doppelkorn spirit distilled from grain

Dornkaat a grain-distilled spirit, slightly flavoured with juniper berries

Eierlikör egg liqueur

Eiskaffee iced coffee

Enzian spirit distilled from gentian root

Exportbier a beer with a higher hops content than lager beer

Flasche bottle

Flaschenbier bottled beer

Franken Franconia; the best vineyards of this wine-producing region around the River Main are situated in the vicinity of Iphofen, Escherndorf, Randersacker, Rödelsee and Würzburg; Franconian white wine is dry, strong and full-bodied; Würzburg produces one of the area's best wines under the name *Steinwein*

Fruchtsaft fruit juice

Gewächs used together with the year on the label of quality wines

gezuckert sugar added, sweetened

Glühwein mulled wine

Himbeergeist spirit distilled from raspberries

Kabinett a term indicating that a wine is of high quality

Kaffee coffee
~ **Hag** caffeine-free
~ **mit Sahne (und Zucker)** with cream (and sugar)
~ **mit Schlag(obers)** served with whipped cream
schwarzer ~ black

Kakao cocoa

Kapuziner coffee with whipped cream and grated chocolate

Kirsch(wasser) spirit distilled from cherries

Klosterlikör herb liqueur

Kognak cognac

Korn(branntwein) spirit distilled from grain

Kümmel(branntwein) caraway flavoured spirit

Likör liqueur, cordial

Limonade 1) soft drink 2) lemon drink

Lindenblütentee lime-blossom tea

Malzbier malt beer, with a low alcoholic content

Märzenbier beer with a high alcoholic content, brewed in March

Maß(krug) a large beer mug holding 1 litre (about 1 quart)

Milch milk
~ **kaffee** half coffee and half hot milk
~ **mix** milk shake

Mineralwasser mineral water

Mosel(–Saar–Ruwer) the official name of the Moselle region; the best Moselle wine is produced in only a part of the region, the mid-Moselle Valley which run from Trittenheim to Traben Trarbach; the best vineyard

are those of Bernkastel, Braune-
berg, Graach, Piesport, Wehlen
and Zeltingen

Most must, young wine

Nahe a wine-producing region,
named after its tributary of the
River Rhine, in the vicinity of
Bad Kreuznach; its white wine
is full-bodied and may be compared to the best wine of Rhenish Hesse; the most celebrated
vineyard is Schloß Böckelheim,
owned by the state; other excellent wine is produced in the
vicinity of Bad Kreuznach,
Bretzenheim, Münster, Nieder-
hausen, Norheim, Roxheim,
Winzerheim

Naturwein unblended, unsweetened wine

Österreich Austria; very little of
its wine is exported; the red—
mainly from Burgenland—is
not especially notable and is
usually drunk only locally; pro-
bably the best-known Austrian
wine is *Gumpoldskirchner*, produced to the south of Vienna, a
good white wine which genera-
tions of Viennese have enjoyed;
along the banks of the River
Danube to the west of Vienna,
good white wine is produced in
the Wachau area (e.g., *Dürn-
steiner, Loibner, Kremser);* in
the immediate vicinity of the
Austrian capital, table wine is
produced (e.g., *Nußberger,
Grinzinger, Badener)* of which
the best is sometimes exported

Perlwein white, semi-sparkling
wine

Pfalz Palatinate; in good years this
region is often first among West

Germany's wine-producing regions in terms of production,
predominantly of white wine;
in medieval times, the Palatinate gained a reputation for
being "the wine cellar of the
Holy Roman Empire"; today's
Palatinate is bounded on the
north by Rhenish Hesse, to the
east by the River Rhine, to
the south and west by Alsace,
and Saarland; some examples
*Dürkheimer, Forster, Deideshei-
mer, Ruppertsberger* for white,
Dürkheimer also for red

Pils(e)ner beer with a particularly
strong aroma of hops

Pfefferminztee peppermint tea

Pflümli(wasser) spirit distilled
from plums

Portwein port (wine)

Rhein Rhine wine is produced in
five regions in the Rhine valley
offering the country's best white
wines

Rheingau region situated at the
foot of the Taunus Mountains
facing the River Rhine; its best
wines are dessert wines which
can be compared to fine Sauternes; a good red wine is produced in Aßmannshausen

Rheinhessen Rhenish Hesse, of
which Mainz is the capital; no
less than 155 villages are dedi-
cated to wine production; some
produce wines of exceptional
quality (Alsheim, Bingen, Bo-
denheim, Dienheim, Gunters-
blum, Ingelheim, Nackenheim,
Nierstein, Oppenheim and
Worms); wine of lesser quality
is sold under the name of *Lieb-
frau(en)milch*

GERMAN

Schillerwein rosé wine

Schloß castle, denotes a wine estate

Schnaps brandy, spirits

Schokolade chocolate

Schweiz Switzerland; the most notable wines (both red and white) are produced in French- and Italian-speaking cantons; German-speaking cantons produce mostly light red wines

Sekt sparkling wine similar to Champagne

Sirup syrup

Sodawasser soda water

Spätlese wine produced from grapes picked late in the season, often resulting in full-bodied wine

Spezialbier more strongly brewed beer than *Vollbier*

Sprudel(wasser) soda water

Starkbier strong beer with a high malt content

Steinhäger juniper-flavoured spirit

Tee tea
  ~ **mit Milch** with milk
  ~ **mit Zitrone** with lemon

trocken dry

Trockenbeerenauslese wine produced from specially selected overripe grapes; usually results in a rich, full-bodied dessert wine

ungezuckert unsweetened

verbessert in reference to wine, "improved" or sweetened

Viertel ¼ litre (about ½ pint) of wine

Vollbier the typical German beer with an alcoholic content of 3–4%

Wachstum used on a wine label with the name of the grower, guarantees natural wine

Wasser water

Wein wine
  Rot~ red
  Schaum~ sparkling
  Süß~ dessert
  Weiß~ white

Weinbrand brandy distilled from wine

Weißbier light beer brewed from wheat

Wermut vermouth

Württemberg wine from this region, rarely exported, must be drunk very young; the term *Schillerwein* is employed in the region to denote rosé wine; best wine is produced at Cannstatt, Feuerbach, Untertürckheim; *Stettener Brotwasser* is a noted wine

Zitronensaft lemon squash (US lemon soda)

Zwetschgenwasser spirit distilled from plums

Greek

Guide to pronunciation

Each Greek word in the following menu reader is followed by a simplified transliteration in our own alphabet to help you to recognize and pronounce the word. However, if you're even more interested in speaking the language, you'll want to obtain a copy of GREEK FOR TRAVELLERS from your favourite bookshop. This Berlitz phrase book uses imitated pronunciation which is read as if it were English.

Letter	Approximate pronunciation	Symbol
Vowels		
α	like the vowel in car, but pronounced further forward in the mouth	a
ε	like e in sell	e
η, ι, υ	like ee in meet	i
o, ω	like o in got	o

Consonants

β	like **v** in **v**ine	v
γ	1) before **α, o, ω, ου** and consonants, a voiced version of the **ch** sound in Scottish lo**ch**	gh
	2) before **ε, αι, η, ι, υ, ει, οι,** like **y** in **y**et	y
δ	like **th** in **th**is	dh
ζ	like **z** in **z**oo	z
θ	like **th** in **th**ing	th
κ	like **k** in **k**it	k
λ	like **l** in **l**emon	l
μ	like **m** in **m**an	m
ν	like **n** in **n**ew	n
ξ	like **x** in si**x**	x
π	like **p** in **p**ot	p
ρ	like **r** in **r**ed	r
σ, ς	1) before **β, γ, δ, ζ, μ, ν, ρ,** like **z** in **z**oo	z
	2) elsewhere, like **s** in **s**ee	s
τ	like **t** in **t**ea	t
φ	like **f** in **f**ive	f
χ	like **ch** in Scottish lo**ch**	kh
ψ	like **ps** in dro**ps**y	ps

Groups of letters

αι	like **e** in g**e**t	e
ει, οι	like **ee** in s**ee**	i
ου	like **oo** in r**oo**t	u
αυ	1) before voiceless consonants (**θ, κ, ξ, π, σ, τ, φ, χ, ψ**), like **uff** in p**uff**ed	af
	2) elsewhere, similar to **ave** in h**ave**	av
ευ	1) before voiceless consonants, like **ef** in l**ef**t	ef
	2) elsewhere, like **ev** in l**ev**el	ev
γγ	like **ng** in li**ng**er	ng
γκ	1) at the beginning of a word, like **g** in **g**o	g
	2) in the middle of a word, like **ng** in li**ng**er	ng

γξ	like **nks** in li**nks**	nx
γχ	like **ng** followed by the **ch** of Scottish lo**ch**	nkh
μπ	1) at the beginning of a word, like **b** in **b**eer	b
	2) in the middle of a word, like **mb** in lu**mb**er	mb
ντ	1) at the beginning of a word, like **d** in **d**ear	d
	2) in the middle of a word, like **nd** in u**nd**er	nd
τζ	like **ds** in see**ds**	dz

Accent marks

These are written in various ways, e.g., ὰ, ά, or ᾶ, but all of them indicate the stressed syllable. The signs for the "breathing" of initial vowels (ἀ, ἀ) can be ignored. A diaeresis (two dots) written over a letter means that the letter is pronounced separately from the previous one.

The alphabet

Here are the characters which comprise the Greek alphabet. The column at left shows the printed capital and small letters, while written letters are shown in the center column. At right you'll find the names of these letters in our simplified transliteration.

A	α	𝒜	α	alfa		N	ν	𝒩	ν	ni
B	β	ℬ	β	vita		Ξ	ξ	𝛯	ξ	xi
Γ	γ	𝒯	γ	ghama		O	o	𝒪	o	omikron
Δ	δ	𝒟	δ	dhelta		Π	π	𝜋	π	pi
E	ε	ℰ	ε	epsilon		P	ρ	𝒫	ρ	ro
Z	ζ	𝒵	ζ	zita		Σ	σ ς	𝛴	ς ς	sighma
H	η	ℋ	η	ita		T	τ	𝒯	τ	taf
Θ	θ	𝛩	θ	thita		Y	υ	𝒴	υ	ipsilon
I	ι	𝰍	ι	iota		Φ	φ	φ	φ	fi
K	κ	𝒦	κ	kapa		X	χ	𝒳	χ	khi
Λ	λ	𝛬	λ	lamdha		Ψ	ψ	ψ	ψ	psi
M	μ	ℳ	μ	mi		Ω	ω	𝒬	ω	omegha

Some useful expressions

Hungry

I'm hungry/I'm thirsty.	Πεινῶ/Διψῶ.	pino/dhipso
Can you recommend a good restaurant?	Μπορεῖτε νά μοῦ ὑπο-δείξετε ἕνα καλό ἑστιατόριο;	borite na mu ipodhixete ena kalo estiatorio
Are there any good, cheap restaurants around here?	Ὑπάρχουν καλά, φθηνά ἑστιατόρια ἐδῶ κοντά;	iparkhun kala fthina estiatoria edho konda
I'd like to reserve a table for…people.	Θά ἤθελα νά κρατήσω ἕνα τραπέζι γιά…	tha ithela na kratiso ena trapezi yia…
We'll come at…	Θά ἔλθουμε στίς…	tha elthume stis

Asking

Good evening, I'd like a table for…people.	Καλησπέρα. Θά ἤθελα ἕνα τραπέζι γιά	kalispera. tha ithela ena trapezi yia…
Could we have a table…?	Θά μπορούσαμε νά ἔχουμε ἕνα τραπέζι…;	tha borusame na ekhume ena trapezi
in the corner	στή γωνία	sti ghonia
by the window	στό παράθυρο	sto parathiro
outside	ἔξω	exo
on the terrace	στή ταράτσα	sti taratsa
May I please have the menu?	Μοῦ δίνετε τό κατάλογο, παρακαλῶ;	mu dhinete to katalogho parakalo
What's this?	Τί εἶναι αὐτό;	ti ine afto
Do you have…?	Ἔχετε…;	ekhete
a set menu	τάμπλ-ντότ	tabl-dot
local dishes	σπεσιαλιτέ τῆς περιοχῆς	spesialite tis periokhis
a children's menu	μενού γιά παιδιά	menu yia pedhia
Waiter/Waitress!	Γκαρσόν!	garson
What do you recommend?	Τί μοῦ προτείνετε;	ti mu protinete
Could I have (a/an)…please?	Θά μπορούσα νά ἔχω… παρακαλῶ;	tha borisae na ekho…parakalo
ashtray	ἕνα στακτοδοχεῖο	ena staktodhokhio
another chair	μία καρέκλα ἀκόμη	mia karekla akomi
fork	ἕνα πηρούνι	ena piruni
glass	ἕνα ποτήρι	ena potiri

knife	ἕνα μαχαίρι	ena makheri
napkin	μία πετσέτα	mia petseta
plate	ἕνα πιάτο	ena piato
pepper mill	μία πιπεριέρα	mia piperiera
serviette	μία πετσέτα	mia petseta
spoon	ἕνα κουτάλι	ena kutali
toothpick	μία ὀδοντογλυφίδα	mia odhondoghlifidha

Ordering

I'd like a/an/some…	Θά ἤθελα …	tha ithela
aperitif	ἕνα ἀπεριτίφ	ena aperitif
appetizer	ἕνα ὀρεκτικό	ena orektiko
beer	μία μπύρα	mia bira
bread	ψωμί	psomi
butter	βούτυρο	vutiro
cheese	τυρί	tiri
chips	πατάτες τηγανιτές	patates tighanites
coffee	ἕνα καφέ	ena kafe
dessert	ἕνα γλυκό	ena ghliko
fish	ψάρι	psari
french fries	πατάτες τηγανιτές	patates tighanites
fruit	φροῦτα	fruta
game	κυνήγι	kiniyi
ice-cream	ἕνα παγωτό	ena paghoto
ketchup	λίγη κέτσαπ	liyi ketsap
lemon	ἕνα λεμόνι	ena lemoni
lettuce	μαρούλι	maruli
meat	κρέας	kreas
mineral water	μεταλλικό νερό	metaliko nero
milk	γάλα	ghala
mustard	μουστάρδα	mustardha
noodles	ζυμαρικά	zimarika
oil	λάδι	ladhi
olive oil	λάδι ἐλιᾶς	ladhi elias
pepper	πιπέρι	piperi
potatoes	πατάτες	patates
poultry	πουλερικά	pulerika
rice	ρύζι	rizi
rolls	ψωμάκια	psomakia
saccharin	ζαχαρίνη	zakharini
salad	σαλάτα	salata
salt	ἁλάτι	alati
sandwich	ἕνα σάντουῖτς	ena sanduïts
seafood	θαλασσινά	thalasina
seasoning	καρύκευμα	karikevma
soup	μία σούπα	mia supa

starter	ἕνα ὀπεκτικό	ena orektiko
sugar	λίγη ζάχαρη	liyi zakhari
tea	ἕνα τσάϊ	ena tsaï
vegetables	λαχανικά	lakhanika
vinegar	ξύδι	xidhi
(iced) water	(παγωμένο) νερό	(paghomeno) nero
wine	κρασί	krasi

ΚΑΛΗ ΣΑΣ ΟΡΕΞΗ

(kali sas orexi)

ENJOY YOUR MEAL!

---

baked	στό φοῦρνο	sto furno
baked in parchment	ψητό στό χαρτί	psito sto kharti
boiled	βραστό	vrasto
braised	μέ σάλτσα	me saltsa
cured	παστό	pasto
fried	τηγανιτό	tighanito
grilled	στή σχάρα	sti skhara
marinated	μαρινάτο	marinato
poached	βραστό	vrasto
roasted	ψητό	psito
sautéed	σωτέ	sote
smoked	καπνιστό	kapnisto
steamed	στόν ἀτμό	ston atmo
stewed	γιαχνί	yiakhni
underdone (rare)	λίγο ψημένο	ligho psimeno
medium	μέτριο	metrio
well-done	καλοψημένο	kalopsimeno
glass	ἕνα ποτήρι	ena potiri
bottle	ἕνα μπουκάλι	ena bukali

ΣΤΗΝ ΥΓΕΙΑ ΣΑΣ

(stin iyia sas)

CHEERS!

---

red	κόκκινο	kokino
white	ἄσπρο	aspro
rosé	ροζέ	roze
very dry	πολύ ξηρό	poli xiro
dry	ξηρό	xiro
sweet	γλυκό	ghliko
light	ἐλαφρό	elafro

full-bodied	πολύ γευστικό	poli yefstiko
sparkling	ἀεριοῦχο	aeriukho
neat (straight)	σκέτο	sketo
on the rocks	μέ παγάκια	me paghakia

The bill

I'd like to pay.	Θά ἤθελα νά πληρώσω.	tha ithela na pliroso
We'd like to pay separately.	Θέλουμε χωριστό λογαριασμό.	thelume khoristo loghariazmo
You've made a mistake in this bill, I think.	Νομίζω ὅτι κάνατε ἕνα λάθος στό λογαριασμό.	nomizó oti kanate ena lathos sto loghariazmo
What's this amount for?	Γιά τί εἶναι αὐτό τό ποσό;	yia ti ine afto to poso
Is service included?	Τό ποσοστό ὑπηρεσίας περιλαμβάνεται;	to pososto ipiresias perilamvanete
Is everything included?	Περιλαμβάνονται τά πάντα;	perilamvanonde ta panda
Do you accept traveller's cheques?	Δέχεστε τράβελερς τσέκ;	dhekheste travelers tsek
Thank you. This is for you.	Εὐχαριστῶ, αὐτό εἶναι γιά σᾶς.	efkharisto afto ine yia sas
Keep the change.	Κρατῆστε τά ψιλά.	kratiste ta psila
That was a very good meal.	Τό γεῦμα ἦταν πολύ ὡραῖο.	to yevma itan poli oreo
We enjoyed it, thank you.	Τό ἀπολαύσαμε, εὐχαριστοῦμε.	to apolafsame efkharistume

Complaints

That's not what I ordered. I asked for...	Δέν παρήγγειλα αὐτό. Ζήτησα ...	dhen paringila afto. zitisa
May I change this?	Μπορῶ νά ἀλλάξω αὐτό;	boro na alakso afto
The meat is...	Τό κρέας εἶναι ...	to kreas ine
overdone	πολύ ψημένο	poli psimeno
underdone	ἄψητο	apsito
too rare	ὠμό	omo
too tough	πολύ σκληρό	poli skliro
This is too...	Αὐτό εἶναι πολύ ...	afto ine poli
bitter/salty/sweet	πικρό/ἁλμυρό/γλυκό	pikro/almiro/ghliko

The food is cold.	Τό φαγητό εἶναι κρύο.	to fayito ine krio
This isn't fresh.	Αὐτό δέν εἶναι φρέσκο.	afto dhen ine fresko
What's taking you so long?	Γιατί ἀργεῖτε τόσο πολύ;	yiati aryite toso poli
Where are our drinks?	Ποῦ εἶναι τά ποτά μας;	pu ine ta pota mas
This isn't clean.	Αὐτό δέν εἶναι καθαρό.	afto dhen ine katharo
Would you ask the head waiter to come over?	Μπορεῖτε νά ζητήσετε στόν ἀρχισερβιτόρο νά ἔλθη ἐδῶ;	borite na zitisete ston arkhiservitoro na elthi edho

Numbers

1	ἕνας, μία, ἕνα	enas, mia, ena
2	δύο	dhio
3	τρία	tria
4	τέσσερα	tesera
5	πέντε	pende
6	ἕξη	exi
7	ἑπτά	epta
8	ὀκτώ	okto
9	ἐννέα	enea
10	δέκα	dheka
11	ἕντεκα	endeka
12	δώδεκα	dhodheka
13	δεκατρία	dhekatria
14	δεκατέσσερα	dhekatesera
15	δεκαπέντε	dhekapende
16	δεκαέξη	dhekaexi
17	δεκαεπτά	dhekaepta
18	δεκαοκτώ	dhekaokto
19	δεκαεννέα	dhekaenea
20	εἴκοσι	ikosi

Food

See also the index of Greek main entries, in Roman characters, on pages 319–321

ἀγγούρι (anguri) cucumber

ἀγκινάρες (anginares) artichoke
- ~ **ἀ λά πολίτα** (a la polita) with potatoes, carrots and chopped dill in oil and lemon dressing
- ~ **γεμιστές** (yemistes) stuffed with rice
- ~ **(μέ)κουκιά** ([me]kukia) with broad beans
- ~ **τηγανιτές** (tighanites) fried

ἀλάτι (alati) salt

ἀλατισμένο (alatizmeno) salted

ἀλεύρι (alevri) flour

ἀλμυρό (almiro) highly salted

ἀμύγδαλο (amighdhalo) almond

ἀμυγδαλωτό (amighdhaloto) marzipan

ἀνάλατο (analato) unsalted

ἄνηθος (anithos) dill

ἀρακᾶς (arakas) peas

ἀραβοσιτέλαιο (aravositeleo) Indian-corn oil (US corn oil)

ἀραχιδέλαιο (arakhidheleo) peanut oil

ἀρνί (arni) lamb
- ~ **ἀτζέμ πιλάφι** (adzem pilafi) lamb and rice stewed in tomato sauce
- ~ **βραστό** (vrasto) boiled lamb
- ~ **(τοῦ) γάλακτος** ([tu] ghalaktos) baby lamb
- ~ **ἐξοχικό** (exohiko) spiced lamb and cheese baked in parchment
- ~ **καπαμᾶς Μωραΐτικος** (kapamas moraïtikos) lamb braised in wine with tomatoes (Peloponnesos)
- ~ **(τῆς) κατσαρόλας** ([tis] katsarolas) lamb casserole with lemon dressing
- ~ **μπούτι** (buti) leg of lamb
- ~ **μπούτι στό χαρτί** (buti sto kharti) leg of lamb baked in parchment
- ~ **σέλινο αὐγολέμονο** (selino avgholemono) lamb braised with celery, served with egg and lemon dressing
- ~ **σκορδοστούμπι ζακυνθινό** (skordhostumbi zakinthino) spiced lamb in tomato and wine gravy (Zakinthos)
- ~ **σούβλας** (suvlas) spit-roasted
- ~ **τάς-κεμπάπ** (tas-kebap) with rice and tomato sauce
- ~ **φρικασέ** (frikase) braised with celery root, spring onions and carrots; served with white sauce
- ~ **ψητό** (psito) roasted

ἀστακός (astakos) lobster
- ~ **μαγιονέζα** (mayioneza) lobster with mayonnaise

ἀτζέμ πιλάφι (adzem pilafi) rice boiled in tomato sauce

(στόν) ἀτμό ([ston] atmo) steamed

αὐγό (avgho) egg
~ βραστό (vrasto) boiled egg
~ μάτι (mati) fried egg
~ μελάτο (melato) soft-boiled egg
~ σφικτό (sfikto) hard-boiled
~ τηγανιτό (tighanito) fried egg
αὐγολέμονο (avgholemono) egg and lemon dressing
ἀχινός (akhinos) sea urchin
ἀχλάδι (akhladhi) pear
βασιλικός (vasilikos) basil
βασιλόπιττα (vasilopita) cake flavoured with orange or mastic; traditionally served on New Year's Eve; a coin baked in the cake is to bring luck to the finder
βατόμουρα (vatomura) blackberries
βερύκοκα (verikoka) apricots
βουτήματα (vutimata) biscuits (US cookies)
βούτυρο (vutiro) butter
βραστό (vrasto) boiled
βυσσινάδα (visinadha) wild-cherry juice
γάλα (ghala) milk
γαλακτομπούρεκο (ghalaktobureko) flaky pastry filled with custard, steeped in syrup
γαλέος (ghaleos) lamprey eel
~ σκορδαλιά (skordhalia) with thick garlic sauce
~ τηγανιτός (tighanitos) fried
γαλοπούλα (ghalopula) turkey
~ γεμιστή (yemisti) stuffed with chestnuts, minced meat and pine nuts; a Christmas speciality
~ ψητή (psiti) roast turkey
γαρίδες (gharidhes) shrimp
~ πιλάφι (pilafi) shrimp with rice in tomato sauce
~ σαλάτα (salata) shrimp cocktail in oil, lemon and parsley

sauce
~ τηγανιτές (tighanites) fried
γεμιστό (yemisto) stuffed
γεῦμα (yevma) meal, lunch
γιαούρτι (yiaürti) yogurt
γιαουρτόπιττα (yiaürtopita) yogurt cake
γιουβαρλάκια αὐγολέμονο (yiuvarlakia avgholemono) rice-and meat-balls in egg and lemon sauce
γιουβέτσι (yiuvetsi) meat with noodles or macaroni, usually baked in a Dutch oven
γλυκά (ghlika) sweets (US candy)
~ τοῦ ταψιοῦ (tu tapsiu) refers to any sweet or pastry baked on a *tapsi* (baking sheet)
γλυκό (ghliko) sweet (adj.)
γλῶσσα (ghlosa) 1) tongue 2) sole
~ πανέ (pane) breaded sole
~ φιλέτο (fileto) fillet of sole
γουρουνόπουλο τοῦ γάλακτος (ghurunopulo tu ghalaktos) sucking pig
~ σούβλας (suvlas) roasted on the spit
γραβιέρα (ghraviera) swiss cheese; best varieties made in Corfu and Crete
γρανίτα (ghranita) water-ice (US sherbet)
δαμάσκηνα (dhamaskina) plums
δάφνη (dhafni) bay leaf
δεῖπνο (dhipno) dinner
δεντρολίβανο (dhendrolivano) rosemary
δίπλες (dhiples) puff pastry with walnuts, steeped in honey syrup
δυόσμος (dhiozmos) mint
ἐλαιόλαδο (eleoladho) olive oil
ἐλιές (elies) olives
~ Καλαμῶν (kalamon) big brown olives from Kalamata

ἐπιδόρπιο (epidhorpio) dessert

ζαμπόν (zambon) ham
~ **καπνιστό** (kapnisto) smoked ham

ζάχαρη (zakhari) sugar

ζελέ φρούτων (zele fruton) fruit jelly, eaten as a dessert

ζεστό (zesto) hot, warm

ζυμαρικά (zimarika) noodles, spaghetti, etc.

ζωμός (zomos) broth
~ **κότας** (kotas) chicken broth
~ **κρέατος** (kreatos) meat broth

θαλασσινά (thalasina) seafood

καβούρι (kavuri) crab

κακαβιά (kakavia) fish stew

καλαμάρια (kalamaria) squid
~ **τηγανιτά** (tighanita) fried

καλαμπόκι (kalamboki) Indian corn (US corn)

καλοψημένο (kalopsimeno) well done

κανέλλα (kanela) cinnamon

καπαμάς (kapamas) the way of braising meat in tomato and wine sauce (Peloponessos)

κάπαρη (kapari) capers

καραβίδα (karavidha) crawfish

(στά) κάρβουνα ([sta]karvuna) the coals, barbecued

καρπούζι (karpuzi) watermelon

καρύδα (karidha) coconut

καρύδια (karidhia) walnuts

καρυδόπιττα (karidhopita) walnut cake
~ **'Αθηναϊκή** (athinaïki) walnut cake steeped in cinnamon syrup (Athens)

καρύκευμα (karikevma) spice

καρότα (karota) carrots

κασέρι (kaseri) light yellow cheese, rich in cream with a soft texture

καταΐφι (kataïfi) a sweet made of sugared thin noodles, almonds, walnuts and syrup

κατάλογος (kataloghos) menu

κατσαρόλα (katsarola) casserole
τῆς ~ ς (tis) in a casserole

κεράσια (kerasia) cherries

κεφτέδες (keftedhes) meatballs
~ **μέ σάλτσα ντομάτα** (me saltsa domata) in tomato sauce
~ **στή σχάρα** (sti skhara) grilled
~ **τηγανιτοί** (tighaniti) fried
~ **φούρνου μέ αὐγά** (furnu me avgha) baked with eggs

κεφαλογραβιέρα (kefaloghraviera) mild yellow cheese, hard texture

κέφαλος (kefalos) mullet

κεφαλοτύρι (kefalotiri) yellow, very strong and salty cheese with tiny holes

κιμᾶς (kimas) minced meat

κόκορας (kokoras) stewing hen
~ **κοκκινιστός** (kokinistos) braised in tomato sauce
~ **μέ κρασί** (me krasi) braised in wine and tomato sauce

κόκκαλο (kokalo) bone

κοκκινιστό (kokinisto) meat or vegetables braised in tomato sauce

κοκορέτσι (kokoretsi) kidneys, tripe and liver grilled on a skewer

κολοκύθα (kolokitha) pumpkin

κολοκύθια (kolokithia) baby marrow (US zucchini)
~ **βραστά σαλάτα** (vrasta salata) as a salad with oil and vinegar dressing, flavoured with oregano
~ **γεμιστά** (yemista) stuffed with rice and/or meat
~ **μουσακᾶς** (musakas) layers of baby marrows (US zucchini) and minced meat topped with a white sauce and oven-browned
~ **μπριάμ** (briam) layers of baby

marrows (US zucchini), potatoes and tomatoes; baked

~ **παπουτσάκια** (paputsakia) baby marrows (US zucchini) stuffed with rice and/or minced meat, topped with sauce; baked

κολοκυθοκεφτέδες (kolokithokeftedhes) baby marrow (US zucchini) croquettes

κομπόστα (kombosta) stewed or tinned (US canned) fruit

~ **ἀχλάδι** (akhladhi) pears

~ **βερύκοκο** (verikoko) apricots

~ **κυδώνι** (kidhoni) quince

~ **μῆλο** (milo) apples

~ **ροδάκινο** (rodhakino) peaches

κοπενχάγη (kopenkhayi) tea bread (US sweet roll) with almond filling, steeped in syrup

κοτολέττα (kotoleta) cutlet, chop

~ **ἀρνίσια** (arnisia) lamb chop

~ **βωδινή** (vodhini) veal cutlet

~ **μοσχαρίσια** (moskharisia) rib or rib-eye steak

~ **πανέ** (pane) breaded cutlet, usually veal

~ **χοιρινή** (khirini) pork chop

κοτόπουλο (kotopulo) chicken

~ **βραστό** (vrasto) boiled

~ **(τῆς) κατσαρόλας** ([tis]katsarolas) in a casserole; served with a butter and lemon sauce

~ **κοκκινιστό** (kokinisto) braised with tomatoes

~ **μέ μπάμιες** (me bamies) braised in tomato sauce with okra

~ **μπούτι** (buti) chicken leg

~ **στή σούβλα** (sti suvla) spit-roasted

~ **στή σχάρα** (sti skhara) grilled

~ **στῆθος** (stithos) breast of chicken

~ **τηγανιτό** (tighanito) fried

~ **ψητό** (psito) roasted

κοτόσουπα (kotosupa) chicken broth

κουζίνα (kuzina) 1) kitchen 2) way of cooking in general

κουνουπίδι (kunupidhi) cauliflower

~ **σαλάτα** (salata) cauliflower salad with oil and lemon sauce

κουκιά (kukia) broad beans

~ **μέ ἀγκινάρες** (me anginares) with artichoke

κουλούρα (kulura) round bread, usually found in villages

κουλουράκια (kulurakia) round biscuits (US cookies)

κουλούρι (kuluri) doughnut-shaped rolls with sesame seeds

κουνέλι (kuneli) rabbit

~ **κρασάτο** (krasato) braised in wine

~ **στιφάδο** (stifadho) braised with spring onions, bay leaf, cloves, red wine and tomato sauce

κουραμπιές (kurambies) almond biscuits (US cookies)

κρέας (kreäs) meat

~ **ἀρνίσιο** (arnisio) lamb

~ **βραστό** (vrasto) boiled meat

~ **βωδινό** (vodhino) veal

~ **μοσχαρίσιο** (moskharisio) beef

~ **χοιρινό** (khirino) pork

~ **ψητό** (psito) roasted meat

κρεατόπιττα (kreätopitta) minced-meat pie

~ **Γιαννιώτικη** (yianiotiki) with eggs, grated cheese, onions and parsley (Yannina)

~ **Κεφαλληνίας** (kefalinias) very spicy meat pie with *feta* cheese, rice, potatoes, onions, garlic (Cephalonia)

κρέμα (krema) cream

~ **καραμελέ** (karamele) caramel mousse (US caramel pudding)

κρεμμύδι (kremidhi) onions

~ **φρέσκο** (fresko) spring onions

κρεμμυδόσουπα (kremidhosoupa) onion soup

κροκέττες (kroketes) meat, vegetable or fish fritters, croquettes

~ **από ψάρι** (apo psari) fish fritters

~ **μέ κρέας** (me kreäs) deep-fried meat fritters

~ **μέ μελιτζάνες** (me melidzanes) fried aubergine (eggplant) croquettes

~ **μέ ρύζι** (me rizi) rice fritters

κρύο (krio) cold

~ **κρέας** (kreäs) cold cuts

κυδόνι (kidhoni) quince

~ **πελτές** (peltes) quince jelly

κυδώνια (kidhonia) clams

κύμινο (kimino) cumin

κυνήγι (kiniyi) fowl

λαγός (laghos) hare

~ **στιφάδο** (stifadho) braised with pearl onions in tomato sauce

~ **στό φούρνο** (sto furno) roasted

λαδερό (ladhero) cooked in oil

~ **φαγητό** (fayito) cooked vegetable dish, usually stuffed with rice and cooked or served with olive oil

λάδι (ladhi) oil

λαδολέμονο (ladholemono) olive oil and lemon dressing

λαδόξυδο (ladhoxidho) olive oil and vinegar dressing

λακέρδα (lakerdha) salted tunny (US tuna)

λαρδί (lardhi) bacon

λαχανικά (lakhanika) vegetables

λάχανο (lakhano) cabbage

~ **ντολμάδες** (dolmadhes) cabbage leaves stuffed with rice and minced meat, braised in white sauce

~ **σαλάτα** (salata) cole slaw

λεμόνι (lemoni) lemon

λίπος (lipos) fat

λουκάνικο (lukaniko) sausage

~ **χωριάτικο** (khoriatiko) hot pork sausage

λουκουμάδες (lukumadhes) light, deep-fried, crisp puffs; served warm in honey syrup

λουκούμι (lukumi) Turkish delight

λυθρίνι (lithrini) grey mullet

~ **στή σχάρα** (sti skhara) grilled

~ **τηγανιτό** (tighanito) fried

μαγειρίτσα (mayiritsa) soup made of minced lamb entrails, dill, egg and lemon sauce; served traditionally at Easter

μαγιονέζα (mayioneza) mayonnaise

μαϊντανός (maïdanos) parsley

μακαρόνια (makaronia) macaroni

~ **μέ κιμά** (me kima) with meat sauce

~ **μέ σάλτσα ντομάτα** (me saltsa domata) in tomato sauce

~ **παστίτσιο** (pastitsio) layers of macaroni and minced meat with white sauce; baked

~ **παστίτσιο μέ φύλλο** (pastitsio me filo) macaroni and minced meat rolled and baked in a crust

μαλακό (malako) soft

μανέστρα (manestra) noodles

~ **σούπα** (supa) noodle and tomato soup

μανιτάρια (manitaria) mushrooms

μανούρι (manuri) a kind of fresh whey cheese, often mixed with honey as a dessert

μανταρίνι (mandarini) tangerine

μάντολες (mandoles) sugared almonds (Cephalonia)

μαντολάτο (mandolato) nougat (Zakinthos)

μαργαρίνη (margharini) margarine

μαρίδες (maridhes) whitebait

μαρινάτο (marinato) marinated

μαρμελάδα (marmeladha) jam

μαρούλι (maruli) lettuce

~ **σαλάτα** (salata) lettuce salad

μεζές (mezes) titbit

μεζεδάκια (mezedhakia) titbits served as appetizers

μέλι (meli) honey

μελιτζάνες (melidzanes) aubergine (eggplant)

~ **γεμιστές μέ ρύζι** (yemistes me rizi) stuffed with rice and onions

~ **ἰμάμ** (imam) stuffed with chopped tomato, onion and parsley and covered with grated cheese and breadcrumbs; baked

~ **κροκέττες** (kroketes) fritters

~ **μέ κρέας** (me kreäs) stewed with meat

~ **μουσακᾶς** (musakas) layers of aubergine (eggplant) and minced meat topped with white sauce, baked

~ **παπουτσάκια** (paputsakia) stuffed with rice and/or meat topped with white sauce; baked

~ **πουρές** (pures) mashed

~ **τηγανιτές** (tighanites) fried

~ **τουρσί** (tursi) pickled

μελιτζανοκεφτέδες (melidzanokeftedhes) fried aubergine (eggplant) and meatballs

μελιτζανοσαλάτα (melidzanosalata) aubergine (eggplant) baked and mashed, flavoured with olive oil, minced onion, garlic and parsley; served chilled as an appetizer or salad

μελοκάρυδο (melokaridho) small cake made of honey and walnuts

μελομακάρονα (melomakarona) pastry steeped in honey syrup

μερίδα (meridha) portion

μέτριο (metrio) medium (of meat)

μῆλο (milo) apple

μηλόπιττα (milopitta) apple tart

μισό (miso) half

μοσχάρι (moskhari) beef

~ **βραστό** (vrasto) boiled beef

~ **καπαμᾶς** (kapamas) braised with tomatoes and wine

~ **κοκκινιστό** (kokinisto) braised with tomatoes

~ **σέλινο αὐγολέμονο** (selino avgholemono) braised with celery in egg and lemon sauce

~ **σουβλάκι** (suvlaki) spit-roasted chunks of beef

~ **φρικασέ** (frikase) braised with celery root, spring onions, carrots and white sauce

~ **ψητό στό φοῦρνο** (psito sto furno) roast beef

μοσχοκάρυδο (moskhokaridho) nutmeg

μουσακᾶς (musakas) layers of vegetables and minced meat topped with white sauce; baked

~ **κολοκύθια** (kolokithia) with baby marrows (US zucchini)

~ **μελιτζάνες** (melidzanes) with aubergine (eggplant)

~ **πατάτες** (patates) with potatoes

μουσταλευριά (mustalevria) grape

jam with almonds and cinnamon

μουστάρδα (mustardha) mustard

μουστοκούλουρα (mustokulura) grape biscuits (US cookies)

μπακαλιάρος (bakaliaros) cod

~ **άλμυρός** (almiros) dried cod

~ **γιαχνί** (yiakhni) dried cod in tomato sauce

~ **σκορδαλιά** (skordhalia) cod with garlic sauce

~ **φιλέττα πανέ** (fileta pane) breaded cod fillets

μπακλαβᾶς (baklavas) flaky pastry filled with nuts and steeped in syrup

μπάμιες (bamies) okra

~ **λαδερές** (ladheres) stewed in oil

~ **μέ κοτόπουλο** (me kotopulo) with chicken

~ **στό φοῦρνο** (sto furno) baked with tomatoes and onions

μπανάνα (banana) banana

μπαρμπούνια (barbunia) red mullet

~ **στή σχάρα** (sti skhara) grilled

~ **τηγανιτό** (tighanito) fried

μπαχαρικά (bakharika) spices

μπεκάτσες (bekatses) woodcock

~ **σαλμί** (salmi) in spicy tomato and wine sauce

μπεσαμέλ (besamel) white sauce

μπιζέλια (bizelia) green peas

μπισκότα (biskota) biscuits (US cookies)

μπιφτέκια (biftekia) meat rissoles (US patties)

~ **στή σχάρα** (sti skhara) grilled

~ **στό φοῦρνο** (sto furno) baked

~ **τηγανιτά** (tighanita) fried

μπουρεκάκια (burekakia) stuffed pasties, rissoles

~ **μέ κιμᾶ** (me kima) minced

meat

~ **μέ σπανάκι** (me spanaki) spinach

~ **μέ τυρί** (me tiri) cheese

μπούτι (buti) leg

μπριάμι (briami) baked casserole of baby marrow (US zucchini), potatoes and tomatoes

μπριζόλα (brizola) cutlet, chop

~ **ἀρνίσια** (arnisia) lamb chop

μυαλά (miala) brains

~ **πανέ** (pane) breaded and fried

~ **τηγανιτά** (tighanita) fried

μύδια (midhia) mussels

~ **μέ πιλάφι** (me pilafi) cooked with rice and tomatoes

~ **τηγανιτά** (tighanita) fried

μυζήθρα (mizithra) soft, salted cheese made from ewe's milk

νεφρά (nefra) kidneys

νεφραμιά (neframia) sirloin steak

ντολμάδες (dolmadhes) cabbage or grape leaves stuffed with rice or minced meat

~ **αὐγολέμονο** (avgholemono) served with egg and lemon dressing

~ **γιαλαντζῆ** (yialandzi) stuffed with rice; steeped in oil

~ **μέ λάχανο** (me lakhano) served with white sauce

~ **μέ φύλλα μαρουλιοῦ** (me fila maruliu) stuffed lettuce leaves

ντομάτες (domates) tomatoes

~ **γεμιστές** (yemistes) baked stuffed tomatoes

~ **μέ κιμᾶ** (me kima) tomatoes stuffed with meat and/or rice

~ **μέ ρύζι** (me rizi) baked tomatoes stuffed with rice and onions

ντοματοσαλάτα (domatosalata) tomato salad

ντοματόσουπα (domatosoupa) tomato soup

ντονέρ (doner) leg of lamb or mutton broiled on a vertical spit; as the meat cooks, thin slices are cut off and served on a flat, round bread

ξυδᾶτο (xidhato) cooked in a vinegar solution

ξύδι (xidhi) vinegar

ὀμελέττα (omeleta) omelet
~ **μέ ζαμπόν** (me zambon) ham
~ **μέ λουκάνικα** (me lukanika) sausage
~ **μέ ντομάτα** (me domata) tomato
~ **μέ πατάτες** (me patates) potato
~ **μέ συκωτάκια πουλιῶν** (me sikotakia pulion) chicken-liver
~ **μέ τυρί** (me tiri) cheese

ὀρεκτικά (orektika) appetizers

ὀρτύκια (ortikia) quail
~ **μέ ντομάτα** (me domata) with tomato sauce

οὐρά βωδινή (ura vodhini) oxtail

παγωμένο (paghomeno) iced

παγωτό (paghoto) ice-cream
~ **ἀνάμικτο** (anamikto) mixed
~ **βανίλλια** (vanilia) vanilla
~ **κασσάτα** (kasata) Neapolitan ice cream (US spumoni)
~ **σοκολάτα** (sokolata) chocolate
~ **φράουλα** (fraula) strawberry

παϊδάκια ἀρνίσια (païdhakia arnisia) lamb chops

πανέ (pane) breaded

πάπια (papia) duck

πάστα (pasta) pastry, plain cake
~ **ἀμυγδάλου** (amighdhalu) almond
~ **σοκολατίνα** (sokolatina) chocolate
~ **φλῶρα** (flora) jam
~ **φρούτου** (frutu) fruit

παστέλι (pasteli) honey and sesame bar

παστιτσάδα (pastitsadha) veal or beef braised with garlic, onions, bay leaves and noodles (Corfu)

παστίτσιο (pastitsio) layers of noodles and minced meat topped with white sauce and baked

παστό (pasto) cured

πατάτες (patates) potatoes
~ **βραστές** (vrastes) boiled
~ **γεμιστές** (yemistes) stuffed with rice and/or minced meat
~ **πουρέ** (pure) mashed
~ **στό φοῦρνο** (sto furno) baked
~ **τηγανιτές** (tighanites) fried
~ **τσίπς** (tsips) crisps (US potato chips)
~ **ψητές** (psites) roasted

πατατοκεφτέδες (patatokeftedhes) fried potato croquettes

πατζάρι (padzari) beetroot
~ **α σκορδαλιά** (a skordhalia) with garlic dressing

πατσᾶς (patsas) tripe

παχύ (pakhi) thick

πεπόνι (peponi) melon

πέρδικα (perdhika) partridge

περιστέρι (peristeri) pigeon

πέρκα (perka) perch

πέστροφα (pestrofa) trout

πηχτή (pikhti) aspic

πιατέλα (piatela) platter

πιάτο (piato) plate, dish

πικρό (pikro) bitter

πιλάφι (pilafi) rice casserole
~ **ἀτζέμ** (adzem) with tomatoes
~ **μέ γαρίδες** (me gharidhes) with shrimp
~ **μέ κιμᾶ** (me kima) with minced meat and tomatoes
~ **μέ μύδια** (me midhia) with mussels
~ **τάς-κεμπάπ** (tas-kebap) with

tomatoes and meat
πιπέρι (piperi) black pepper
πιπεριά (piperia) sweet pepper
~ **πράσινη** (prasini) green pepper
πιπεριές γεμιστές (piperies yemistes) green peppers stuffed with rice
πιτσούνια (pitsunia) young pigeon, squab
~ **γεμιστά** (yemista) stuffed
~ **σαλμί** (salmi) braised with tomatoes and wine in a spicy broth
πίττα (pitta) a flat, round bread
πληγούρι (plighuri) cracked-wheat noodles
~ **γιουβέτσι** (yiuvetsi) roasted leg of lamb or mutton served with tomatoes and cracked-wheat noodles
ποδαράκια αρνίσια αυγολέμονο (podharakia arnisia avgholemono) leg of lamb with egg and lemon dressing
ποικιλία ὀρεκτικῶν (pikilia orektikon) assorted appetizers
πορτοκάλι (portokali) orange
πουλερικά (pulerika) fowl
πουρές (pures) mashed or puréed vegetables or fruit
~ **μελιτζάνες** (melidzanes) aubergines (eggplant)
~ **πατάτες** (patates) mashed potatoes
~ **σπανάκι** (spanaki) spinach
πράσσα (prassa) leeks
~ **μέ ρύζι** (me rizi) with rice
πρόγευμα (proyevma) breakfast
προϊόντα (proïonda) products
~ **κατεψυγμένα** (katepsighmena) frozen food
~ **φρέσκα** (freska) fresh produce
ραδίκια (radhikia) dandelion

greens
ραπανάκια (rapanakia) radishes
ρεβανί (revani) kind of sponge cake steeped in syrup
ρεβίθια (revithia) chick-peas
ρέγγα (renga) herring
~ **καπνιστή** (kapnisti) smoked herring
ρίγανη (righani) oregano
ροδάκινο (rodhakino) peach
ρόδι (rodhi) pomegranate
ρολλό μέ αυγά (rollo me avgha) meatloaf stuffed with eggs
ρύζι (rizi) rice
ρυζόγαλο (rizoghalo) rice pudding
σαγανάκι (saghanaki) cheese croquette with lemon and butter dressing
σαλάμι (salami) salami
σαλάτα (salata) salad
~ **ἀγγούρι** (anguri) cucumber
~ **γαρίδες** (gharidhes) shrimp
~ **λάχανο** (lakhano) cole slaw with lemon and olive oil dressing
~ **μελιτζάνες** (melidzanes) aubergine (eggplant)
~ **ντομάτα** (domata) tomato
~ **πατζάρια** (padzaria) beetroot
~ **σατζίκι** (sadziki) salad made of yogurt, cucumber, garlic, olive oil and mint
~ **σκορδαλιά** (skordhalia) crushed garlic combined with mashed potatoes and olive oil
ταραμο ~ (taramo~) cod or mullet roe combined with bread, olive oil, lemon juice seasoning
~ **φρούτων** (fruton) fruit cocktail
~ **χόρτα** (khorta) greens, such as endive (US chicory) or dandelion, boiled and served cold with an olive oil and lemon

dressing

~ **χωριάτικη** (khoriatiki) salad of tomatoes, cucumber, onion, peppers, olives, *feta* cheese, parsley and oregano

σάλτσα (saltsa) sauce

~ **άσπρη** (aspri) white sauce

~ **αυγολέμονο** (avgholemono) egg and lemon dressing

~ **λαδολέμονο** (ladholemono) oil and lemon dressing

~ **λαδόξυδο** (ladhoxidho) vinegar and oil dressing

~ **μαγιονέζα** (mayioneza) mayonnaise

~ **ντομάτα** (domata) tomato sauce with parsley and onions

~ **πράσινη** (prasini) parsleyed mayonnaise

~ **ψητού** (psitu) gravy

σαντιγύ (sandiyi) whipped cream

σαρδέλλες (sardheles) sardines

σβίγγοι (svingi) fritters

σέλινο (selino) celery

~ **κρέας αυγολέμονο** (kreās avgholemono) meat with celery in egg and lemon dressing

σιμιγδάλι (simighdhali) farina

σιρόπι (siropi) syrup

σκαλτσουνάκια σιφνέϊκα (skaltsunakia sifneïka) a turnover stuffed with fruit, chopped almonds or nuts and cinnamon (Sifnos)

σκέτο (sketo) plain

σκληρό (skliro) hard

σκορδαλιά (skordhalia) a salad of minced garlic, potatoes or bread with onions

σκόρδο (skordho) garlic

σοκολάτα (sokolata) chocolate

σοκολατάκια (sokolatakia) assorted chocolates

σολομός (solomos) salmon

(στή) σούβλα ([sti]suvla) on a spi

σουβλάκι (suvlaki) meat on a spi

~ **μέ πίττα** (me pitta) snack consisting of pieces of meat grilled on a spit with tomatoes, onions and parsley wrapped in round, flat bread (*pitta*)

~ **χωριάτικο** (khoriatiko) meat on a spit served at counters with a slice of bread

σούπα (supa) soup

~ **αυγολέμονο** (avgholemono) poultry or meat broth with rice, egg, lemon juice

~ **βραστό** (vrasto) broth meat

~ **κακαβιά** (kakavia) fish stew

κοτό~ (koto~) chicken broth

~ **μαγειρίτσα** (mayiritsa) Easter soup made of minced lamb entrails, dill, egg and lemon juice

~ **ντομάτα** (domata) tomato

~ **πατσάς** (patsas) tripe

~ **ρεβύθια** (revithia) chick-pea

~ **τραχανάς** (trakhanas) made with yoghurt or sour cream with cracked-wheat dumplings

~ **φακή** (faki) lentil

~ **φασόλια** (fasolia) butter bean (US navy-bean)

χορτό~ (khorto~) vegetable

~ **χυλοπίττες** (khilopites) tomato with square noodles

ψαρό ~ (psaro~) fish

σουπιές (supies) cuttlefish

~ **μέ σπανάκι** (me spanaki) braised with spinach

σουτζουκάκια σμυρνέϊκα (sudzukakia smirneïka) cumin-flavoured meat-balls braised with tomato sauce

σοφρίτο (sofrito) meat stewed in a wine-vinegar with garlic (Corfu)

σπανάκι (spanaki) spinach

σπανακόπιττα (spanakopita) spinach pasty

σπανακόρυζο (spanakorizo) spinach cooked with rice

σπαράγγια (sparangia) asparagus

σπιτικό (spitiko) homemade

σπλήνα (splina) spleen

~ γεμιστή (yemisti) stuffed with rice, onions, pine nuts and tomatoes; baked

σταφίδα (stafidha) raisins

~ σουλτανιά (sultania) sultanas, raisins

σταφύλι (stafili) grapes

~ άσπρο (aspro) green grapes

~ κόκκινο (kokino) red grapes

~ μαύρο (mavro) black grapes

~ σουλτανιά (sultania) seedless grapes

στήθος (stithos) breast

στιφάδο (stifadho) a method of braising meat with spring onions, tomatoes and wine

~ κουνέλι (kuneli) with rabbit

στό φούρνο (sto furno) baked

στρείδια (stridhia) oysters

~ τηγανιτά (tighanita) fried

σύκα (sika) figs

συκώτι (sikoti) liver

~ στή σχάρα (sti skhara) grilled

~ τηγανιτά (tighanita) fried

~ τάς-κεμπάπ (tas-kebap) sliced liver in tomato sauce, usually served with rice

συναγρίδα (sinaghridha) sea bream

σφυρίδα (sfiridha) whiting

σφολιάτα ζύμη (sfoliata zimi) crust, short-pastry dough

(στή) σχάρα ([sti] skhara) grilled

ταραμάς (taramas) cod or mullet roe

ταραμοκεφτέδες (taramokeftedhes) balls of cod or mullet roe

ταραμοσαλάτα(taramosalata) cod or mullet-roe salad with bread, olive oil and lemon juice

ταψί (tapsi) baking sheet

~ γλυκά τοῦ ταψιοῦ (ghlika tu tapsiu) refers to any sweet or pastry baked on a *tapsi*

τουρσί (tursi) pickles (US pickled vegetables)

τηγανίτα (tighanita) fritter

τηγανιτό (tighanito) fried

τῆς ὥρας (tis oras) made to order

τιμή (timi) price

~ καθωρισμένη (kathorizmeni) set price

τόννος (tonos) tunny (US tuna)

τριμμένο (trimeno) chopped or grated

τρόφιμα (trofima) food

τρυφερό (trifero) tender

τσάï (tsaï) tea

τσιπούρα (tsipura) gilthead (fish)

τσουρέκι (tsureki) bun

τυρί (tiri) cheese

τυρόπιττα (tiropita) cheese tart

τυροπιττάκια (tiropitakia) small cheese tarts

φάβα (fava) yellow lentils

φακή (faki) lentils

φασιανός (fasianos) pheasant

φασόλια (fasolia) beans

~ γιαχνί (yiakhni) butter beans (US navy beans) in tomato sauce

~ ξερά (xera) dried butter beans (US navy beans)

~ πράσινα (prasina) green beans

~ σαλάτα μπιάζ (salata biaz) butter beans (US navy beans) with tomatoes, onions and parsley

φέτα (feta) 1) slice; 2) the best

known Greek cheese, made of goat's or ewe's milk, white and crumbly

φιδές (fidhes) thin noodles

~ **σούπα** (supa) noodle soup

φιλέτο (fileto) fillet

φιλοδώρημα (filodhorima) tip

φουντούκια (fundukia) hazelnuts

φράουλες (fraüles) strawberries

φράπα (frapa) grapefruit

φρατζόλα (fradzola) white bread; like English or American white bread

φρέσκο (fresko) fresh

φρικασέ (frikase) cooked with onions and carrots in a creamy sauce

φρούτα (fruta) fruit

~ **ἐποχῆς** (epokhis) fruit of the season

φρουτοσαλάτα (frutosalata) fruit cocktail

φτερούγα (fterugha) wing

φυστίκια (fistikia) nuts

~ **Αἰγίνης** (eyinis) pistachios

~ **ἀράπικα** (arapika) peanuts

χαλβᾶς (khalvas) a sugary loaf made from farina and almonds

~ **τῆς Ρήνας** (tis rinas) flavoured with cinnamon

χέλι (kheli) eel

~ **τηγανιτό** (tighanito) fried

χήνα (khina) goose

~ **γεμιστή** (yemisti) stuffed

χοιρινή μπριζόλα (khirini brizola) pork chop

χοιρινό (khirino) pork

~ **μέ σέλινα** (me selina) with celery in egg and lemon

χόρτα (khorta) herbs

~ **σαλάτα** (salata) greens, such as endive (US chicory) or dandelion, boiled and served cold with an olive oil and lemon dressing

χορτόπιττα (khortopita) herb tart

χορτόσουπα (khortosupa) vegetable soup

χουρμάδες (khurmadhes) dates

χταπόδι (khtapodhi) octopus

~ **βραστό** (vrasto) boiled

~ **κρασσάτο** (krasato) stewed in wine

~ **μέ πιλάφι** (me pilafi) stewed with rice and tomatoes

~ **στιφάδο** (stifadho) braised with onions and tomatoes

χυλοπίττες (khilopittes) square noodles

ψάρι (psari) fish

~ **βραστό** (vrasto) poached

~ **μαγιονέζα Ἀθηναϊκή** (mayioneza athinaïki) fish salad

~ **μαρινάτο** (marinato) marinated

~ **πανέ** (pane) breaded, fried

~ **πλακί** (plaki) baked sliced with tomatoes, parsley and bread crumbs

~ **στή σχάρα** (sti skhara) grilled

~ **φούρνου** (furnu) baked

~ **φούρνου σπετσιώτικο** (furnu spetsiotiko) braised with tomatoes, olive oil, parsley and spices (Spetse)

ψαρόσουπα (psarosupa) fish soup

ψητό (psito) roasted

~ **τῆς κατσαρόλας** (tis katsarolas) pot roasted, baked in a Dutch oven

ψωμί (psomi) bread

~ **ἡμίλευκο** (imilefko) white bread, using unblanched flour

~ **μαῦρο** (mavro) wholemeal bread (US wholewheat bread)

~ **μέ σουσάμι** (me susami) sesame bread

~ **χωριάτικο** (khoriatiko) rye

bread, called village bread because in the villages it's still | homemade
ὠμό (omo) raw, cured

Drink

ἀεριοῦχο (aeriukho) sparkling

Ἄλφα (alfa) one of the best-known brands of Greek beer

ἀναψυκτικό (anapsiktiko) soft drink

Ἀττική (attiki) Attica, the vicinity of Athens; nearly all the country's resinated wine is produced here; most of it white but there is some rosé

Βερντέα (verndea) dry white wine (Zakinthos)

βυσσινάδα (vissinadha) morellocherry juice

γάλα (ghala) milk

~ **ἀποβουτυρωμένο** (apovutiromeno) skim milk

γκαζόζα (gazoza) soda water

γλυκό (ghliko) sweet

ζεστό (zesto) warm

Ζίτσα (zitsa) sparkling white wine (Epirus)

Ἤπειρος (ipiros) Epirus, the northwestern part of Greece bordering on the Ionian Sea, produces much white table wine

θερμοκρασία δωματίου (thermokrasia domatiu) room temperature

Ἰόνιοι Νήσοι (ionii nisi) Ionian Islands; vineyards are found on most of the islands in the Ionian Sea; the white table wine of Cephalonia (its *Rombola*) and of Zakinthos (its *Verdea*) are con-

sidered quite good; Corfu and Levkas (*Santa Mavra*) have red table wine

κακάο (kakao) cocoa

καράφα (karafa) carafe

καφές (kafes) coffee

~ **(μέ) γάλα** ([me]ghala) white

~ **ἐξπρέσσο** (expreso) espresso

τούρκικος ~ (turkikos) "Turkish coffee"; boiled

~ **φραπέ** (frape) iced

~ **χωρίς καφεΐνη** (khoris kafeïni) caffeine-free

κίτρο (kitro) lemon liqueur (Naxos)

κοκτέϊλ (kokteïl) cocktail

κονιάκ (koniak) brandy

κουμ-κουάτ (kum-kuat) kumquat liqueur (Corfu)

κρασί (krasi) wine

~ **ἀεριοῦχο** (aeriukho) sparkling

~ **ἀρετσίνωτο** (aretsinoto) nonresinated

~ **ἄσπρο** (aspro) white

~ **γλυκό** (ghliko) dessert wine

~ **κόκκινο** (kokkino) red

~ **μοσχάτο** (moskhato) muscat wine

~ **ξηρό** (xiro) dry

~ **ρετσίνα** (retsina) resinated wine; about half of the Greek wines contain sandarac, a pine resin; the best resinated wine is produced in the Attica region

~ **ροζε** (rose) rosé wine

Κρήτη (kriti) Crete, an important island to the south of Athens, produces predominantly red table wine

κρύο (krio) cold

λεμονάδα (lemonadha) lemon drink

~ **μέ ἀνθρακικό**(me anthrakiko) lemon soda

λικέρ (liker) liqueur

λίτρο(litro) litre

Μακεδονία (makedhonia) Macedonia, the region to the north of Greece, produces mostly red table wine

μαστίχα(mastikha) mastic liqueur (Chios)

μαυροδάφνη (mavrodhafni) red dessert wine (Peloponnesus)

Μεταξᾶ (metaxa) the best-known brand of Greek brandy

μηλίτης (militis) apple cider

μισό (miso) half

μπουκάλι (bukali) bottle

μπύρα (bira) beer

νερό (nero) water

μεταλλικό ~ (metaliko) mineral water

Νήσοι Αἰγαίου (nisi egheu) Aegean Islands; nearly all the islands scattered throughout the Aegean produce table wine, some of it of very good quality; Samos is noted for its white muscat wine; either red or white table wine is found on islands like Andros, Kos, Milos or Naxos while Karpathos, Chios and Rhodes produce white table wine; red wine is produced on the islands of Ikaria and Lemnos

οἰνοπνευματώδες (inopnevmato-dhes) alcoholic drink

οὖζο (uzo) aniseed-flavoured liqueur; best brands: *San Rival Masters, Achaia Clauss, 22 Tyrnavos*

παγάκια (paghakia) ice cubes

(μέ) πάγο ([me] pagho) on the rocks

πάγος (paghos) ice

παγωμένο (paghomeno) iced, chilled

Πελοπόννησος (peloponisos) Peloponnesus, the peninsula forming the southern part of the Greek mainland; the nation's most important wine-growing region; over a third of Greece's vineyards are located here; the Peloponnesus is noted for its red dessert wine like *Malvasia, Mavrodaphni,* a sweet red wine, is considered the region's most notable wine

πικρό (pikro) bitter

πορτοκαλάδα (portokaladha) orangeade

~ **(μέ) ἀνθρακικό** ([me] anthrakiko) orange soda

ποτήρι(potiri) glass

ποτό (poto) drink

ρακί (raki) aniseed-flavoured liqueur

ρετσίνα (retsina) resinated wine; about half of the Greek wines contain sandarac, a pine resin; the best resinated wine is produced in the Attica region

Ρομπόλα(rombola) dry white wine produced on the island of Cephalonia

ροῦμι (rumi) rum

σαμπάνια (sambania) a sparkling, champagne-like wine; best brands: *Cuvée Réservée, Achaia*

Clauss] *Côte d'Or*

Σάντα Μαύρα (santa mavra) red dry wine produced in the island of Levkas

σκέτο (sketo) neat (US straight)

σοκολάτα (sokolata) chocolate

σουμάδα (sumadha) soft drink made with almonds

Στερεά Ἑλλάς (stereä elas) Sterea Ellas, the region to the north-west of Athens, has red table wine

τσάϊ (tsaï) tea

~ **(μέ) γάλα** ([me] ghala) with milk

~ **(μέ) λεμόνι** ([me] lemoni) with lemon

Φίξ (fiks) best-known brand of Greek beer

Θεσσαλία (thesalia) Thessaly, located between Sterea Ellas and Macedonia; has mainly red table wine

Θράκη (thraki) Thrace, on the northeastern corner of Greece, produces principally red table wine

φλυτζάνι (flidzani) cup

χυμός (himos) juice

~ **μανταρινιοῦ** (mandariniu) tangerine

~ **μήλου** (milu) apple juice

~ **πορτοκαλιοῦ** (portokaliu) orange

~ **ντομάτας** (domatas) tomato

~ **φρούτου** (frutu) fruit

Italian

Guide to pronunciation

Letter	Approximate pronunciation
Consonants	
b, d, f, k, l, m, n, p, qu, t, v	are pronounced as in English
c	1) before **e** and **i**, like **ch** in **ch**ip
	2) elsewhere, like **c** in **c**at
ch	like **c** in **c**at
g	1) before **e** and **i**, like **j** in **j**et
	2) elsewhere, like **g** in **g**o
gh	like **g** in **g**o
gl	like **lli** in mi**lli**on
gn	like **ni** in o**ni**on
h	always silent
r	trilled like a Scottish **r**
s	1) generally like **s** in **s**it
	2) sometimes like **z** in **z**oo

ITALIAN

sc	1) before **e, i,** like **sh** in **sh**ut
	2) elsewhere, like **sk** in **sk**in
z or **zz**	1) generally like **ts** in hi**ts**
	2) sometimes like **ds** in roa**ds**

Vowels

a	1) short, like **a** in c**a**r, but shorter
	2) long, like **a** in c**a**r
e	1) can always be pronounced like **ay** in g**ay**
	2) in correct speech, it's sometimes pronounced like **e** in g**e**t or, when long, more like **ai** in h**ai**r
i	like the **ee** in m**ee**t
o	1) can always be pronounced like **oa** in g**oa**t
	2) in correct speech, it's sometimes pronounced like **o** in g**o**t or, when long, more like **aw** in l**aw**
u	like the **oo** in f**oo**t

Two or more vowels

In groups of vowels, **a, e** and **o** are strong, and **i** and **u** are weak. When two strong vowels are next to each other, they're pronounced as two separate syllables, e.g., *beato*. When a strong and weak vowel are next to each other, the weak one is pronounced more quickly and with less stress (less loudly) than the strong one, e.g., *piede;* such sounds are diphthongs and constitute only one syllable. If the weak vowel is stressed, then it's pronounced as a separate syllable, e.g., *due*. Two weak vowels together are pronounced as a diphthong, and it's generally the second one that's more strongly stressed, e.g., *guida*.

Stressing of words

Generally, the vowel of the next to the last syllable is stressed. When a final vowel is stressed, it has an accent written over it (´ or `). Normally an accent is used only when the stress falls on a final vowel and not when it falls on syllables before the next to the last one.

Some useful expressions

Hungry

I'm hungry/I'm thirsty. — **Ho fame/Ho sete.**

Can you recommend a good restaurant? — **Può consigliarmi un buon ristorante?**

Are there any good, cheap restaurants around here? — **Vi sono dei buoni ristoranti economici qui vicino?**

I'd like to reserve a table for ... people. — **Vorrei riservare un tavolo per ... persone.**

We'll come at ... o'clock. — **Verremo alle ...**

Asking

Good evening. I'd like a table for ... people. — **Buona sera. Vorrei un tavolo per ... persone.**

Could we have a table...? — **Potremmo avere un tavolo...?**

in the corner — **d'angolo**
by the window — **vicino alla finestra**
outside — **all'aperto**
on the terrace — **sulla terrazza**

May I please have the menu? — **Per favore, mi può dare il menù?**

What's this? — **Cos'è questo?**

Do you have...? — **Avete...?**

a set menu — **un menù a prezzo fisso**
local dishes — **piatti locali**
a children's menu — **un menù per bambini**

Waiter/Waitress! — **Cameriere/Cameriera!**

What do you recommend? — **Cosa consiglia?**

Could I have (a/an)... please? — **Posso avere... per favore?**

ashtray — **un portacenere**
another chair — **un'altra sedia**
finger bowl — **una vaschetta lavadita**
fork — **una forchetta**
glass — **un bicchiere**
knife — **un coltello**

ITALIAN

napkin	un tovagliolo
plate	un piatto
pepper mill	un macinapepe
serviette	un tovagliolo
spoon	un cucchiaio
toothpick	uno stuzzicadenti

Ordering

I'd like a/an/some...	Vorrei...
aperitif	un aperitivo
appetizer	un antipasto
beer	una birra
bread	del pane
butter	del burro
cheese	del formaggio
chips	delle patatine fritte
coffee	un caffè
dessert	un dolce
fish	del pesce
french fries	delle patatine fritte
fruit	della frutta
game	della cacciagione
ice-cream	un gelato
lemon	un limone
lettuce	della lattuga
meat	della carne
mineral water	dell'acqua minerale
milk	del latte
mustard	della mostarda
noodles	della pasta asciutta
oil	dell'olio
olive oil	dell'olio d'oliva
pepper	del pepe
potatoes	delle patate
poultry	del pollo
rice	del riso
rolls	dei panini
saccharin	della saccarina
salad	dell'insalata
salt	del sale

ITALIAN

sandwich	**un sandwich**
seafood	**dei frutti di mare**
seasoning	**dei condimenti**
soup	**una minestra**
starter	**un antipasto**
sugar	**dello zucchero**
tea	**un tè**
vegetables	**delle verdure**
vinegar	**dell'aceto**
(iced) water	**dell'acqua (ghiacciata)**
wine	**del vino**

BUON APPETITO!
ENJOY YOUR MEAL!

---

baked	**al forno**
baked in parchment	**al cartoccio**
boiled	**lesso**
braised	**brasato**
cured	**salato**
fried	**fritto**
grilled	**ai ferri**
marinated	**marinato**
poached	**affogato**
roasted	**arrostito**
sautéed	**fritto in padella**
smoked	**affumicato**
steamed	**cotto a vapore**
stewed	**in umido**
underdone (rare)	**al sangue**
medium	**a puntino**
well-done	**ben cotto**

ITALIAN

CIN-CIN!
CHEERS!

---

glass	**un bicchiere**
bottle	**una bottiglia**

red	**rosso**
white	**bianco**
rosé	**rosatello**
very dry	**molto secco**
dry	**secco**
sweet	**dolce**
light	**leggero**
full-bodied	**pieno**
sparkling	**spumante**
neat (straight)	**liscio**
on the rocks	**con ghiaccio**

The bill

I'd like to pay.	**Vorrei pagare.**
We'd like to pay separately.	**Vorremmo pagare separatamente.**
You've made a mistake in this bill, I think.	**Penso che abbiate fatto un errore nel conto.**
What's this amount for?	**Per che cos'è questo importo?**
Is service included?	**È compreso il servizio?**
Is everything included?	**È tutto compreso?**
Do you accept traveller's cheques?	**Accettate i traveller's checques?**
Thank you. This is for you.	**Grazie, questo è per lei.**
Keep the change.	**Tenga la moneta.**
That was a very good meal.	**È stato un pasto molto buono.**
We enjoyed it, thank you.	**Ci è piaciuto, grazie.**

Complaints

That's not what I ordered.	**Non è ciò che avevo ordinato.**
I asked for...	**Avevo chiesto...**
May I change this?	**Posso cambiare questo?**
The meat is...	**La carne è...**
overdone	**troppo cotta**
underdone	**poco cotta**
too rare	**troppo al sangue**
too tough	**troppo dura**

This is too...	Questo è troppo...
bitter/salty/sweet	amaro/salato/dolce
The food is cold.	Il cibo è freddo.
This isn't fresh.	Questo non è fresco.
What's taking you so long?	Perchè avete impiegato tanto tempo?
Where are our drinks?	Dove sono le nostre bevande?
This isn't clean.	Questo non è pulito.
Would you ask the head waiter to come over?	Vuole chiedere al capo cameriere di venire qui?

Numbers

1	uno, una	11	undici
2	due	12	dodici
3	tre	13	tredici
4	quattro	14	quattordici
5	cinque	15	quindici
6	sei	16	sedici
7	sette	17	diciassette
8	otto	18	diciotto
9	nove	19	diciannove
10	dieci	20	venti

Food

abbacchio grilled lam

~ **alla cacciatora** pieces of lamb, often braised with garlic, rosemary, white wine, anchovy paste and hot peppers

(all') abruzzese Abruzzi style; with red peppers and sometimes ham

acciughe anchovies

~ **al limone** fresh anchovies served with a sauce of lemon, oil, breadcrumbs and oregano

(all')aceto (in) vinegar

acetosella sorrel

acquacotta soup of bread and vegetables, sometimes with eggs and cheese

affettati sliced cold meat, ham and salami (US cold cuts)

affumicato smoked

agliata garlic sauce; garlic mashed with breadcrumbs

aglio garlic

agnello lamb

agnolotti kind of ravioli with savoury filling of vegetables, chopped meats, sometimes with garlic and herbs

(all')agro dressing of lemon juice and oil

agrodolce sweet-sour dressing of caramelized sugar, vinegar and flour to which capers, raisins or lemon may be added

al, all', alla in the style of: with

ala wing

albicocca apricot

alice anchovy

allodola lark

alloro bay leaf

ananas pineapple

anguilla eel

~ **alla veneziana** braised with tunny (tuna) and lemon sauce

anguria watermelon

anice aniseed

animelle (di vitello) (veal) sweetbreads

anitra duck

~ **selvatica** wild duck

annegati slices of meat in white wine or Marsala wine

antipasto hors-d'oeuvre

~ **di mare** seafood

~ **a scelta** to one's own choosing

arachide peanuts

aragosta spiny lobster

arancia orange

aringa herring

arista loin of pork

arrosto roast(ed)

arsella kind of mussel

asiago cheese made of skimmed milk, semi hard to hard, sweet when young

asparago asparagus

assortito assorted

astice lobster

attorta flaky pastry filled with fruit and almonds

avellana hazelnut

babbaluci snails in olive-oil sauce with tomatoes and onions

baccalà stockfish, dried cod

~ **alla fiorentina** floured and fried in oil

~ **alla vicentina** poached in milk with onion, garlic, parsley, anchovies and cinnamon

(con) bagna cauda simmering sauce of butter, olive oil, garlic and chopped anchovies, into which raw vegetables and bread are dipped

barbabietola beetroot

basilico basil

beccaccia woodcock

Bel Paese smooth cheese with delicate taste

ben cotto well-done

(alla) besciamella (with) white sauce

bigoli in salsa noodles with an anchovy or sardine sauce

biscotto rusk, biscuit (US zwieback, cookie)

bistecca steak, usually beef, but may be another kind of meat

~ **di manzo** beef steak

~ **(alla) pizzaiola** with tomatoes, basil and sometimes garlic

~ **di vitello** veal scallop

bocconcini diced meat with herbs

bollito 1) boiled 2) meat or fish stew

(alla) bolognese in a sauce of tomatoes and meat or ham and cheese

(alla) brace on charcoal

braciola di maiale pork chop

bracioletta small slice of meat

~ **a scottadito** charcoal-grilled lamb chops

braciolone alla napoletana breaded rumpsteak with garlic, parsley, ham and currants; rolled, sautéed and stewed

branzino bass

brasato braised

broccoletti strascinati brocoli sautéed with pork fat and garlic

brodetto fish soup with onions and tomato pulp

brodo bouillon, broth, soup

~ **vegetale** vegetable broth

bruschetta a thick slice of countrystyle bread, grilled, rubbed with garlic and sprinkled with olive oil

budino blancmange, custard

bue beef

burrida fish casserole strongly flavoured with spices and herbs

burro butter

~ **maggiordomo** with lemon juice and parsley

busecca thick tripe and vegetable soup

cacciagione game

(alla) cacciatora often with mushrooms, herbs, shallots, wine, tomatoes, strips of ham and tongue

cacciucco spicy fish soup, usually with onions, green pepper, garlic and red wine topped with garlic flavoured croutons

caciocavallo firm, slightly sweet cheese from cow's or sheep's milk

calamaretto young squid

calamaro squid

caldo hot

calzone pizza dough envelope with ham, cheese, herbs and baked

(alla) campagnola with vegetables, especially onions and tomatoes

canederli dumplings made from ham, sausage and breadcrumbs

cannella cinnamon

cannelloni tubular dough stuffed with meat, cheese or vegetables, covered with a white sauce and baked

~ **alla Barbaroux** with chopped ham, veal, cheese and covered with white sauce

~ **alla laziale** with meat and onion filling and baked in tomato sauce

~ **alla napoletana** with cheese and ham filling in tomato and herb sauce

cannolo rolled pastry filled with sweet, white cheese, sometimes nougat and crystallized fruit

capitone large eel

capocollo smoked salt pork

caponata aubergine, green pepper, tomato, vegetable marrow, garlic, oil and herbs; usually served cold

cappelletti small ravioli filled with meat, herbs, cheese and eggs

cappero caper

cappon magro pyramid of cooked vegetables and fish salad

cappone capon

capretto kid

~ **ripieno al forno** stuffed with herbs and roasted

caprino a soft goat's cheese

~ **romano** hard goat's milk cheese

capriolo roebuck

caramellato caramelized

(alla) carbonara *pasta* with smoked ham, cheese, eggs and olive oil

carbonata 1) grilled pork chop 2) beef stew in red wine

carciofo artichoke

~ **alla romana** stuffed, sautéed in oil, garlic and white wine

carciofino small artichoke

cardo cardoon

carne meat

~ **a carrargiu** spit-roasted

carota carrot

carpa, carpione carp

(della) casa chef's speciality

(alla) casalinga home-made

cassata ice-cream with a crystallized fruit filling

~ **(alla) siciliana** sponge cake garnished with sweet cream cheese, chocolate and crystallized fruit

(in) casseruola (in a) casserole

castagnaccio chestnut cake with pine kernels, raisins, nuts, cooked in oil

castagne chestnuts

caviale caviar

cavolfiore cauliflower

cavolino di Bruxelles brussels sprout

cavolo cabbage

cazzoeula a casserole of pork, celery, onions, cabbage and spices

cece chick-pea

cena dinner, supper

cerfoglio chervil

cervella brains

cervo stag
cetriolino gherkin (US pickle)
cetriolo cucumber
chiodo di garofano cloves
ciambella ringshaped bun
cicoria endive (US chicory)
ciliegia cherry
cima cold, stuffed veal
   ~ alla genovese stuffed with eggs, sausage and mushrooms
cinghiale (wild) boar
cioccolata chocolate
cipolla onion
cipollina pearl onion
ciuppin thick fish soup
cocomero watermelon
coda di bue oxtail
colazione lunch
composta stewed fruit
coniglio rabbit
   ~ all'agro stewed in red wine, with the addition of lemon juice
contorno garnish
copata small wafer of honey and nuts
coppa kind of raw ham, usually smoked
corda lamb tripes roasted or braised in tomato sauce with peas
cornetti 1) string beans 2) crescent rolls
cosce di rana frogs' legs
coscia leg, thigh
cosciotto leg
costata beef steak or chop, entrecôte
   ~ alla fiorentina grilled over an olive-wood fire, served with lemon juice and parsley
   ~ alla pizzaiola braised in sauce with tomatoes, marjoram, parsley and *mozzarella* cheese
   ~ al prosciutto with ham,

cheese and truffles; breaded and fried
costoletta cutlet, chop (veal or pork)
   ~ alla bolognese breaded veal cutlet topped with a slice of ham, cheese and tomato sauce
   ~ alla milanese veal cutlet, breaded, then fried
   ~ alla parmigiana breaded and baked with parmesan cheese
   ~ alla valdostana with ham and *fontina* cheese
   ~ alla viennese breaded veal scallop, wiener schnitzel
cotechino spiced pork sausage, served hot in slices
cotto cooked
   ~ a puntino medium (done)
cozza mussel
cozze alla marinara mussels cooked in white wine with parsley and garlic
crauti sauerkraut
crema cream, custard
cremino 1) soft cheese 2) type of ice-cream bar
crescione watercress
crespolino spinach-filled pancake baked in cheese sauce
crocchetta potato or rice croquette
crostaceo shellfish
crostata pie, flan
crostini small pieces of toast, croutons
   ~ in brodo broth with croutons
   ~ alla provatura diced bread and *provatura* cheese toasted on a spit
crostino alla napoletana small toast with anchovies and melted cheese
crudo raw
culatello type of raw ham, cured

in white wine

cuore heart

~ **di sedano** celery heart

cuscusu di Trapani fish soup with semolina flakes

dattero date

datteri di mare mussels, small clams

dentice dentex (Mediterranean fish, similar to sea bream)

(alla) diavola usually grilled with a lavish amount of pepper, chili pepper or pimento

diverso varied

dolce 1) sweet 2) sweet, dessert

dolci pastries, cakes

(alla) Doria with cucumbers

dragoncello tarragon

fagiano pheasant

fagiolino French bean (US green bean)

fagiolo haricot bean

faraona guinea hen

farcito stuffed

farsumagru rolled beef or veal stuffed with bacon, ham, eggs, cheese, parsley and onions; braised with tomatoes

fatto in casa home-made

fava broad bean

favata casserole of beans, bacon, sausage and seasoning

fegatelli di maiale alla Fiorentina pork liver grilled on a skewer with bay leaves

fegato liver

~ **alla veneziana** slices of calf's liver fried with onions

(ai) ferri on the grill, grilled

fesa round cut taken from leg of veal

~ **in gelatina** roast veal in aspic jelly

fettina small slice

fettuccine flat narrow noodles

~ **verdi** green noodles

fico fig

filetto fillet

finocchio fennel

~ **in salsa bianca** in white sauce

(alla) fiorentina with herbs, oil and often spinach

focaccia 1) flat bread, sprinkled with olive oil, sometimes with fried chopped onions or cheese 2) sweet ring-shaped cake

~ **di vitello** veal patty

fondo di carciofo artichoke heart (US bottom)

fonduta melted cheese with egg-yolk, milk and truffles

fontina a soft, creamy cheese from Piedmont, chiefly used in cooking

formaggio cheese

(al) forno baked

forte hot, spicy

fra diavolo with a spicy tomato sauce

fragola strawberry

~ **di bosco** wild

frattaglie giblets

fregula soup with semolina and saffron dumplings

fresco cool, fresh, uncooked

frittata omelet

~ **semplice** plain

frittatina di patate potato omelet

frittella fritter, pancake, often filled with ham and cheese or with an apple

fritto deep-fried

~ **alla milanese** breaded

~ **misto** deep-fried bits of seafood, vegetables or meat

~ **alla napoletana** fried fish, vegetables and cheese

~ **alla romana** sweetbread, artichokes and cauliflower

~ **di verdura** fried vegetables

frutta fruit

~ **candita** crystallized (US candied)

~ **cotta** stewed

frutti di mare shellfish

fungo mushroom

galantina tartufata truffles in aspic jelly

gallina hen

gallinaccio 1) chanterelle mushroom 2) woodcock

gallinella water-hen

gallo cedrone grouse

gamberetto shrimp

gambero crayfish, crawfish

garofolato beef stew with cloves

(in) gelatina (in) aspic jelly

gelato ice-cream; iced dessert

(alla) genovese with basil and other herbs, pine kernels, garlic and oil

ghiacciato iced, chilled

ginepro juniper (berry)

girello round steak from the leg

gnocchi dumplings

gorgonzola most famous of the Italian blue-veined cheese, rich with a tangy flavour

grana hard cheese; also known as *parmigiano(-reggiano)*

granchio crab

grasso rich with fat or oil

(alla) graticola grilled

gratinata sprinkled with breadcrumbs and grated cheese and oven-browned

grattugiato grated

(alla) griglia from the grill

grissino breadstick

gruviera mild cheese with holes, Italian version of Swiss *gruyère*

guazzetto meat stew with garlic, rosemary, tomatoes and pimentos

incasciata layers of dough, meat sauce, hard-boiled eggs and grated cheese

indivia chicory (US endive)

insalata salad

~ **all'americana** mayonnaise and shrimps

~ **russa** diced boiled vegetables in mayonnaise

~ **verde** green

~ **di verdura cotta** boiled vegetables

involtino stuffed meat or ham roll

lampone raspberry

lampreda lamprey

lardo bacon

lasagne thin layers of generally green noodle dough alternating with tomato, sausage meat, ham, white sauce and grated cheese; baked in the oven

latte alla portoghese baked custard with liquid caramel

lattuga lettuce

lauro bay leaf

(alla) laziale with onions

legume vegetable

lenticchia lentil

lepre hare

~ **al lardo con funghi** with bacon and mushrooms

~ **in salmì** jugged

leprotto leveret

lesso 1) boiled 2) meat or fish stew

limone lemon

lingua tongue

linguine flat noodles

lista dei vini wine list

lodigiano kind of parmesan cheese

lombata loin

luganega pork sausage

ITALIAN

lumaca snail
lupo di mare sea perch
maccheroni macaroni
macedonia di frutta fruit salad
maggiorana marjoram
magro 1) lean 2) dish without meat
maiale pork
  ~ al latte cooked in milk
  ~ ubriaco cooked in red wine
maionese mayonnaise
mandarino mandarin
mandorla almond
manzo beef
  ~ arrosto ripieno stuffed roast
  ~ lesso boiled
  ~ salato corned beef
(alla) marinara sauce of tomatoes, olives, garlic, clams and mussels
marinato marinated
maritozzo soft roll
marmellata jam
  ~ d'arance marmalade
marrone chestnut
mascarpone soft, butter-coloured cheese, often served as a sweet dish
medaglione round fillet of beef or veal
mela apple
  ~ cotogna quince
melanzana aubergine (US eggplant)
melanzane alla parmigiana aubergines baked with tomatoes, parmesan cheese and spices
melanzane ripiene stuffed with various ingredients and gratinéed
melone melon
  ~ con prosciutto with cured ham
menta mint
meringa meringue

merlano whiting
merluzzo cod
messicani veal scallops rolled around a meat, cheese or herb stuffing
midollo marrow (bone)
miele honey
(alla) milanese 1) Milanese style of cooking 2) breaded (of meat)
millefoglie custard slice (US napoleon)
minestra soup
  ~ in brodo bouillon with noodles or rice and chicken liver
  ~ di funghi cream of mushroom
minestrone thick vegetable soup
  ~ alla genovese with spinach, basil, macaroni
  ~ verde with French beans and herbs
mirtillo bilberry (US blueberry)
misto mixed
mitilo mussel
(alla) montanara with different root vegetables
montone mutton
mora blackberry, mulberry
mortadella bologna (sausage)
mostarda mustard
  ~ di frutta spiced crystallized fruits (US candied fruits) in a sweet-sour syrup
mozzarella soft, unripened cheese with a bland, slightly sweet flavour, made from buffalo's milk in southern Italy, elsewhere with cow's milk
(alla) napoletana with cheese, tomatoes, herbs and sometimes anchovies
nasello whiting
naturale plain, without sauce or

filling
navone yellow turnip
nocciola hazelnut
noce nut
~ **di cocco** coconut
~ **moscata** nutmeg
nostrano local, home-grown
oca goose
olio oil
~ **d'arachide** peanut oil
~ **di semi** seed oil
olive agrodolci olives in vinegar and sugar
olive ripiene stuffed olives (e.g. with meat, cheese, pimento)
ombrina umbrine (fish)
orata John Dory (fish)
origano oregano
osso bone
~ **buco** veal shanks cooked in various ways depending on the region
ostrica oyster
ovalina small *mozzarella* cheese from buffalo's milk
ovolo egg mushroom
(alla) paesana with bacon, potatoes, carrots, vegetable marrow and other root vegetables
pagliarino medium-soft cheese from Piedmont
palomba wood-pigeon, ring-dove
pan di Genova almond cake
pan di Spagna sponge cake
pan tostato toasted Italian bread
pancetta bacon
pandolce heavy cake with dried fruit and pine kernels
pane bread
~ **casareccio** home-made
~ **scuro** dark
~ **di segale** rye
panettone tall light cake with a few raisins and crystallized fruit

panforte di Siena flat round slab made mostly of spiced crystallized fruit
pangrattato breadcrumbs
panicielli d'uva passula grapes wrapped in citron leaves and baked
panino roll
~ **imbottito** sandwich
panna cream
~ **montata** whipped
panzarotti fried or baked large dough envelopes often with a filling of pork, eggs, cheese, anchovies and tomatoes
pappardelle long, broad noodles
~ **con la lepre** garnished with spiced hare
parmigiano(-reggiano) parmesan, a hard cheese generally grated for use in hot dishes
passatelli pasta made from a mixture of egg, parmesan cheese, breadcrumbs, often with a pinch of nutmeg
passato purée, creamed
~ **di verdura** mashed vegetable soup, generally with croutons
pasta the traditional Italian first course; essentially a dough consisting of flour, water, oil (or butter) and eggs; produced in a variety of shapes and sizes (e.g. spaghetti, macaroni, broad noodles, ravioli, shell- and star-shaped *pasta*); may be eaten on its own, in a bouillon, seasoned with butter or olive oil, stuffed or accompanied by a savoury sauce, sprinkled with grated cheese
~ **asciutta** any pasta not eaten in a bouillon; served with any of various dressings

ITALIAN

pasticcino tart, cake, small pastry
pasticcio 1) pie 2) type of *pasta* like *lasagne*
pastina small *pasta* in various shapes used principally as a bouillon or soup ingredient
pasto meal
patate potatoes
~ **fritte** deep fried
~ **lesse** boiled
~ **novelle** new
~ **in padella** fried in a pan
~ **rosolate** roasted
~ **saltate** sliced and sautéed
patatine small, new potatoes
pecorino a hard cheese made from sheep's milk
pepato peppered
pepe pepper
peperonata stew of peppers, tomatoes and sometimes onions
peperone green or red sweet pepper
~ **arrostito** roasted sweet pepper
~ **ripieno** stuffed, usually with rice and chopped meat
pera pear
pernice partridge
pesca peach
~ **melba** peach-halves poached in syrup over vanilla ice-cream, topped with raspberry sauce and whipped cream
pescatrice angler fish, frog fish
pesce fish
~ **spada** swordfish
pesto sauce of basil leaves, garlic, cheese and sometimes with pine kernels and majoram; used in *minestrone* or with *pasta*
petto breast
(a) piacere to your own choosing
piatto dish

~ **del giorno** the day's speciality
~ **principale** main course
primo ~ first course
piccante highly seasoned
piccata thin veal scallop
~ **al marsala** braised in Marsala sauce
piccione pigeon (US squab)
piede trotter (US foot)
(alla) piemontese Piedmontese style; with truffles and rice
pignoli pine kernels
pinoccate pine kernel and almond cake
pisello pea
pistacchi pistachio nuts
piviere plover (bird)
pizza flat, open(-faced) pie, tart, flan; bread dough bottom with any of a wide variety of toppings
pizzetta small *pizza*
polenta pudding of maizemeal (US cornmeal)
~ **pasticciata** *polenta*, sliced and served with meat sauce, mushrooms, white sauce, butter and cheese
~ **e uccelli** small birds spit-roasted and served with *polenta*
pollame fowl
pollo chicken
~ **alla diavola** highly spiced and grilled
~ **novello** spring chicken
polpetta di carne meatball
polpettone meat loaf of seasoned beef or veal
polpo octopus
~ **in purgatorio** sautéed in oil with tomatoes, parsley, garlic and peppers
(salsa di) pommarola tomato sauce

for *pasta*
...omodoro tomato
...ompelmo grapefruit
...opone melon
...orchetta roast suck(l)ing pig
...orcini boletus mushrooms
...orro leek
...ranzo lunch or dinner
...rezzemolo parsley
...rezzo price
~ **fisso** fixed price
...rima colazione breakfast
...rimizie spring fruit or vegetables
...rofiterole filled cream puff
~ **alla cioccolata** with chocolate frosting
...rosciutto ham
~ **affumicato** cured, smoked
~ **di cinghiale** smoked wild boar
~ **di Parma** cured ham from Parma
...rovatura soft, mild and slightly sweet cheese made from buffalo's milk
...rovolone white, medium-hard cheese
...rugna plum
~ **secca** prune
...unte di asparagi asparagus tips
...urè di patate mashed potatoes
quaglia quail
...abarbaro rhubarb
...afano horse-radish
...agù meat sauce for *pasta*
...agusano hard and slightly sweet cheese
...apa turnip
...avanello radish
...aviggiolo cheese made from sheep's or goat's milk
...azza ray
...ibes currants
~ **neri** blackcurrants

~ **rossi** redcurrants
riccio di mare sea urchin
ricotta soft cow's or sheep's milk cheese
rigaglie giblets
rigatoni 1) type of *pasta* similar to *cannelloni* 2) type of macaroni
ripieno stuffing, stuffed
risi e bisi rice and peas cooked in chicken bouillon
riso rice
~ **in bianco** white rice with butter
risotto dish made of boiled rice served as a first course, with various ingredients according to the region
(brodo) ristretto consommé
robiola soft, rich and sweet sheep's milk cheese
robiolina goat's or sheep's milk cheese
rognoni kidneys
(alla) romana with vegetables, particularly onions, mint and sometimes anchovies
rombo turbot, brill
rosbif roast beef
rosmarino rosemary
rotolo rolled, stuffed meat
salame salami
salato salted
sale salt
salmone salmon
salsa sauce
salsiccia any spiced pork sausage to be served cooked
saltimbocca veal slices with ham, sage, herbs and wine
~ **alla romana** veal cutlet flavoured with ham and sage, sautéed in butter and white wine
(al) sangue underdone (US rare)
sarda pilchard, sardine

ITALIAN

sardina small sardine

sardo sheep's milk cheese, hard, pungent and aromatic

sartù oven-baked rice with tomatoes, meat balls, chicken giblets, mushrooms and peas

scalogno shallot

scaloppa, scaloppina veal scallop
~ **alla fiorentina** with spinach and white sauce

scamorza aged *mozzarella*, firmer and saltier

scampi Dublin Bay prawns

scapece fried fish preserved in white vinegar with saffron

(allo) sciroppo in syrup

scorfano rascasse, a Mediterranean fish, used for fish soup

scorzonera salsify

sedano celery

selvaggina game

senape mustard

seppia cuttlefish, squid

servizio (non) compreso service (not) included

sfogliatelle puff pastry with custard or fruit-preserve filling

sgombro mackerel

silvano chocolate meringue or tart

soffritto sautéed

sogliola sole
~ **arrosto** baked in olive oil, herbs and white wine
~ **dorata** breaded and fried
~ **ai ferri** grilled
~ **alla mugnaia** sautéed in butter with lemon juice and parsley

soppressata 1) sausage 2) preserved pig's head with pistachio nuts

sottaceti pickled vegetables

sottaceto pickled

spaghetti spaghetti

~ **aglio e olio** with olive oil and fried garlic

~ **all'amatriciana** with tomato sauce, garlic and parmesan cheese

~ **alla carbonara** with oil, cheese, bacon and eggs

~ **pomodoro e basilico** fresh tomatoes and basil leaves

~ **alle vongole** with clam or mussel sauce, tomatoes, garlic and pimento

spalla shoulder

specialità speciality

spezzatino meat or fowl stew

spiedino pieces of meat grilled or roasted on a skewer
~ **di mare** pieces of fish and seafood skewered and roasted

(allo) spiedo (on a) spit

spigola sea bass

spinaci spinach

spugnola morel mushroom

spumone foamy ice-cream dessert with crystallized fruit, whipped cream and nuts

(di) stagione (in) season

stellette star-shaped *pasta*

stinco knuckle (of veal), shin (of beef)

stoccafisso stockfish, dried cod

storione sturgeon

stracchino creamy, soft to medium-soft cheese

stracciatella consommé with semolina or breadcrumbs, eggs and grated cheese

stracotto meat stew, slowly cooked for several hours

strascinati shell-shaped fresh *pasta* with different sauces

stufato 1) stew(ed) 2) beef stew

succu tunnu soup with semolina and saffron dumplings

sufflé soufflé
sugo sauce, gravy
(carne di) suino pork
suppli rice croquettes with *mozzarella* cheese and meat sauce
suprema di pollo in gelatina chicken breast in aspic jelly
susina plum
tacchino turkey
tagliatelle flat noodles
tagliolini thin flat noodles
taleggio medium-hard cheese with a mild flavour
tartaruga turtle
tartina open(-faced) sandwich
tartufo truffle
tartufi di mare cockles or small clams
(al) tegame sautéed
(alla) teglia fried in a pan
testa di vitello calf's head
timo thyme
tinca tench (fish)
tonnato in tunny (tuna) sauce
tonno tunny (US tuna)
topinambur Jerusalem artichoke
tordo thrush
torrone nougat
torta pie, tart, flan
tortelli small fritters
tortellini ringlets of dough filled with seasoned minced meat
tortiglione almond cake
tortino savoury tart filled with cheese and vegetables
  ~ **di carciofi** fried artichokes mixed with beaten eggs
(alla) toscana with tomatoes, celery and herbs
tostato toasted
totano young squid
tramezzino small sandwich
trenette noodles
triglia red mullet

trippe alla fiorentina slowly braised tripe and minced beef with tomato sauce, marjoram, parmesan cheese
trippe alla milanese tripe stewed with onions, leek, carrots, tomatoes, beans, sage and nutmeg
trippe alla romana cooked in sweet-and-sour sauce with cheese
tritato minced
trota trout
  ~ **alle mandorle** stuffed, seasoned, baked in cream and topped with almonds
  ~ **di ruscello** river trout
tutto compreso everything included
uccelletti, uccelli small birds, usually spit-roasted
  ~ **in umido** stewed
uovo egg
  ~ **affogato nel vino** poached in wine
  ~ **al burro** fried in butter
  ~ **in camicia** poached
  ~ **alla coque** boiled
  ~ **alla fiorentina** fried, served on a bed of spinach
  ~ **(al) forno** baked
  ~ **fritto** fried
  ~ **molle** soft-boiled
  ~ **ripieno** stuffed
  ~ **sodo** hard-boiled
  ~ **strapazzato** scrambled
uva grape
vaniglia vanilla
vario assorted
(alla) veneziana with onions or shallots, white wine and mint
verdura green vegetables
vermicelli thin noodles
verza green cabbage
vitello veal

ITALIAN

~ **all'uccelletto** diced veal, sage, simmered in wine
vongola small clam
zaba(gl)ione dessert of egg-yolks, sugar and Marsala wine; served warm
zampone pig's trotter filled with seasoned pork, boiled and served in slices
zèppola fritter, doughnut
zimino fish stew
zucca pumpkin, gourd
zucchero sugar

zucchino small vegetable marrow (US zucchini)
zuppa soup
~ **fredda** cold
~ **di frutti di mare** seafood
~ **inglese** sponge cake steeped in rum with candied fruit and custard or whipped cream
~ **alla pavese** consommé with poached egg, croutons and grated cheese
~ **di vongole** clam soup with white wine

Drink

abboccato medium dry (wine)
acqua water
~ **fredda** ice-cold
~ **gasata** soda water
acquavite brandy, spirits
Aleatico a dessert wine made from muscat grapes
amabile slightly sweet (wine)
Americano a popular aperitif made with *Campari*, vermouth, angostura and lemon peel
aperitivo aperitif
aranciata orangeade
asciutto dry (wine)
Asti Spumante the renowned sparkling white wine from Piedmont
Aurum an orange liqueur
Barbaresco a red wine from Piedmont resembling *Barolo*, but lighter and slightly drier
Barbera a dark red, full-bodied

wine from Piedmont and Lombardy with a rich bouquet
Bardolino a very pale red wine, from the Lago di Garda near Verona
Barolo a high quality red wine from Piedmont, can be compared to wines from the Rhone Valley
bibita beverage, drink
birra beer
~ **di barile** draught (US draft)
~ **chiara** lager, light
~ **scura** dark
~ **alla spina** draught (US draft)
caffè coffee
~ **corretto** espresso laced with a shot of liquor or brandy
~ **freddo** iced
~ **macchiato** with a few drops of warm milk
~ **nero** black

~ **ristretto** small and concentrated

caffellatte coffee with milk

Campania the region around Naples is noted for its fine red and white wines like *Capri, Falerno* and *Lacrima Christi*

Campari a reddish bitter aperitif with a quinine taste

cappuccino black coffee and whipped milk, sometimes with grated chocolate

caraffa carafe

Castelli Romani a common dry white wine from south-east of Rome

Centerbe a strong, green herb liqueur

Cerasella a cherry liqueur

Certosino a yellow or green herb liqueur

Chianti the renowned red and white table wines of Tuscany, traditionally bottled in a *fiasco;* there are many different qualities depending on the vineyards

Chiaretto one of Italy's most famous rosé wines; best when drunk very young; produced south of Lago di Garda

Cortese a dry white wine from Piedmont with limited production

dolce sweet (wine)

Emilia-Romagna the region around Bologna produces chiefly red wine like *Lambrusco*, which is sparkling and has a certain tang, and *Sangiovese*, a still type

Est! Est! Est! a semi-sweet white wine from the region north of Rome

Etna wines from the west slopes of Mount Etna (Sicily)

Falerno red and white dry wines produced in Campania

Fernet-Branca a bitter digestive

fiasco a straw-covered flask

frappè milk shake

Frascati a *Castelli Romani* white wine which can be dry or slightly sweet

Freisa red wines from Piedmont; one type is dry and fruity, the other is lighter and can be slightly sweet or semi-sparkling; one of Italy's best red wines produced south-west of Lago Maggiore

frizzante semi-sparkling (wine)

Gattinara a red, high-quality full-bodied wine from Piedmont, south-east of Lago Maggiore

granatina, granita fruit syrup or coffee served over crushed ice

grappa spirit distilled from grape mash

Grignolino good quality red wine with a special character and scent; often with a high alcoholic content

Lacrima Christi the most well-known wine from the Vesuvian slopes (Campania); the white wine is the best, but there are also red and rosé versions

Lago di Caldaro light red wine produced in the Italian Tyrol

Lagrein Rosato a good rosé from the region around Bolzano in the Italian Tyrol

Lambrusco a sparkling and tingling red wine from Emilia-Romagna

latte milk

~ **al cacao** chocolate drink

Lazio Latium; the region princi-

ITALIAN

pally to the south of Rome produces chiefly white wine like *Castelli Romani*, *Est! Est! Est!* and *Frascati*

limonata lemonade

Lombardia Lombardy; the region around Milan produces various red wines like the *Bonarda*, *Inferno*, *Spanna* and *Valtellina*, the rosé *Chiaretto* and the white *Lugana*

Lugana a good dry white wine from the region of Lago di Garda

Marsala the renowned red dessert wine from Sicily

Martini a brand-name of white and red vermouth

Millefiori a liqueur distilled from herbs and alpine flowers

Moscatello, Moscato muscatel; name for different dessert and table wines produced from the muscat grapes; there are some red, but most are white

Orvieto light, white wine from Umbria; three versions exist: dry, slightly sweet and sweet

Piemonte Piedmont; the north-western region of Italy reputedly produces the highest quality wine in the country and is best known for its sparkling wine *Asti Spumante;* among its red wines are *Barbaresco*, *Barbera*, *Barolo*, *Dolcetto*, *Freisa*, *Gattinara*, *Grignolino*, *Nebbiolo; Cortese* is a light white wine

porto port (wine)

Puglia Apulia; at the south-eastern tip of Italy, this region produces the greatest quantity of the nation's wine, mainly table wine and some dessert wine

Punt e Mès a brand-name vermouth

Sangiovese a red table wine from Emilia-Romagna

Santa Giustina a good red table wine from the Italian Tyrol

Santa Maddalena a good quality red wine from the Italian Tyrol, light in colour and rather fruity

sciroppo fruit syrup diluted with water

secco dry (wine)

Sicilia Sicily; this island is noted for its dessert wine, particularly the celebrated *Marsala;* among many table wines the red, white and rosé *Etna* wines are the best known

sidro cider

Silvestro a herb and mint liqueur

Soave very good dry white wine, which is best when drunk young (from the east ov Verona)

spremuta fresh fruit drink

spumante sparkling

Stock a wine-distilled brandy

Strega a strong herb liqueur

succo juice

tè tea

~ **al latte** with milk

~ **al limone** with lemon

Terlano Tyrolean white wine, renowned, well balanced, greenish yellow in colour and with a delicate taste

Toscana Tuscany; the region around Florence is particularly noted for its red and white *Chianti*, a good table wine, and the dessert wines *Aleatico* and *Vin Santo*

Traminer a Tyrolean white wine from the region which gave the grape and the name to the renowned Alsatian *Traminer* and *Gewürztraminer* white wines

Trentino-Alto Adige the alpine region produces red wines like *Lago di Caldaro, Santa Giustina, Santa Maddalena; Terlano* and *Traminer* are notable white wines; *Lagrein Rosato* is a rosé to remember while *Vin Santo* is a good dessert wine

Valpolicella a light red wine with a rich cherry colour and a trace of bitterness; it is best when drunk young

Valtellina region near the Swiss border which produces good, dark red wine

Vecchia Romagna a wine-distilled brandy

Veneto the north-eastern region of Italy produces high quality wines; among its red wines are *Amarone, Bardolino, Merlot, Pinot Nero, Valpolicella;* among the whites, *Pinot Grigio, Soave. Recioto* is a sparkling red wine

Vin Santo (Vinsanto) a fine dessert wine produced chiefly in Tuscany but also in Trentino, the Italian Tyrol

vino wine

- ~ **aperto** open
- ~ **bianco** white
- ~ **del paese** local
- ~ **rosatello, rosato** rosé
- ~ **rosso** red

Norwegian

Guide to pronunciation

Letter	Approximate pronunciation
Consonants	
b, d, f, h, m, n, p, t, v	as in English
g	1) before **i, y** or **ei**, like **y** in yet 2) otherwise, like **g** in go
j, gj, hj, lj	like **y** in yet
k	1) before **i, y** or **j**, like **ch** in German i**ch** or something like **ch** in Scottish lo**ch**; it's similar to the first sound of huge 2) otherwise, like **k** in kit
l	always as in lee, never as in be**ll**
r	in southwestern Norway, it's pronounced in the back of the mouth (as in French), elsewhere it's slightly rolled in the front of the mouth
rs	is generally pronounced like **sh** in **sh**ut in eastern Norway

NORWEGIAN

s	always as in **so**
sj, skj, sk	when followed by **i, y** or **øy**, like **sh** in **shut**

Notice that in groups **rd, rl, rn** and **rt**, the **r** tends not to be pronounced but influences the pronunciation of the following consonant, which is then pronounced with the tongue behind the upper teeth ridge (turned upwards at the front). The letters **c, q, w, z** are only found in foreign words and tend to be pronounced as in the language of origin.

Vowels

A vowel is generally long in stressed syllables when it's the final letter or followed by only one consonant. If followed by two or more consonants, or in unstressed syllables, the vowel is generally short.

a	1) when long, like **a** in **car** 2) when short, very much like **u** in **cut**
e	1) when long, like **ay** in **say**, but a pure sound, *not* a diphthong 2) when short, like **e** in **get** 3) when followed by **r**, like **a** in **bad**; long or short 4) when unstressed, like **er** in **other**
i	1) when long, like **ee** in **see**, but with the tongue more raised and the lips more drawn back at the sides 2) when short, like **ee** in **meet**
o	1) when long, like **oo** in **soon**, but with the lips more rounded (when followed by **-rt, -st, -m** and **-nd**, it can be short) 2) when short, generally like **o** in **hot**
u	a difficult sound; something like the **ew** in **few** or Scottish **oo** in **good**; you'll find it very hard to distinguish from Norwegian **y**
y	put your tongue in the position for the **ee** in **bee** and then round your lips as for the **oo** in **pool**; the vowel you pronounce like this should be more or less correct
æ	1) before **r**, like **a** in **bad**; usually long but sometimes short 2) otherwise, like **ay** in **say**
å	1) when long, like **aw** in **saw** 2) when short (which is rare), more like **o** in **hot**
e, ö	like **u** in **fur**; either long or short

Diphthongs

au	this sounds like **ow** in n**ow**, but in fact the first part is a Norwegian **ø** sound
ei	like **ay** in s**ay** but often reminiscent of **igh** in s**igh**
øy	fairly like **oy** in b**oy**

Silent letters

1) The letter **g** is generally silent in the endings **-lig** and **-ig**.
2) The letter **d** is generally silent after **l** or **n** or after **r** at the end of a word (with lengthening of the vowel) or often after a long vowel, e.g., **holde, land, gård.**
3) The letter **v** is silent in a few words, e.g., **selv, tolv, halv, sølv.**

Some useful expressions

Hungry

I'm hungry/I'm thirsty.	**Jeg er sulten/Jeg er tørst.**
Can you recommend a good restaurant?	**Kan De anbefale en bra restaurant?**
Are there any good, cheap restaurants around here?	**Finnes det en bra og rimelig restaurant i nærheten?**
I'd like to reserve a table for ... people.	**Jeg vil gjerne bestille et bord til ...**
We'll come at ... o'clock.	**Vi kommer klokken ...**

Asking

Good evening. I'd like a table for ... people.	**God aften, jeg vil gjerne ha et bord til ...**
Could we have a table...?	**Kan vi få et bord...?**
in the corner	**i hjørnet**
by the window	**ved vinduet**
outside	**ute**
on the terrace	**på terrassen**
May I please have the menu?	**Kan jeg få se spisekortet?**
What's this?	**Hva er dette?**

Do you have...?	**Har De...?**
a set menu	en fast meny
local dishes	stedets spesialiteter
a children's menu	en barnemeny
Waiter/Waitress!	**Kelner/Frøken!**
What do you recommend?	**Hva kan De anbefale?**
Could I have (a/an/some) ... please?	**Kunne De gi meg...?**
ashtray	et askebeger
another chair	en stol til
finger bowl	en skylleskål
fork	en gaffel
glass	et glass
knife	en kniv
napkin	en serviett
plate	en tallerken
pepper mill	en pepperkvern
serviette	en serviett
spoon	en skje
toothpicks	noen tannpirkere

NORWEGIAN

Ordering

I'd like a/an/some...	**Jeg vil gjerne ha...**
aperitif	en aperitiff
appetizer	en forrett
beer	en øl
bread	brød
butter	smør
cheese	ost
chips	pommes frites
coffee	kaffe
dessert	en dessert
fish	fisk
french fries	pommes frites
fruit	frukt
game	vilt
ice-cream	en iskrem
lemon	sitron
lettuce	en salat

meat	**kjøtt**
mineral water	**mineralvann**
milk	**melk**
mustard	**sennep**
noodles	**nudler**
oil	**olje**
olive oil	**olivenolje**
pepper	**pepper**
potatoes	**poteter**
poultry	**fugl**
rice	**ris**
rolls	**rundstykker**
saccharin	**sakkarin**
salad	**en salat**
salt	**salt**
sandwich	**et smørbrød**
seafood	**fisk og skalldyr**
seasoning	**krydder**
soup	**en suppe**
starter	**en forrett**
sugar	**sukker**
tea	**te**
vegetables	**grønnsaker**
vinegar	**eddik**
(iced) water	**(is)vann**
wine	**vin**

NORWEGIAN

VELBEKOMME!
ENJOY YOUR MEAL!

---

baked	**ovnsbakt**
baked in parchment	**ovnsbakt i smørpapir**
boiled	**kokt**
braised	**stekt**
cured	**spekt**
fried	**stekt**
grilled	**grillstekt, griljert**
marinated	**marinert**
poached	**pochert**

roasted	**stekt**
sautéed	**ristet**
smoked	**røkt**
steamed	**dampkokt**
stewed	**surret i gryte**
underdone (rare)	**råstekt**
medium	**medium stekt**
well-done	**godt stekt**

SKÅL!
CHEERS!

---

glass	**glass**
bottle	**flaske**
red	**rød**
white	**hvit**
rosé	**rosé**
very dry	**ekstra tørr**
dry	**tørr**
sweet	**søt**
light	**lett**
full-bodied	**fyldig**
sparkling	**musserende**
neat (straight)	**bar**
on the rocks	**med is**

NORWEGIAN

The bill

I'd like to pay.	**Jeg vil gjerne betale.**
We'd like to pay separately.	**Vi vil gjerne betale hver for oss.**
You've made a mistake in this bill, I think.	**Jeg tror De har gjort en feil på regningen.**
What's this amount for?	**Hva står dette beløpet for?**
Is service included?	**Er service inkludert?**
Is everything included?	**Er alt inkludert?**
Do you accept traveller's cheques?	**Tar De reisesjekker?**

Thank you. This is for you.	**Takk skal De ha, dette er til Dem.**
Keep the change.	**Behold resten.**
That was a very good meal.	**Det var et deilig måltid.**
We enjoyed it, thank you.	**Det smakte meget godt.**

Complaints

That's not what I ordered. I asked for...	**Det er ikke det jeg bestilte, jeg ba om...**
May I change this?	**Kan jeg få byttet dette?**
The meat is...	**Kjøttet er...**
overdone	**for mye stekt**
underdone	**for lite stekt**
too rare	**for rått**
too tough	**for seigt**
This is too...	**Dette er for...**
bitter/salty/sweet	**bittert/salt/søtt**
The food is cold.	**Maten er kald.**
This isn't fresh.	**Dette er ikke ferskt.**
What's taking you so long?	**Hvorfor tar det så lang tid?**
Where are our drinks?	**Har De glemt drinkene våre?**
This isn't clean.	**Dette er ikke rent.**
Would you ask the head waiter to come over?	**Vil De be hovmesteren komme hit?**

Numbers

1	**en**		11	**elleve**
2	**to**		12	**tolv**
3	**tre**		13	**tretten**
4	**fire**		14	**fjorten**
5	**fem**		15	**femten**
6	**seks**		16	**seksten**
7	**sju**		17	**sytten**
8	**åtte**		18	**atten**
9	**ni**		19	**nitten**
10	**ti**		20	**tjue**

NORWEGIAN

Food

Please note that Norwegian alphabetical order is **a-z, æ, ø, å**.

NORWEGIAN

agurk cucumber
ananas pineapple
and duck
ansjos marinated sprats
appelsin orange
aprikos apricot
arme riddere French toast; slices of bread dipped in batter and fried, served with jam
asparges asparagus
  ~**bønne** French bean (US green bean)
  ~**topp** asparagus tip
bakt baked
banan banana
bankebiff slices or chunks of beef simmered in gravy
bekkørret river trout
benløse fugler rolled slices of veal stuffed with minced meat
betasuppe thick soup of meat, bone marrow and vegetables
biff beefsteak
  ~**med løk** with fried onions
  ~**tartar** steak tartare, minced raw beef
bjørnebær blackberry
blandede grønnsaker mixed vegetables
blodpudding black pudding (US blood sausage)
blomkål cauliflower

bløtkake rich sponge layer cake
blåbær bilberry (US blueberry)
blåskjell mussel
brekkbønne French bean (US green bean)
bringebær raspberry
brisling sprat
broiler specially fed 2-months-old chicken
brød bread
buljong broth, consommé
bønne bean
daddel (pl **dadler**) date
dagens meny day's menu
dagens rett day's special
drue grape
dyrestek roast venison
eddik vinegar
egg egg
  ~**og bacon** bacon and eggs
  bløtkokt ~ soft-boiled
  forlorent ~ poached
  hårdkokt ~ hard-boiled
  kokt ~ boiled
  speil~ fried (US sunny side up)
eggerøre scrambled eggs
elgstek roast elk (US moose)
eple apple
  ~**kake** apple cake
ert pea
ertesuppe pea soup

estragon tarragon
fasan pheasant
fenalår cured leg of mutton
fersken peach
ferskt kjøtt og suppe meat-and-vegetable soup
fiken fig
fisk fish
fiskebolle fish ball
fiskegrateng fish casserole
fiskekabaret fish and shellfish in aspic
fiskekake fried fish ball
fiskepudding fish pudding
fiskesuppe fish soup
flatbrød thin wafer of rye and sometimes barley
fleskepannekake thick oven-baked pancake with bacon
fleskepølse pork sandwich spread
flyndrefilet fillet of flounder
fløte cream
  ~ **ost** cream cheese
  ~ **vaffel** cream-enriched waffle often served with Arctic cloud-berries or jam
forrett first course, starter
frokost breakfast
fromasj mousse, blancmange
frukt fruit
  ~ **is** water-ice, sherbet
  ~ **salat** fruit salad
  ~ **terte** fruit tart
fugl fowl
fyll stuffing, forcemeat
fårefrikassé mutton or lamb fricassee
fårekjøtt mutton
fårestek leg of lamb
fårikål mutton or lamb in cabbage stew
gaffelbiter salt- and sugar-cured herring fillets
gammelost a semi-hard cheese

with grainy texture and strong flavour
geitekilling kid
geitost a bitter-sweet brown cheese made from goat's milk
gjedde pike
grapefrukt grapefruit
gravet ørret salt-cured trout flavoured with dill
gravlaks salt- and sugar-cured salmon flavoured with dill, often served with creamy dill-and-mustard sauce
gressløk chive
griljert breaded
grillet grilled
grovbrød brown bread
grønnsak vegetable
grøt porridge, cereal
gudbrandsdalsost a slightly sweet brown cheese made from goat's and cow's milk
gulrot (pl **gulrøtter**) carrot
gås goose
gåselever(postei) goose liver (paste)
gåsestek roast goose
hasselnøtt hazelnut
havre oats
  ~ **grøt** oatmeal (porridge)
  ~ **kjeks** oatmeal biscuit (US oatmeal cookie)
helkornbrød wholemeal (US whole-wheat) bread
hellefisk halibut
helstekt roasted whole
hjemmelaget home-made
hoffdessert layers of meringue and whipped cream, topped with chocolate sauce and toasted almonds
honning honey
hummer lobster
hvalbiff steak of whale

hvetebolle sweet roll, bun
~ **med rosiner** with raisins
hvitløk garlic
hvitting whiting
hønsefrikassé chicken fricassée
is ice, water ice (US sherbet)
~ **krem** ice-cream
italiensk salat salad of diced cold meat or ham, apples, potatoes, gherkins and other vegetables in mayonnaise
jordbær strawberry
julekake rich fruit cake (Christmas speciality)
kake cake, tart
kalkun turkey
kalvekjøtt veal
kalvekotelett veal chop
kalvemedaljong a small round fillet of veal
kalvetunge calf's tongue
kanel cinnamon
karamellpudding caramel blancmange (US pudding)
karbonadekake hamburger steak
kardemomme cardamom
karri curry
karve caraway seed
kastanje chestnut
kirsebær cherry
kjeks biscuit (US cracker or cookie)
kjøtt meat
~ **bolle** meat ball
~ **deig** minced meat
~ **kake** small hamburger steak
~ **pudding** meat loaf
~ **suppe** broth with diced meat or sausage
klippfisk salted and dried cod
knekkebrød crisp bread (US hardtack)
kokosmakron coconut macaroon
kokosnøtt coconut

kokt cooked, boiled
koldtbord a buffet of cold dishes such as fish, meat, salad, cheese and dessert
kolje haddock
korint currant
kotelett chop, cutlet
krabbe crab
kransekake cone-shaped pile of almond-macaroon rings
krem whipped cream
kreps crayfish
kringle ring-twisted bread with raisins
kryddersild soused herring
kumle potato dumpling
kylling chicken
~ **bryst** breast
~ **lår** leg, thigh
~ **vinge** wing
kål cabbage
~ **ruletter** cabbage leaves stuffed with minced meat
laks salmon
lammebog shoulder of lamb
lammebryst brisket of lamb
lammekotelett lamb chop
lapskaus thick stew of diced or minced meat (generally beef, lamb or pork), potatoes, onions and other vegetables
lefse thin pancake (without eggs)
lettstekt sautéed
lever liver
~ **postei** liver paste
loff white bread
lompe kind of potato pancake
lungemos hash of pork lungs and onions
lutefisk boiled stockfish, served with white sauce or melted butter and potatoes
løk onion
makrell mackerel

mandel (pl **mandler**) almond
marengs meringue
marinert marinated
medisterkake hamburger steak made of pork
meny bill of fare, menu
middag dinner
morell morello cherry
morkel (pl **morkler**) morel mushroom
multe Arctic cloudberry
musling mussel
mysost a brown whey cheese similar to *gudbrandsdalsost*
mørbrad rumpsteak
napoleonskake custard slice (US napoleon)
normannaost blue cheese
nype rose hip
nyre kidney
nøtt nut
oksefilet fillet of beef
oksehalesuppe oxtail soup
oksekjøtt beef
okserull rolled stuffed beef, served cold
oksestek roast beef
omelett med sjampinjonger button mushroom omelet
ost cheese
pai pie
pale young coalfish
panert breaded
pannekake pancake
pepperkake ginger biscuit (US ginger snap)
pepperrot horse-radish
~ **saus** horse-radish sauce
persille parsley
pinnekjøtt salted and fried ribs of mutton roasted on twigs (Christmas speciality)
pir small mackerel
pisket krem whipped cream

plomme plum
~ **grøt med fløtemelk** stewed plums and cream
plukkfisk poached fish (usually dried cod or haddock) in white sauce
pommes frites potato chips (US French fries)
postei 1) vol-au-vent 2) meat or fish pie
potet potato
~ **chips** crisps (US chips)
~ **gull** crisps (US chips)
~ **kake** potato fritter
pultost a soft, sometimes fermented cheese, usually flavoured with caraway seeds
purre leek
pyttipanne diced meat and potatoes fried with onions, sometimes topped with a fried egg
pære pear
pølse sausage
rabarbra rhubarb
rakørret salt-cured trout
rapphøne partridge
reddik radish
regnbueørret rainbow trout
reinsdyrstek roast reindeer
reke shrimp
remuladesaus mayonnaise mixed with cream, chopped gherkins and parsley
rips redcurrant
ris rice
risengrynsgrøt rice pudding sprinkled with cinammon and sugar, served warm
riskrem boiled rice mixed with whipped cream, served with raspberry or strawberry sauce
rislapp small sweet rice cake
ristet grilled, sautéed, toasted

rogn roe
rosenkål brussels sprout
rosin raisin
rundstykke roll
rype ptarmigan, snow grouse
rødbete beetroot
rødgrøt fruit pudding served with vanilla custard or cream
rødkål red cabbage
rødspette plaice
røkelaks smoked salmon
røkt smoked
rømme thick sour cream
  ~ **grøt** boiled and served with sugar
rørte tyttebær cranberry jam made without cooking
rå raw
  ~ **stekt** underdone
saus sauce
sei coalfish
selleri celery
sennep mustard
service inkludert service included
sild herring
sildekake herring patty
sildesalat salad of diced salt herring, cucumber, onions, vegetables, spices and mayonnaise
sirupssnipp ginger biscuit (US ginger snap)
sitron lemon
  ~ **fromasj** lemon blancmange (US lemon custard)
sjampinjong button mushroom, champignon
sjokolade chocolate
sjøtunge sole
sjøørret sea trout
skalldyr shellfish
skilpaddesuppe turtle soup
skinke ham
skive slice
slangeagurk cucumber

smør butter
  ~ **brød** open-faced sandwich
småkake biscuit (US cookie)
snittebønner sliced French beans
solbær blackcurrant
sopp mushroom
speilegg fried egg
spekemat cured meat (beef, mutton, pork, reindeer), often served with scrambled eggs and chives
spekepølse large air-dried sausage
spekesild salted herring, often served with cabbage, potatoes and pickled beetroot
spekeskinke cured ham
spinat spinach
stangselleri branch celery
stek roast
stekt fried, roasted
stikkelsbær gooseberry
stuet 1) stewed (of fruit) 2) creamed (of vegetables)
sukker sugar
  ~ **brød** sponge cake
  ~ **ert** sugar pea
suppe soup
surkål boiled cabbage flavoured with sugar, vinegar and caraway seeds
sursild soused herring
svinekjøtt pork
svinekotelett pork chop
svineribbe spare-rib
svinestek roast pork
sviske prune
  ~ **grøt** stewed prunes
sylte brawn (US head cheese)
  ~ **agurk** pickled gherkin (US pickle)
syltelabb boiled and salt-cured pig's trotter (US pig's foot)
syltetøy jam
terte tart, cake

tilslørte bondepiker dessert made from layers of apple sauce and bread-crumbs, topped with whipped cream

timian thyme

torsk cod

torskerogn cod roe

torsketunge cod tongue

trøffel (pl **trøfler**) truffle

tunfisk tunny (US tuna)

tunge tongue

tyttebær kind of cranberry

vaffel waffle

vaktel quail

valnøtt walnut

vannbakkels cream puff

vannis water-ice (US sherbet)

vilt game

voksbønne butter bean (US wax bean)

vørterkake spiced malt bread

wienerbrød Danish pastry

ørret (salmon) trout

østers oyster

ål eel

årfugl black grouse

Drink

akevitt spirits distilled from potatoes or grain, often flavoured with aromatic seeds and spices

alkoholfri non-alcoholic

aperitiff aperitif

appelsinbrus orangeade

bar neat (US straight)

brennevin brandy, spirit

brus fizzy (US carbonated) fruit drink

dobbel double

dram shot of spirit

eplemost applejuice

fløte cream

fruktsaft fruit juice

gløgg similar to mulled wine, with spirits and spices

is ice

  med ~ on the rocks

kaffe coffee

  ~ med fløte with cream

  ~ uten fløte black

  ~ likør coffee-flavoured liqueur

  is~ iced

kakao cocoa

kefir kefir, a kind of yoghurt

konjakk cognac

likør liqueur

linjeakevitt *akevitt* which is stored in oak casks in the holds of Norwegian ships; the rolling motion of the ship is said to produce a unique taste

melk milk

  kald ~ cold

  varm ~ warm

mineralvann mineral water

pils lager

pjolter long drink of whisky or brandy and soda water

portvin port (wine)

rom rum

rødvinstoddi mulled wine
saft squash (US fruit drink)
sjokolade chocolate drink
te tea
   ~ **med sitron** with lemon
vann water
vin wine
   het~ fortified
   hvit~ white

musserende ~ sparkling
rød~ red
tørr ~ dry
øl beer
   bayer~ medium-strong, dark
   bokk~ bock
   export~ strong, light coloured
   lager~ light lager
   vørter~ non-alcoholic beer

NORWEGIAN

Polish

Guide to pronunciation

Letter	Approximate pronunciation
Consonants	
b, f, k, l, m, p, z	are pronounced as in English
cz	like **ch** in **ch**urch
dż	like **j** in **j**am
g	as in **g**irl
j	like **y** in **y**et
ł	like **w** in **w**in
n	as in English but put your tongue against the front teeth and not the teeth ridge
s	as in **s**it
sz	like **sh** in **sh**ine
t, d	as in English but put your tongue against the front teeth and not against the teeth ridge

| w | like v in van |
| ż or rz | like s in pleasure |

Sounds distinctly different

An often recurring phenomenon in the Slavic languages is "softening" or the "softened" pronunciation of consonants. Examples of this in Polish are **ć, dź, ń, ś** and **z**. A similar effect can be produced by pronouncing **y** as in yet–but very, very short—after the consonant.

c	like the English sequence **ts** in **ts**et**s**e pronounced quickly
ć	pronounced like the Polish c but with "softening"
dz	like the English sequence **ds** in be**ds** pronounced quickly
dź or dzi	pronounced like the Polish dz but with "softening"
h or ch	similar to English **h** but with much more friction
ń or ni	pronounced like the English **n** with considerable "softening"
r	like the Scottish **r** (vibration of the tip of the tongue); note that it's also pronounced at the end of words
ś or si	pronounced like the English **s** but with "softening"
ź or zi	pronounced like the English **z** but with "softening"

Notice that voiced sounds become completely devoiced at the end of a word or in combination with voiceless sounds, i.e., they're pronounced like their voiceless counterparts (e.g., **b** of chleb is pronounced like **p; w** of rów is pronounced like **f; rz** and **z** in przez like **sz** and **s**, etc.).

Vowels

a	like English **u** in c**u**lt
e	like **e** in t**e**n
i	like **ee** in f**ee**t
y	like **i** in f**i**t
o	like **o** in c**o**t
u or ó	a sound between the English **u** in p**u**t and **oo** in b**oo**ts
ą	is pronounced **on** before a consonant; when it's the final letter, it's pronounced like French **an** in fiancé
ę	is pronounced **en** before a consonant or like **e** in b**e**d when it's the final letter

Some diphthongs

ej	like **a** in take
aj	like **i** in like

Stress

The stress falls in Polish on the next to the last syllable.

Some useful expressions

Hungry

I'm hungry/I'm thirsty.

Jestem głodny/Chce mi się pić.

Can you recommend a good restaurant?

Czy może pan/pani polecić mi dobrą restaurację?

Are there any good, cheap restaurants around here?

Czy jest tu gdzieś blisko tania i dobra restauracja?

I'd like to reserve a table for ... people.

Chciałbym zarezerwować stolik dla ... osób.

We'll come at ... o'clock.

Przyjdziemy o ...

Asking

Good evening. I'd like a table for ... people.

Dobry wieczór. Proszę o stolik dla ... osób.

Could we have a table...?

Proszę stolik...

in the corner
by the window
outside
on the terrace

w rogu
przy oknie
na zewnątrz
na tarasie

May I please have the menu?

Czy mogę prosić o kartę?

What's this?

Co to jest?

Do you have...?

Czy jest...?

a set menu
local dishes
a children's menu

obiad firmowy
dania regionalne
danie dla dziecka

Waiter/Waitress!	Proszę pana/Proszę pani!
What do you recommend?	Co pan/pani poleca?
Could I have (a/an)… please?	Proszę…

ashtray	popielniczkę
another chair	jeszcze jedno krzesło
finger bowl	miseczkę do mycia rąk
fork	widelec
glass	szklankę
knife	nóż
napkin	serwetkę
plate	talerz
pepper mill	młynek do pieprzu
serviette	serwetkę
spoon	łyżkę
toothpick	wykałaczkę

| I'd like a/an/some… | Proszę |

aperitif	aperitif
appetizer	zakąskę
beer	piwo
bread	chleb
butter	masło
cheese	ser
chips	frytki
coffee	kawę
dessert	deser
fish	rybę
french fries	frytki
fruit	owoce
game	dziczyznę
ice-cream	lody
lemon	cytrynę
lettuce	sałatę
meat	mięso
mineral water	wodę mineralną
milk	mlekb
mustard	musztardę
noodles	makaron
oil	olej
olive oil	oliwę
pepper	pieprz

potatoes	**ziemniaki**
poultry	**drób**
rice	**ryż**
rolls	**bułeczki**
saccharin	**sacharynę**
salad	**sałatkę**
salt	**sól**
sandwich	**kanapkę**
seafood	**frutti di mare**
seasoning	**przyprawy**
soup	**zupę**
starter	**zakąskę**
sugar	**cukier**
tea	**herbatę**
vegetables	**jarzynę**
vinegar	**ocet**
(iced) water	**wodę (z lodem)**
wine	**wino**

SMACZNEGO!
ENJOY YOUR MEAL!

---

baked	**zapiekane**
baked in parchment	**pieczone w pergaminie**
boiled	**gotowane**
braised	**gotowane**
cured	**peklowane**
fried	**smażone**
grilled	**z rusztu**
marinated	**marynowane**
poached	**z wody**
roasted	**pieczone**
sautéed	**sauté**
smoked	**wędzone**
steamed	**gotowane**
stewed	**duszone**
underdone (rare)	**po angielsku**
medium	**średnio wysmażone**
well-done	**mocno wysmażone**

NA ZDROWIE!
CHEERS!

glass	**lampka**
bottle	**butelka**
red	**czerwone**
white	**białe**
rosé	**rosé**
very dry	**wytrawne**
dry	**półwytrawne**
sweet	**słodkie**
light	**jasne**
full-bodied	**wytrawne**
sparkling	**musujące**
neat (straight)	**czysta**
on the rocks	**z lodem**

The bill

I'd like to pay.	**Chciałbym zapłacić.**
We'd like to pay separately.	**Chcielibyśmy zapłacić oddzielnie.**
You've made a mistake in this bill, I think.	**Chyba się pan pomylił w rachunku.**
What's this amount for?	**Czego dotyczy ta suma?**
Is service included?	**Czy obsługa jest wliczona?**
Is everything included?	**Czy rachunek obejmuje wszystko?**
Do you accept traveller's cheques?	**Czy pan/pani przyjmuje czeki podróżne?**
Thank you. This is for you.	**Dziękuję, to dla pana/pani.**
Keep the change.	**Reszty nie trzeba.**
That was a very good meal.	**Jedzenie było bardzo dobre.**
We enjoyed it, thank you.	**Smakowało nam. Dziękuję.**

Complaints

That's not what I ordered.	**Tego nie zamawiałem.**
I asked for...	**Prosiłem o...**
May I change this?	**Czy mogę to zamienić?**
The meat is...	**Mięso jest...**
overdone	**przesmażone**
underdone	**niedosmażone**
too rare	**za surowe**
too tough	**za twarde**
This is too...	**To jest za...**
bitter/salty/sweet	**gorzkie/słone/słodkie**
The food is cold.	**To danie jest zimne.**
This isn't fresh.	**To nie jest świeże.**
What's taking you so long?	**Dlaczego to trwa tak długo?**
Where are our drinks?	**Gdzie są nasze napoje?**
This isn't clean.	**To nie jest czyste.**
Would you ask the head waiter to come over?	**Czy można prosić kierownika sali?**

Numbers

1	jeden	11	jedenaście
2	dwa	12	dwanaście
3	trzy	13	trzynaście
4	cztery	14	czternaście
5	pięć	15	piętnaście
6	sześć	16	szesnaście
7	siedem	17	siedemnaście
8	osiem	18	osiemnaście
9	dziewięć	19	dziewiętnaście
10	dziesięć	20	dwadzieścia

Food

Please note that Polish alphabetical order is **a, ą, b, c, ć, d, e, ę, f, g, h, i, j, k, l, ł, m, n, ń, o, ó, p, r, s, ś, t, u, w, y, z, ź, ż.**

agrest gooseberries
ananas pineapple
antrykot rib steak
arbuz watermelon
(w) auszpiku (in) gelatine
babka drożdżowa a yeast cake with a hole in the centre
  ~ **piaskowa** a yeast cake with a hole in the centre, usually with raisins and almonds added
bakalie exotic or non-Polish fruits such as raisins, almonds
bakłażany eggplant, aubergine
  ~ **faszerowane mięsem** stuffed with meat
baleron large ham sausage
banany bananas
baranina mutton
  ~ **duszona w kapuście** stewed mutton with cabbage
  ~ **duszona z kminkiem** stewed mutton with cumin
barszcz czerwony borsch, beetroot soup; served hot
  ~ **ukraiński** Ukrainian-style borsch, soup with vegetables
bażant pheasant
  ~ **pieczony** broiled pheasant
befsztyk beefsteak
  ~ **tatarski** raw chopped meat, anchovies, egg, onion, oil, pepper, salt
  ~ **z cebulą** beefsteak with fried onions

bezy meringue
biała kiełbasa pork sausage
białko egg white
bigos a mixture of cabbage and sauerkraut with a variety of boiled meats
  ~ **z dorsza** browned slices of cod, mixed with cabbage, boiled mushrooms, tomato paste, paprika and other seasonings
biszkoptowe ciasto sponge cake
biszkopty fancy biscuits (US cookies)
bita śmietana whipped cream
  ~ **z rodzynkami** whipped cream with raisins
bliny Russian-style pancakes; small and thick yeast pancakes
boczek bacon
  ~ **wędzony** smoked bacon
boeuf Stroganoff beef stroganoff; thin slices of beef braised in a sour-cream sauce
borowiki boletus mushrooms
borówki bilberries, blueberries
  ~ **z chrzanem** bilberries with horseradish
botwina beet greens
bób broad beans
  ~ **z wody** stewed broad beans
brizol grilled beefsteak
brukiew turnips

brukselka brussels sprouts

bryndza kind of sheep's milk cheese, strong flavour and salty

brzoskwinie peaches

budyń milk pudding

bukiet z jarzyn mixed vegetables

bulion z diablotką consommé with meat-fillet, ravioli-type noddles

~ **z żółtkiem** consommé with raw egg

bułki rolls

~ **mleczne** bread rolls or sweet rolls

buraczki beetroot

camembert imitation camembert; a soft cheese with a tangy flavour

cebula onion

cebulka marynowana pickled onion

cena price

chałwa halvah; a sugary loaf, made with honey and often pistachio nuts

chińska półsurówka z selerem half raw and half cooked salad of celery root, seasoned with oil and mustard

chleb bread

~ **czerstwy** stale bread

~ **pszenny** wholemeal (US wholewheat) bread

~ **razowy** black bread (US pumpernickel)

~ **świeży** fresh bread

~ **żytni** rye bread

chłodnik chilled cream of beetroot soup with vegetables

chrzan horseradish

ciastka kruche biscuits (US cookies)

~ **drożdżowe** yeast cake

~ **tortowe** layer cake with flavoured butter-cream filling

ciastko cake

cielęcina veal

~ **duszona w jarzynach** veal and vegetable stew

(w) cieście 1) pasty 2) pastry

cietrzew duszony w śmietanie black grouse braised in sour cream

comber barani saddle of mutton

comber sarni loin of venison

cukier sugar

cukierki sweets (US candy)

cykoria endive (US chicory)

cynaderki kidneys

~ **cielęce** veal kidneys

cynamon cinnamon

cytryna lemon

czarna rzepa black radish

czarne porzeczki blackcurrants

czekolada chocolate

czekoladki chocolate biscuits (US chocolate sandwich cookies) with different fillings

czereśnie cherries

czernina soup made of duck blood broth and vinegar

czosnek garlic

ćwikła salad of beetroot with horseradish

daktyle dates

danie meal

deser dessert

diablotka a kind of dumpling or meatball served with soup

dorsz cod

~ **po grecku** cod, marinated with vegetables; grilled

~ **w galarecie** cod in gelatine

drożdże yeast

drożdżowe ciastko sugared tea cake (US Danish pastry)

drób fowl

~ **w kokilce** dressed with white sauce

duszone stewed, braised

dynia pumpkin

dziczyzna game

dzik boar

dzika kaczka pieczona roast wild duck

dżem jam

~ **owocowy** fruit jam

~ **śliwkowy** plum jam

edamski ser imitation edam cheese; mild flavour, yellow colour

eklerka chocolate cake with whipped-cream filling

ementalski ser swiss cheese; imitation *Emmental*, with holes and mild, nutty flavour

eskalop schabowy loin of pork

estragon tarragon

fasola beans

~ **po bretońsku** butter (US navy) beans in tomato sauce

~ **szparagowa** haricot beans

faworki a kind of light, sugared fritter

figi figs

filet fillet

~ **cielęcy** veal scallop

~ **wieprzowy** pork fillet

~ **z polędwicy** beef fillet

~ **z ryby** fish fillet

flaki tripe with seasoning

~ **cielęce** veal tripe

~ **po warszawsku** Warsaw-style tripe with marjoram and pepper seasoning

flaki jarskie "vegetable tripe"; different kinds of spiced, stewed vegetables

flądra flounder

~ **wędzona** smoked flounder

forszmak veal in tomato sauce

fricassée z dorsza oven-browned cod, with mushrooms, cauliflower, french beans

frytki chips (US french fries)

(w) galarecie (in) gelatine

galaretka owocowa jam

galaretka z nóżek cielęcych calf's trotters (US feet) in gelatine

galaretka z nóżek wieprzowych pig's trotters (US feet) in gelatine

gąski marynowane marinated chanterelle mushrooms

gęś goose

~ **pieczona z jabłkami** roast goose with apples

~ **w maladze** goose braised in red dessert wine

gicz leg

główka cielęca calf's head

golonka shoulder of pork

~ **gotowana** boiled

~ **peklowana** pickled

~ **z kapustą** with sauerkraut

gołąbki cabbage

~ **z kaszą i mięsem** stuffed cabbage with cooked groats and meat

~ **z ryżu i grzybami** stuffed with rice and mushrooms

gołębie pieczone roast pigeon

gorące hot

gorczyca Russian mustard, sharp

gotowane braised

Gouda imitation Dutch-style cheese, mild

goździki cloves

grejpfrut grapefruit

grochówka pea soup

groszek green peas

~ **w majonezie** green peas in mayonnaise

gruszki pears

~ **w czekoladzie** pears in chocolate sauce

grzanki toast

~ **do zupy** sippets, croutons

grzyby mushrooms

gulasz goulash; chunks of beef braised in a savoury paprika sauce

~ **po węgiersku** a hotter and spicier goulash dish

halibut halibut

~ **w sosie śliwkowym** halibut in plum sauce

herbatniki biscuits (US cookies)

homar lobster

imbir ginger

indyk turkey

~ **nadziewany** stuffed turkey braised in dessert wine

~ **pieczony** roast turkey

jabłka apples

~ **nadziewane z konfiturami** apples filled with jam

~ **pieczone** baked apples

~ **w cieście** apple fritters

jadłospis set menu

jagody bilberries, blueberries

jajecznica scrambled eggs

~ **na boczku** with bacon

~ **z szynką** with ham

jajka eggs

~ **faszerowane** stuffed eggs

~ **na miękko** soft-boiled eggs

~ **na twardo** hard-boiled eggs

~ **sadzone** soft-boiled eggs, shelled, served in a glass

~ **w galarecie** eggs lightly poached and served in gelatine

~ **w majonezie** egg salad

~ **w sosie chrzanowym** hard-boiled eggs with horseradish sauce

~ **w sosie musztardowym** hard-boiled eggs with mustard sauce

~ **w szklance (po wiedeńsku)** soft-boiled eggs, shelled, served in a glass

jarzyny vegetables

jeleń venison

jesiotr sturgeon

jeżyny blackberries

kabaczki vegetable marrow (US zucchini)

kabanosy very thin dried pork sausage

kaczka duck

~ **pieczona** roast duck

~ **z jabłkami** duck stuffed with apples

kajzerka bread roll

kalafior cauliflower

kalamary squid

~ **w majonezie** squid with mayonnaise

kalarepka kohlrabi

kanapka sandwich

~ **z serem** cheese

~ **z szynką** jam

kaparki capers

kapusta cabbage

~ **czerwona** red cabbage

~ **kiszona** sauerkraut

~ **na słodko z kminkiem** cabbage seasoned with cumin

~ **włoska** savoy

kapuśniak sauerkraut and cabbage soup

karaś crucian, a freshwater fish

karmazyn haddock

karp carp

~ **na słodko z migdałami** carp in almond sauce

~ **po królewsku** "king's carp"; baked carp balls with almonds and raisins

~ **w szarym sosie z grzybami** carp in sweet-and-sour sauce with mushrooms

kartoflanka potato soup

kartofle potatoes

~ **w mundurkach** boiled potatoes in their jackets

kasza groats, porridge

~ **gryczana** buckwheat groats

~ **jaglana** millet groats

~ **manna** wheat groats

~ **perłowa** pearl barley

~ **ze słoniną** groats with bacon bits

kaszanka z cebulą black pudding (US blood sausage) braised with onions

kasztany chestnuts

kawior caviar

ketchup ketchup

kiełbasa sausage

~ **na gorąco** hot sausage

~ **na rożnie** grilled sausage

~ **parówkowa** kind of frankfurter, wiener

kisiel jam

~ **żurawinowy** cranberry sauce

kiszka krwawa black pudding (US blood sausage)

~ **wątrobiana** liver sausage

kleik gruel, porridge

klops z cielęciny veal meatballs

kluski dumplings

~ **kładzione** poached dumplings

~ **lane** dumplings

~ **śląskie ze słoniną** bacon dumplings

~ **z makiem** poppy seed dumplings

~ **z serem** cream cheese dumplings

kminek cumin

knedle dumplings

~ **czeskie ze słoniną** a type of dumpling made of white rolls and bacon

~ **ze śliwkami** plum dumplings

kogel-mogel beaten egg yolk with sugar; especially given to children as a tonic

kolacja supper

kołduny litewskie dumpling o meat, suet, marjoram an onions

kompot stewed fruit

~ **z gruszek** stewed pears

~ **z jabłek** stewed apples

~ **z wiśni** stewed cherries

~ **ze śliwek** stewed plums

koncentrat pomidorowy tomat paste

konfitura jam

konina horse meat

konserwa tin (US can)

koper dill

kopytka potato dumplings, serve with bacon bits

korki ze śledzia small rolled her ring

korniszony gherkins

kości bones

kotlet chop, hamburger, chicke breast

~ **de volaille** chicken breas filled with melted butter

~ **mielony** hamburger steak

~ **schabowy** pork chop

krem 1) whipped cream 2) a kin of dessert made of whippe cream with the addition o other ingredients, e.g. raisin fruit, etc.

~ **czekoladowy** whipped crean with chocolate

~ **pomarańczowy** whippe cream with orange

~ **sułtański** whipped cream wit raisins

krewetki shrimp

królik rabbit

~ **w śmietanie** rabbit braised i sour cream

krupnik barley soup

kukurydza maize (US corn)

kulebiak pasty, pie
~ **z grzybami** mushroom pasty
~ **z kapustą** cabbage pasty
~ **z rybą** fish pasty
kura w potrawce chicken fricassee
~ **w rosole** stewed chicken
kurczę chicken
~ **po polsku** roast chicken stuffed with chicken livers and white bread
kurki chanterelle mushrooms
kwaśne sour
leniwe pierogi white-cheese dumpling
leszcz bream
~ **w galarecie** bream in gelatine
lin tench
listek laurowy laurel
lody ice-cream
~ **bakaliowe** tutti-frutti ice-cream
~ **mieszane** mixed ice-cream
~ **truskawkowe** strawberry ice-cream
~ **waniliowe** vanilla ice-cream
łazanki thin noodles, often served with soup on special occasions, e.g. Christmas
łopatka shoulder
łosoś salmon
~ **wędzony** smoked salmon
majeranek marjoram
majonez mayonnaise
mak poppy seed
makaron macaroni, noodles
~ **z jajkami** noodles with fried eggs
~ **z serem** macaroni and cheese
makowiec poppy seed cake
makrela mackerel
maliny raspberries
mała small
mandarynki tangerines
manna kasza cream of wheat

Marago a brand-name instant coffee
marchewka carrot
marmolada jam
marynowane marinated
marynowane grzyby marinated mushrooms
masło butter
maślaki boletus mushrooms
~ **ze śmietaną** with sour cream
mazurek a square cake
~ **bakaliowy** usually with raisins, almonds
~ **figowy** with figs
~ **orzechowy** with chestnuts
mąka flour
medalion small, round or oval cut of meat
~ **cielęcy** small, round or oval cut of veal
melba ice-cream with fruit
melon melon
mieszane (a), (y) mixed
mięso meat
~ **mocno wysmażone** well-done
~ **po angielsku** underdone (US rare)
~ **wysmażone** medium
~ **zimne w galarecie** cold meat in gelatine
mięta peppermint
migdały almonds
miód pszczeli honey
mirabelki yellow plums
mizeria chopped cucumbers with sour cream and dill
mleczko waniliowe vanilla custard pudding
młode young, spring
~ **kartofle** spring potatoes
morele apricots
mortadela bologna sausage
mostek breast portion of meat with a savoury stuffing

~ **barani** stuffed breast of mutton

~ **cielęcy** stuffed breast of veal

móżdżek cielęcy calf's brains

~ **w cieście** pasty of calf's brains

mus z jabłek apple sauce

musztarda mustard

myśliwska kiełbasa kind of dry pork sausage

nabiał dairy products

nadzienie stuffing

naleśniki pancakes

~ **z kapustą i grzybami** filled with cabbage and mushrooms

~ **z marmoladą** with jam

~ **z mięsem** with meat

~ **z serem** with cottage cheese

~ **ze szpinakiem** with spinach

napoleonka napoleon

nerki kidney

~ **cielęce duszone** stewed veal kidneys

nerkówka cielęca nadziewana roast veal stuffed with kidneys

nerkówka cielęca pieczona roast veal with kidneys

Neska a brand-name instant coffee

nóżki cielęce calf's trotters (US feet)

~ **w cieście** calf's trotters (US feet) in pasty

~ **w galarecie** calf's trotters (US feet) in gelatine

obiad dinner

~ **firmowy** menu

obsługa wliczona service included

ocet vinegar

ogórek cucumber

~ **kiszony** pickled cucumber

~ **konserwowy** gherkins

olej oil

oliwa olive oil

oliwki olives

omlet omelet

~ **z dżemem** jam

~ **z groszkiem** peas

~ **z grzybami** mushrooms

~ **z szynką** ham

~ **ze szczawiem** sorrel

orzechy chestnuts

~ **laskowe** hazelnuts

~ **włoskie** walnuts

ostrygi oysters

oszczypek smoked sheep's milk cheese

owoce fruit

ozór tongue

~ **cielęcy** veal tongue

~ **po polsku** in sweet-and-sour sauce

~ **wołowy** beef tongue

panierowane breaded

parmezan parmesan cheese

parówki wiener, frankfurter

papryka pepper, sweet pepper, pimento

~ **czerwona** red sweet pepper

~ **zielona** green pepper

paprykarz stew

~ **cielęcy** veal stew

~ **z królika** rabbit stew

~ **z ryby** fish stew

paszteciki rissole (US patty), croquette

~ **z kapustą** cabbage rissole

~ **z mięsem** meat croquette

~ **z ryby** fish croquette

pasztet moulded pâté; meatloaf

~ **w auszpiku** meatloaf in gelatine

~ **z cielęciny** veal

~ **z drobiu** chicken

~ **z dziczyzny** game

~ **z gęsich wątróbek** goose-liver pâté

~ **z indyka** turkey

~ **z królika** rabbit

~ **z zająca** hare
pączki doughnut
perliczki pieczone roast guinea fowl
pieczarki button mushrooms
~ **w śmietanie** in sour-cream
~ **z patelni** sautéed
pieczeń barania roast mutton
~ **cielęca** roast veal
~ **wieprzowa** roast pork
~ **wołowa** roast beef
~ **z dzika** roast wild boar
pieczeń z ryb morskich a loaf of saltwater fish, served with potatoes and salad, or cold with marinated mushrooms and plums
pieczone roasted
pieczywo bread and rolls
pieprz pepper
piernik spice cake
pierogi dumplings
~ **ruskie ze słoniną** dumplings with bacon bits
~ **z grzybami** mushroom dumplings
~ **z jagodami** bilberry, blueberry dumplings
~ **z kiszonej kapusty** sauerkraut dumplings
~ **z mięsem** meatballs
~ **z serem** cheese dumplings
~ **z wiśniami** cherry dumplings
pieróg pasty
~ **ruski ze słodką kapustą** cabbage pasty
~ **z mięsem** meat pasty
pietruszka parsley
pigwa quince
pilaw steamed rice
piwna zupa beer soup with cinnamon, cloves and sometimes cream
placek drożdżowy z owocami yeast cake with fresh fruit
placki ziemniaczane potato fritters
płastuga dab
~ **pieczona w słoninie** baked dab with salt bacon
płatki owsiane z mlekiem porridge
płucka cielęce z winem veal lights in wine
podroby giblets
polewka buttermilk soup
polędwica beef
~ **duszona ze śmietaną** braised with sour cream
~ **po angielsku** roast
~ **wędzona** smoked
pomarańcze oranges
pomidory tomatoes
ponczowe ciastko sponge cake steeped in rum
pory leeks
porzeczki currants
powidła damson (plum) jam
poziomki wild strawberries
przepiórka quail
przyprawy seasoning, spices
przystawki appetizers
pstrąg trout
~ **sauté** sautéed trout
ptysie z bitą śmietaną cream puff
pulardy fattened pullet
pulpety croquette of meat, fish, vegetables or dough, coated with breadcrumbs or butter and deep-fried
pumpernikiel black bread (US pumpernickel)
purée purée, mashed
~ **z jarzyn** purée of vegetables
~ **z ziemniaków** mashed potatoes
pyzy meat pie
rabarbar rhubarb
racuszki drożdżowe a kind of yeast doughnut

ragout z baraniny mutton stew
raki freshwater crayfish
  ~ **z wody** poached crayfish
rakowa zupa crayfish soup
renklody greengage
rizotto rice casserole
  ~ **z baraniny** mutton and rice casserole
  ~ **z drobiu** chicken and rice casserole
rodzynki raisins
rogaliki crescent roll
rolada a slice of meat rolled around minced meat or other stuffing
rolmops marinated herring rolled around chopped onions or gherkins
rosół broth
  ~ **z cielęciny** veal
  ~ **z kury** chicken
  ~ **z wołowiny** beef
rostbef roast beef
roztrzepaniec sour milk
(z) rożna grilled
rumsztyk rumpsteak
rurki francuskie z bitą śmietaną tube-like waffles filled with whipped cream
(z) rusztu grilled
ryba fish
  ~ **po grecku** fish marinated with vegetables in tomato sauce, grilled and served chilled
rydze orange agaric or meadow mushrooms
  ~ **z patelni** fried orange agaric mushrooms
ryż rice
  ~ **z masłem** with butter
  ~ **zapiekany z jabłkami** baked with apples
  ~ **z mlekiem** with milk

rzodkiewki radishes
sago sago
salami salami
salceson brawn (US headcheese)
sałata lettuce
sałatka
  ~ **jarzynowa** cooked vegetables in mayonnaise
  ~ **śledziowa** cooked vegetables in mayonnaise with herring
  ~ **z ryby** fish salad
sałatki z ryb wędzonych smoked-fish salad with marinated plums, mayonnaise, paprika
sandacz perch
  ~ **polski** with eggs
  ~ **w galarecie** in gelatine
  ~ **z pieczarkami** perch-pike with mushrooms
sardynki sardines
  ~ **w oliwie** sardines in oil
sarna roe deer, venison
sarnina venison
schab pieczony roast pork tenderloin steak
schab po wiedeńsku breaded pork chop
seler celery
ser cheese
  ~ **biały** fresh curd cheese
  ~ **owczy** cheese from sheep's milk
  ~ **żółty** semi-hard, robust yellow cheese
serce heart
sernik wiedeński cheesecake
sękacz a layer cake
siekane minced, hashed
sielawa whiting
słodkie sweet
słodycze sweets (US candy)
słodzone sweetened
słonina salt bacon
smalec lard

~ **gęsi** goose fat
smażone fried
soja soya beans
sola sole
  ~ **zapiekana z pomidorami** baked in tomatoes
solone salted
solone śledzie salted herring
sos sauce
  ~ **cebulowy** onion
  ~ **chrzanowy** horseradish
  ~ **cumberland** sauce of orange juice and redcurrant jelly
  ~ **grzybowy** mushroom
  ~ **holenderski** tangy mayonnaise
  ~ **koperkowy** dill
  ~ **musztardowy** mustard
  ~ **pomidorowy** tomato
  ~ **sojowy** soy
  ~ **szary** sweet-and-sour sauce with raisins, almonds; served with fish
  ~ **tatarski** mayonnaise with gherkins, chives, capers
  ~ **węgierski** hot tomato sauce with paprika
sól salt
stefanka a long layer cake with butter-cream filling
stek steak, fillet
  ~ **barani** mutton fillet
  ~ **cielęcy** veal fillet
  ~ **wieprzowy** pork fillet
  ~ **z polędwicy** beefsteak
strucla long white plain cake (US coffee cake); Christmas speciality
strudel thin layers of pastry alternating with apples, nuts, raisins
sucha kiełbasa dried pork sausage
sucharki crackers
sułtanki sultanas, raisins

sum sheatfish (type of large cat-fish)
  ~ **duszony** stewed sheatfish
surowe raw
surówka salad
  ~ **z cykorii** chicory (US endive)
  ~ **z kapusty kiszonej** sauerkraut
  ~ **z marchwi** carrot
  ~ **z ogórków** cucumber
  ~ **z pomidorów** tomato
  ~ **z rzodkiewki** radish
suszone grzyby dried mushrooms
suszone owoce dried fruit
szafran saffron
szarlotka apple cake
szaszłyk shashlik; grilled chunks of meat on a skewer
  ~ **barani** mutton shashlik
  ~ **z polędwicy** beef shashlik with onions
szczaw sorrel
szczupak pike
  ~ **gotowany z jajami** poached with hard-boiled eggs
  ~ **w galarecie** in gelatine
szczypiorek chives
sznycel cielęcy veal scallop
sznycel jarski "vegetarian scallop"; a kind of potato fritter
szparagi asparagus tips
szpinak spinach
  ~ **zasmażany** spinach thickened with browned butter
szprotki sprats
sztufada marinated and larded roast beef
sztuka mięsa boiled beef
szynka ham
  ~ **gotowana** boiled
  ~ **konserwowa** tinned (US canned)
  ~ **wędzona** smoked
szynkowa sausage which resembles ham in taste

śledź herring

~ **marynowany** marinated

~ **po śląsku** a paste of herring, sausage and apples

~ **po wileńsku** marinated herring, served with a sauce made of onions, mushrooms, gherkins, sprats, tomato paste and pepper

~ **w oleju** in oil

~ **w śmietanie** in sour cream

śliwki plums

~ **suszone** prunes

śmietana cream

~ **bita** whipped and sweetened cream

~ **kwaśna** sour

~ **słodka** fresh

śniadanie breakfast

świeży fresh

talerz plate

tapioka tapioca

tłuste fat (adj)

topiony ser melted cheese

torcik waflowy waffle sandwich; two waffles with a sweet filling

tort layer cake

~ **czekoladowy** chocolate

~ **kawowy** mocha

~ **makowy** poppy-seed

~ **marcepanowy** marzipan

~ **orzechowy** walnut

~ **pomarańczowy** orange

trufle truffles

truskawki strawberries

~ **ze śmietaną** with cream

tuńczyk tunny (US tuna)

twaróg fresh curd cheese

~ **z kminkiem** flavoured with cumin

~ **ze słodką śmietaną** flavoured with sweet cream

~ **ze szczypiorkiem i rzodkiewką** flavoured with chives

and radishes

tylżycki ser firm, pale yellow cheese with mild taste

tymianek thyme

udziec leg

~ **sarni** leg of venison

uszka do barszczu dough envelopes served in hot borsch (beetroot soup)

~ **z grzybami** with mushroom filling

~ **z mięsem** with meat filling

wafelki waffles

wanilia vanilla

warzywa vegetables

wątróbka liver

~ **cielęca duszona** sautéed calf's liver

~ **z dorsza w oliwie** cod liver in oil

wędliny cured pork sausages and beef products

wędzone smoked

wędzonka smoked bacon

węgorz eel

~ **w marynacie** eel in vegetable gelatine

~ **wędzony** smoked eel

wieprzowina pork

winogrona grapes

wiśnie cherries

(z) wody poached

wołowina beef

W–Z (wuzetka) a small cake, with a filling of chocolate, jam and custard

zając hare

~ **duszony po myśliwsku** stewed in wine with mushrooms and sour cream

~ **pieczony** roast hare

~ **po polsku** braised in sour cream

~ **w śmietanie** roast hare served

in sour cream
zakąska appetizer
zapiekane baked
ziemniaki potatoes
  ~ **purée** creamed
  ~ **smażone** roast
  ~ **z wody** boiled
zimne cold
zrazy chop, slice of meat
  ~ **baranie** mutton chop
  ~ **bite** pounded fillet
  ~ **siekane** chop, cutlet
  ~ **w sosie pomidorowym** in tomato sauce
  ~ **wieprzowe z ryżem** pork chop with rice
  ~ **z grzybami i ze śmietaną** with mushrooms and sour cream
  ~ **zawijane** an escalope of meat which has been filled and rolled
zupa soup
  ~ **fasolowa** bean
  ~ **grzybowa** mushroom

  ~ **jarzynowa** vegetable
  ~ **ogórkowa** cucumber
  ~ **pomidorowa** tomato
  ~ **rybna** fish
  ~ **szczawiowa** sorrel
  ~ **szparagowa** asparagus
  ~ **w proszku** packaged soup
zupa mleczna cream soup
  ~ **z kaszki manny** cream of semolina soup
  ~ **z płatków owsianych** porridge
  ~ **z ryżu** cream of rice soup
zupa owocowa fruit soup
  ~ **śliwkowa** plum
  ~ **z rabarbaru** rhubarb
  ~ **z wiśni** cherry
żeberka wieprzowe spare ribs
  ~ **duszone** stewed
  ~ **w jarzynach** with vegetables
żurawiny cranberries
żurek sour rye-flour soup, usually with cream
żytni chleb rye bread

Drink

advocat egg brandy
alkoholowe napoje spirits
anyżówka aniseed-flavoured vodka
aperitif aperitif
butelka bottle
Cassis blackcurrant liqueur
coctail mleczny milkshake
  ~ **jabłkowy** apple
  ~ **jagodowy** blackberry
  ~ **kawowy** mocha
  ~ **truskawkowy** strawberry
cytrynówka lemon-flavoured vodka
ćwiartka wódki a quarter of a litre

(about ½ pint) of vodka
Egri-Bikaver "bull's blood"; a full-bodied red wine from Hungary
eierkoniak egg brandy
gazowane sparkling
gorąca czekolada hot chocolate, often with the addition of a beaten egg, topped with whipped cream
grog toddy, hot tea to which rum and spices are added
grzane mulled
  ~ **piwo** ale
  ~ **wino** wine

herbata tea
  ~ **z cytryną** with lemon
jabłecznik cider
jałowcówka home-distilled liquor
jarzębiak vodka flavoured with rowanberries (mountain ashberries)
jogurt yoghurt
kakao cocoa
karafka carafe
kawa coffee
  ~ **duża** large cup
  ~ **mała** small cup
  ~ **mrożona** iced coffee
  ~ **po arabsku** a strong, boiled coffee flavoured with cinnamon
  ~ **po malajsku** a strong, boiled coffee flavoured with vanilla
  ~ **po staropolsku** coffee with whipped cream and cinnamon, and laced with brandy
  ~ **po turecku** a strong, boiled coffee
  ~ **z mlekiem** white coffee
  ~ **zbożowa** coffee substitute, like Postam
  ~ **ze śmietanką** coffee with cream
kefir sour milk
koniak brandy, cognac
krupnik liqueur made from mead (a fermented mixture of water, honey, malt and yeast)
kryniczanka a mineral water
lampka wina a glass of wine
lemoniada soft drink
likier liqueur
(z) lodem on the rocks
lód ice
Madera imitation madeira wine
maślanka buttermilk
mineralna woda mineral water
miód pitny mead, a fermented drink of water, malt, honey,

yeast
  ~ **grzany** mulled mead
mleko milk
  ~ **gorące** hot
  ~ **kwaśne** sour
  ~ **zimne** cold
Myśliwska wódka "hunter's vodka"; has a flavour rather like gin
nalewka na świerzych owocach fruit liqueur
napoje drinks
  ~ **alkoholowe** alcoholic drinks
  ~ **mleczne** dairy drinks
  ~ **niealkoholowe** soft drinks
  ~ **orzeźwiające** refreshments
napój juice, nectar
  ~ **firmowy** home-made
  ~ **jabłeczny** apple
  ~ **malinowy** raspberry
  ~ **z porzeczek** raisin
okocimskie piwo full, light beer (Okocim)
oranżada orangeade
Ovomaltina Ovaltine
pieprzówka pepper-flavoured vodka
Pilsner beer from Pilsen, Czechoslovakia; a light beer with a strong hops flavour
piwo beer
  ~ **beczkowe** draught (draft) beer
  ~ **ciemne** dark beer
  ~ **grzane** mulled beer
  ~ **jasne** light beer
  ~ **z jajkiem** with an egg yolk
  ~ **z sokiem** with syrup
poncz punch, usually a mulled rum drink diluted with water
porter strong, stout beer; 12% alcoholic content
Radeberger East German light beer from Radeberg
Rizling imitation Riesling; dry

white wine from Hungary or Yugoslavia

rum kubański Cuban rum

sok juice

~ **ananasowy** pineapple

~ **grejpfrutowy** grapefruit

~ **jabłkowy** apple

~ **naturalny** fruit

~ **pomarańczowy** orange

~ **pomidorowy** tomato

~ **z czarnej porzeczki** blackcurrant

soplica a dry and fine golden-coloured vodka

spirytus distilling alcohol

syrop syrup

szampan champagne, sparkling wine

śliwowica plum brandy

~ **paschalna** strong plum brandy, especially drunk during Jewish passover

Tokaj sweet golden or dry white wine from Hungary

tonic tonic water

Trójniak a very popular mead (a mixture of water, honey, malt, yeast) liqueur

vermouth vermouth

winiak brandy, distilled from grapes, like cognac

wino wine

~ **białe** white wine

~ **czerwone** red wine

~ **grzane** mulled wine

~ **musujące** sparkling wine

~ **owocowe** apple cider

~ **półwytrawne** slightly dry

~ **słodkie** sweet wine

~ **w temperaturze pokojowej** wine at room temperature

~ **wytrawne** dry wine

~ **zimne** chilled wine

wiśniówka cherry liqueur

woda water

~ **mineralna** mineral water

~ **sodowa** soda water

wódka vodka

~ **wyborowa** the finest clear vodka

żubrówka vodka flavoured with the grass the bison feeds on

żytnia wódka top-quality rye vodka

Żywieckie piwo full light beer from Zywiec

Portuguese

Guide to pronunciation

Letter	Approximate pronunciation
Consonants	
f, k, l, p, t, v	as in English
b	as in English, but often less decisive (more like **v**)
c	1) before **e** and **i**, like **s** in sit 2) elsewhere, like **k** in kill
ç	like **s** in sit
ch	like **sh** in shut
d	as in English, but often less decisive (more like **th** in **this**)
g	1) before **a, o** and **u** or a consonant or after **l, n** and **r**, like **g** in go 2) between vowels, like a soft version of the **ch** in Scottish lo**ch** 3) before **e** and **i**, like **s** in pleasure
h	always silent
j	like **s** in pleasure

lh	like **lli** in million
m	1) between a vowel and a consonant or at the end of a word, it indicates that the vowel is nasalized (see "Nasal vowels") 2) elsewhere, like **m** in met
n	1) when the initial letter or between vowels, like **n** in no 2) in a consonant group and in plural endings it nasalizes the preceding vowel, but is generally silent
nh	like **ni** in onion
q	like **k** in kill
r	strongly trilled as in Scottish speech
s	1) when the initial letter, after a consonant or written **ss**, like **s** in sit 2) between vowels (not necessarily in the same vowels), like **z** in razor 3) when final or before **c, f, p, q, t**, like **sh** in shut 4) elsewhere, like **s** in pleasure
x	1) generally, like **sh** in shut 2) in **ex-** before a vowel, like **z** in razor 3) sometimes like **x** in exit
z	1) when the initial letter, or between vowels, like **z** in razor 2) when final or before **c, f, p, q, s** or **t**, like **sh** in shut 3) elsewhere, like **s** in pleasure

Vowels

a	1) when stressed (see under "Stress"), it's like a blend of the **u** in cut and the **a** in party 2) when unstressed or before **m, n** or **nh** but not in the same syllable, like **a** in about
e	1) when stressed, generally like **e** in get 2) when stressed, sometimes like **a** in late 3) when unstressed, like **er** in other 4) at the beginning of a word and in certain other cases, like **i** in hit
é	like **e** in get
ê	like **a** in late
i	1) when stressed, like **ee** in seed 2) when unstressed, like **i** in coming
o	1) when stressed, like **o** in rod 2) when unstressed, usually like **oo** in foot 3) sometimes, either stressed or unstressed like **o** in note (most common **o** sound)

ô	like **o** in n**o**te
u	1) generally like **oo** in s**oo**n
	2) silent in **gu** and **qu** before **e** or **i**

Diphthongs

A diphthong is two vowels pronounced as a single vowel sound, e.g., in English **boy** there is a diphthong consisting of **o** plus a weak **i** sound. In Portuguese diphthongs, **a**, **e** and **o** are strong vowels and **i** and **u** are weak vowels. In diphthongs the strong vowels are pronounced with more stress (louder) than the weak ones, e.g., **ai** is pronounced like **igh** in s**igh**, and **au** like **ow** in h**ow**. Sometimes the weak vowels can combine to make a diphthong. Apart from these generalizations the exact pronunciation of Portuguese diphthongs isn't easy to predict.

Nasal vowels

These are pronounced through the mouth and through the nose at the same time, just as in the French nasal vowels (e.g., in the French **bon**) and quite similar to the nasal twang heard in some areas of America and Britain.

ã, am, an	something like **ung** in l**ung** or like **an** in French d**an**s
em, en	something like **ing** in s**ing**, but recalling also the **a** in l**a**te
im, in	a nasalized version of the **ea** in l**ea**rn
om, on	like **orn** in c**orn**cob or like **on** in French b**on**
um, un	something like the pronunciation in the North of England of **ung** in l**ung** (a nasalized version of **u** in p**u**t)

Semi-nasalized diphthongs

In these, the first element is nasalized and combined with a weak **i** (pronounced like **y** in yet) or **u** pronounced like **w** in was.

ãe, ãi, êm, final en, usually final em	pronounced as **ã** followed by **y** in yet
ão, final unstressed am	pronounced as **ã** followed by **w** in was
õe, oi	like **orn** in c**orn**cob or like **on** in French b**on**, followed by **y** in yet
ui	like nasal vowel **u** followed by **y** in yet

Stress

1) If a word ends with **a, e** or **o**, the stress falls on the next to the last syllable. Plural endings **m** and **s** are generally disregarded.
2) All other words are stressed on the last syllable.

Words not stressed in accordance with these rules have an accent ('or') over the vowel of the stressed syllable.

Some useful expressions

Hungry

I'm hungry/I'm thirsty.	**Tenho fome/Tenho sede.**
Can you recommend a good restaurant?	**Pode aconselhar um bom restaurante?**
Are there any good, cheap restaurants around here?	**Há algum restaurante bom, barato por aqui?**
I'd like to reserve a table for ... people.	**Queria reservar uma mesa para ... pessoas.**
We'll come at ... o'clock.	**Chegamos às ...**

Asking

Good evening. I'd like a table for ... people.	**Boa noite. Queria uma mesa para ... pessoas.**
Could we have a table...?	**Podemos ter uma mesa...?**
in the corner	**ao canto**
by the window	**perto da janela**
outside	**ao ar livre/fora**
on the terrace	**no terraço**
May I please have the menu?	**Pode dar-me a ementa [o cardápio]?**
What's this?	**O que é isto?**
Do you have...?	**Tem...?**
a set menu	**uma ementa [cardápio] fixa**
local dishes	**pratos típicos**
a children's menu	**uma ementa [cardápio] para crianças**

(Brazilian variations are shown in brackets)

PORTUGUESE

Waiter/Waitress!	**Por favor [Garçom/Garçonete]!**
What do you recommend?	**O que me aconselha?**
Could I have (a/an)... please?	**Pode dar-me... por favor?**
ashtray	**um cinzeiro**
another chair	**outra cadeira**
finger bowl	**uma taça para os dedos**
fork	**um garfo**
glass	**um copo**
knife	**uma faca**
napkin	**um guardanapo**
plate	**um prato**
pepper mill	**o moinho da pimenta**
serviette	**um guardanapo**
spoon	**uma colher**
toothpick	**um palito**

Ordering

I'd like a/an/some...	**Queria...**
aperitif	**um aperitivo**
appetizer	**uns acepipes [aperitivos]**
beer	**uma cerveja**
bread	**pão**
butter	**manteiga**
cheese	**queijo**
chips	**batatas fritas**
coffee	**café**
dessert	**uma sobremesa**
fish	**peixe**
french fries	**batatas fritas**
fruit	**fruta**
game	**caça**
ice-cream	**um gelado [sorvete]**
lemon	**limão**
lettuce	**alface**
meat	**carne**
mineral water	**uma água mineral**
milk	**leite**

mustard	**mostarda**
noodles	**massa**
oil	**óleo**
olive oil	**azeite**
pepper	**pimenta**
potatoes	**batatas**
poultry	**aves**
rice	**arroz**
rolls	**uns pãezinhos**
saccharin	**sacarina**
salad	**uma salada**
salt	**sal**
sandwich	**uma sanduíche**
seafood	**mariscos**
seasoning	**tempero**
soup	**uma sopa**
starter	**uns acepipes [aperitivos]**
sugar	**açúcar**
tea	**chá**
vegetables	**legumes**
vinegar	**vinagre**
(iced) water	**água (com gelo)**
wine	**vinho**

BOM APETITE!
ENJOY YOUR MEAL!

---

baked	**no forno**
baked in parchment	**envolto em papel**
boiled	**cozido**
braised	**estufado**
cured	**salgado/curado**
fried	**frito**
grilled	**grelhado**
marinated	**marinado**
poached (of fish or meat)	**cozido**
poached (of eggs)	**escalfado**
roasted	**assado**
sautéed	**salteado**
smoked	**fumado [defumado]**

steamed	**cozido a vapor**
stewed	**guisado**
underdone (rare)	**muito mal passado**
medium	**mal passado**
well-done	**bem passado**

SAÚDE!
CHEERS!

---

glass	**um copo**
bottle	**uma garrafa**
red	**tinto**
white	**branco**
rosé	**rosé/palhete**
very dry	**extra-seco**
dry	**seco**
sweet	**doce**
light	**ligeiro**
full-bodied	**encorpado**
sparkling	**espumante**
neat (straight)	**puro**
on the rocks	**com gelo**

The bill

I'd like to pay.	**Queria pagar.**
We'd like to pay separately.	**Queríamos pagar cada um separadamente.**
You've made a mistake in this bill, I think.	**Creio que se enganou na conta.**
What's this amount for?	**A que corresponde esta importância?**
Is service included?	**O serviço está incluído?**
Is everything included?	**Está tudo incluído?**
Do you accept traveller's cheques?	**Aceita cheques de viagem?**
Thank you. This is for you.	**Obrigado/a, isto é para si.**

PORTUGUESE

Keep the change.	**Guarde o troco.**
That was a very good meal.	**A refeição estava muito boa.**
We enjoyed it, thank you.	**Apreciámos, obrigado/a.**

Complaints

That's not what I ordered.	**Não é o que eu encomendei.**
I asked for…	**Eu pedi…**
May I change this?	**Posso trocar isto?**
The meat is…	**A carne está…**
overdone	**passada demais**
underdone	**mal passada**
too rare	**mal passada demais**
too tough	**dura demais**
This is too…	**Isto está muito…**
bitter/salty/sweet	**amargo/salgado/doce**
The food is cold.	**A comida está fria.**
This isn't fresh.	**Isto não está fresco.**
What's taking you so long?	**Porque demora tanto?**
Where are our drinks?	**Esqueceu-se de nos trazer as bebidas.**
This isn't clean.	**Isto não está limpo.**
Would you ask the head waiter to come over?	**Pode chamar o Chefe de Mesa [maitre], por favor?**

Numbers

1	**um (fem. uma)**	11	**onze**
2	**dois (fem. duas)**	12	**doze**
3	**três**	13	**treze**
4	**quatro**	14	**catorze**
5	**cinco**	15	**quinze**
6	**seis**	16	**dezasseis**
7	**sete**	17	**dezassete**
8	**oito**	18	**dezoito**
9	**nove**	19	**dezanove**
10	**dez**	20	**vinte**

Food

à, à moda de in the style of
abacate avocado pear
abacaxi pineapple
abóbora pumpkin (US winter squash)
açafrão saffron
acará, acarajé portion of fritters made of black-eyed bean purée, ground, dried shrimps and hot peppers
acelga swiss chard
acepipes hors d'œuvre
acompanhamento vegetables, side dish
açorda thick soup or side dish where bread is a principal ingredient
  ~ alentejana with poached eggs, garlic, coriander leaves and olive-oil
  ~ de bacalhau with dried cod, sliced and fried in garlic-flavoured olive-oil
  ~ à moda de Sesimbra with fish, garlic and coriander leaves
açúcar sugar
agrião watercress
aipim cassava root
aipo celeriac

alcachofra artichoke
  fundo de ~ bottom
alcaparra caper
alecrim rosemary
aletria 1) vermicelli, thin noodles 2) dessert made with vermicelli
alface lettuce
alheira garlic sausage made of breadcrumbs and different kinds of minced meat
  ~ à transmontana served with fried eggs, fried potatoes and cabbage
alho garlic
  ~ francês/-porro leek
almoço lunch
almôndega ball of fish or meat
alperce apricot
amargo bitter
amêijoas baby clams
  ~ à bulhão pato fried in olive-oil with garlic and coriander
  ~ à espanhola baked in the oven with onions, tomatoes, peppers, garlic and herbs
  ~ ao natural steamed with herbs and served with melted butter and lemon juice
ameixa plum
  ~ seca prune

amêndoa almond
amendoim peanut
amora blackberry
ananás pineapple
anchova anchovy
angu cassava-root flour or maize boiled in water and salt
ao in the style of
arenque herring
arroz rice
  ~ de Cabidela kind of risotto with giblets and chicken blood, flavoured with vinegar
  ~ doce pudding flavoured with cinnamon
  ~ de frango baked with chicken
  ~ de manteiga cooked in water and butter
  ~ de pato no forno duck cooked with bacon and *chouriço* then baked with rice
  ~ tropeiro with *carne de sol*
aspargo asparagus
assado roast
atum tuna fish
  bife de ~ cutlet (US steak) marinated in white wine and fried in olive-oil
aveia oats
avelã hazelnut
aves fowl
azeda sorrel
azedo sour
azeite olive-oil
  ~ de dendê palm-oil
azeitona olive
  ~ preta black
  ~ verde (de Elvas) green
babá de moça dessert made of egg yolks poached in coconut milk and syrup
bacalhau cod, usually dried and salted

  ~ à Brás fried with onions and potatoes, then baked with a topping of beaten eggs
  ~ de caldeirada braised with chopped onions, tomatoes, parsley, garlic and coriander (or saffron)
  ~ cozido com todos poached and served with boiled cabbage, onions, potatoes, chickpeas and eggs
  ~ à Gomes de Sá fried with onions, boiled potatoes, garlic and garnished with hard-boiled eggs and black olives
  ~ com leite de coco poached in coconut milk seasoned with coriander
  ~ com natas no forno boiled, then baked with potatoes in a white sauce with cream
  ~ à provinciana a gratin of poached cod, potatoes and *grelos* (or broccoli), topped with minced hard-boiled eggs, flour and port wine
  ~ à transmontana braised with cured pork or *chouriço,* white wine, parsley, garlic and tomatoes
batata potato
  ~ doce yam, sweet potato
  ~ frita chip (US french fry)
  ~ palha matchstick
baunilha vanilla
berbigão type of cockle
beringela aubergine (US eggplant)
besugo sunfish, type of sea-bream
beterraba beetroot
bifana slice of pork tenderloin usually served in a bun
bife steak, escalope

~ **a cavalo** of beef topped with a fried egg

~ **à cortador** of beef fried in garlic-flavoured butter

~ **de espadarte** swordfish cutlet (US steak) fried with onions and potatoes

~ **à milanesa** breaded escalope of veal

bifinhos de vitela slices of veal fillet served with a Madeira wine sauce

biscoito biscuit (US cookie)

bobó dish made of dried shrimps, onions, cassava root, fish stock, palm-oil, coconut milk and served with bananas and grated coconut

boi beef

bola de Berlim doughnut

bolacha biscuit (US cookie)

~ **de água e sal** cracker

bolinho de bacalhau deep-fried croquette of dried cod and mashed potatoes flavoured with eggs and parsley

bolo cake

~ **caseiro** home-made

~ **podre** flavoured with honey and cinnamon

borracho young pigeon

borrego lamb

(na) brasa charcoal-grilled

brioche yeast bun

broa 1) thick maize-(US corn-). meal cracker 2) type of gingerbread

brócolos broccoli

cabrito kid

~~**montês** roebuck

~ **à ribatejana** marinated and roasted with herbs and paprika

caça game

(à) caçador(a) simmered in white wine with carrots, onions, herbs and sometimes tomatoes

cachorro (quente) hot-dog

cachucho small sea-bream

café da manhã breakfast

caju cashew nut

calamar (sliced) squid

caldeirada fish stewed with potatoes, onions, tomatoes, pimentos, spices, wine and olive-oil

~ **de enguias** eel simmered with potatoes, onions, garlic, bay leaf and parsley

~ **à fragateira** fish, shellfish and mussels simmered in a fish stock with tomatoes and herbs; served on toast

~ **à moda da Póvoa** hake, skate, sea-bass and eel simmered with tomatoes in olive-oil

caldo clear soup, consommé

~ **verde** thick soup made from shredded cabbage, potatoes and *chouriço*

camarões shrimps

~ **à baiana** served in a spicy tomato sauce with boiled rice

~ **grandes** Dublin Bay prawns (US jumbo shrimps)

cambuquira tender shoots of pumpkin (US squash) stewed with meat

canapé small open sandwich

canela cinnamon

canja chicken-and-rice soup

canjica dessert made of peanuts and sweet-corn cooked in milk with cloves and cinnamon and served in fresh coconut milk

capão capon

caqui persimmon

caracóis snails

caracol 1) snail 2) a spiral-shaped bun filled with currants

caranguejo crab

carapau horse mackerel
~ **de escabeche** fried and dipped in a sauce made of vinegar, olive-oil, fried onions and garlic

cardápio menu

caril curry

carne meat
~ **de porco à alentejana** cubes of marinated pork fried with clams
~ **de sol** salted and dried in the sun

carneiro mutton
~ **guisado** stewed with tomatoes, garlic, bay leaf, parsley and often potatoes

carnes frias cold meat (US cold cuts)

caruru 1) green amaranth 2) a dish of minced herbs stewed in oil and spices

castanha chestnut
~ **de caju** cashew nut

(na) cataplana steamed in a copper pan shaped like a big nutshell

cavala mackerel

cebola onion

cebolada fried-onion garnish

cenoura carrot

cereja cherry

cherne black grouper

chicória endive (US chicory)

chispalhada pig's trotters (US feet) stewed with navy beans, cabbage, bacon and blood sausage

chispe pig's trotter (US foot)

chocos com tinta cuttlefish cooked in their own ink

chouriça, chouriço smoked pork sausage flavoured with paprika

chuchu type of marrow (US summer squash)

churrasco charcoal-grilled meat served in Brazil with *farofa* and a hot-pepper sauce

cocada coconut macaroon

coco coconut

codorniz quail

coelho rabbit

coentro coriander

cogumelo (button) mushroom

colorau paprika (used for colouring)

cominho caraway seed

compota compote, stewed fruit

congro conger eel

conta bill (US check)

coração heart

cordeiro lamb

corvina croaker (fish)

costeleta chop, cutlet

couve cabbage
~-**de-bruxelas** brussels sprouts
~-**flor** cauliflower
~ **galega** galician (with a long stem, big dark green leaves and a slightly bitter taste)
~ **lombarda** savoy
~ **portuguesa** portuguese (like the galician but smaller)
~ **roxa** red

cozido 1) boiled stew 2) boiled 3) cooked
~ **em lume brando** simmered
~ **à portuguesa** beef and pork boiled with *chouriço*, carrots, turnips and cabbage *(couve portuguesa)*

creme cream
~ **de leite** fresh

criação fowl

croissant crescent roll

cru raw

curau mashed sweet-corn cooked in coconut milk with sugar and cinnamon

damasco apricot

dióspiro persimmon

dobrada, dobradinha tripe

doce 1) sweet 2) jam
~ **de laranja** marmalade

dourada guilt-head (fish)

eiró eel

eiroses fritas fried eel

ementa 1) menu 2) set menu

empada small type of pie

empadão large type of pie
~ **de batata** shepherd's pie (with minced meat and mashed potato topping)

enchidos assorted pork products made into sausages

endívia chicory (US endive)

enguia eel

ensopado meat or fish casserole served on (or with) slices of bread

entrecosto sparerib

ervilha green pea

escabeche sauce of fried onions, garlic, olive-oil and vinegar

escalfado poached

escalope de vitela escalope of veal, thin, flattened breaded slice of veal

espadarte swordfish

espargo asparagus
ponta de ~ tip

esparregado purée of assorted greens in cream

especiaria spice

espetada kebab

(no) espeto spit-roasted

espinafre spinach

estragão tarragon

estufado braised

esturjão sturgeon

farofa cassava-root meal browned in oil or butter

farófias floating island

fatias slices
~ **da China** cold, baked egg yolks topped with syrup flavoured with lemon and cinnamon
~ **douradas** slices of bread dipped into milk and egg yolk, fried and sprinkled with sugar (US french toast)

favas broad beans
~ **guisadas com chouriço** stewed with *chouriço* and coriander leaves

febras de porco à alentejana pieces of pork fillet grilled with onions, *chouriço* and bacon

feijão bean
~ **branco** navy
~ **catarino** pink
~ **encarnado** red
~ **frade** black-eyed
~ **guisado** stewed with bacon in a tomato sauce
~ **preto** black
~ **tropeiro** black beans fried with chopped *carne de sol* and served with *farofa*
~ **verde** runner (US green)

feijoada dish of dried beans stewed with pig's head and trotters (US feet) bacon, sausages and sometimes vegetables; served in Brazil with *farofa,* rice, sliced oranges and a hot-pepper sauce

fiambre cooked (US boiled) ham

fígado liver
~ **de aves** chicken

figo fig

filete fillet of fish

filhó fritter

  ~ **de abóbora** of pumpkin
purée

fios de ovos dessert of fine golden
strands made from beaten egg
yolk and melted sugar

folhado sweet puff-pastry
delicacy

(no) forno baked

framboesa raspberry

frango chicken

  ~ **com farofa** served with
farofa mixed with olives,
hard-boiled eggs and giblets

  ~ **na púcara** chicken cassserole
flavoured with port wine,
prepared in a special earthenware pot

fresco fresh

fressura de porco guisada
casserole of pork offal (US
variety meat), sometimes with
navy beans

fricassé casserole, usually of
lamb or veal in a cream sauce

(na) frigideira sautéed

frio cold

fritada de peixe deep-fried fish

frito 1) fried 2) fritter

fruta fruit

  ~ **em calda** in syrup

  ~ **do conde** variety of tropical
fruit

  ~ **cristalizada** candied

fubá maizeflour (US cornflour)

fumado smoked

galantina pressed meat in gelatine

galinha boiling chicken

galinhola woodcock

ganso goose

garoupa large grouper (fish)

gaspacho chilled soup with diced
tomatoes, sweet peppers,
onions, cucumber and
croutons

gelado 1) ice-cream 2) chilled

geleia 1) jelly 2) jam (Brazil)

gengibre ginger

ginja morello cherry

goiaba guava

goiabada guava paste

gombo okra (GB lady's finger)

grão(-de-bico) chickpeas

  ~ **com bacalhau** stew made of
chickpeas, potatoes and dried-
cod fillets

gratinado oven-browned

grelhado grilled

grelos turnip greens

groselha red currant

guaraná very sweet tropical fruit

guisado 1) stew 2) stewed

hortaliça fresh vegetables

hortelã mint

incluído included

inhame yam, variety of sweet
potato

iscas thinly sliced liver

  ~ **à portuguesa** marinated in
white wine with herbs and
garlic then fried

jabuticaba bing cherry

jambu variety of cress

jantar dinner

jardineira mixed vegetables

javali wild boar

lagosta spiny lobster

  ~ **americana** fried with onions
and garlic, flambéed in brandy
and served in a sauce flavoured
with Madeira wine

  ~ **suada** with onions, garlic,
tomatoes and flavoured with
port wine

lagostim Norwegian lobster,
langoustine

  ~**-do-rio** fresh-water crayfish

lampreia lamprey

~ **à moda do Minho** marinated in "green" wine, port wine, brandy, blood and spices then poached in the marinade and served with rice

lanche snack

laranja orange

lavagante lobster

lebre hare

legumes vegetables
~ **variados** mixed

leitão suck(l)ing pig
~ **à Bairrada** coated with spicy lard and roasted on a spit in a very hot bread-oven
~ **recheado** stuffed with a spicy, brandy-flavoured mince of bacon, *chouriço* and giblets and then roasted

leite-creme blancmange (US pudding) often sprinkled with caramelised sugar

lentilha lentil

lima lime

limão lemon
~ **verde** lime

língua tongue

linguado sole
~ **à meunière** sautéed in butter, served with parsley and lemon-juice
~ **com recheio de camarão** filled with shrimps in a white sauce

linguiça thin pork sausage flavoured with paprika

lista dos vinhos wine list

lombo loin

louro bay leaf

lulas squid
~ **de caldeirada** simmered with white wine, olive-oil, diced potatoes, tomatoes, onions and parsley

~ **recheadas** braised with a stuffing of eggs, onions and *chouriço*

maçã apple
~ **assada** baked

maçapão, massapão 1) marzipan 2) almond macaroon

macarrão macaroni

macaxeira cassava root

maionese mayonnaise

malagueta hot pepper

mamão papaya

mandioca cassava root

manjar de coco coconut blanc-mange (US pudding) topped with plum syrup

manjericão basil

manteiga butter

mãozinhas de vitela guisadas calves' trotters (US feet) braised with onions, parsley and vinegar, served with vegetables

maracujá passion fruit

marinado marinated
(à) marinheira with white wine, onions, parsley and sometimes tomatoes

marisco seafood

marmelada quince paste

marmelo quince

massa 1) dough, pastry 2) pasta, all types of noodle

medalhão medallion, small choice cut of meat

medronho arbutus berry

meia desfeita poached pieces of dried cod fried with chickpeas, onions and vinegar, topped with hard-boiled eggs and chopped garlic

mel honey

melancia watermelon

melão melon, usually a honeydew

PORTUGUESE

melon
~ **com vinho do Porto** with
port wine
merengue meringue
mero red grouper (fish)
mexilhão mussel
mexerica tangerine
migas meat or fish fried in olive-
oil with onions and garlic and
thickened with bread
mil-folhas flaky pastry with
cream filling (US napoleon)
milho doce sweet-corn
mioleira brains
miolos brains
~ **mexidos com ovos** of
lamb fried and served with
scrambled eggs
misto mixed
miúdos de galinha chicken giblets
mocotós stewed calves' trotters
(US feet), usually served with
farofa and a hot-pepper sauce
molho sauce
~ **branco** white
~ **de manteiga** with butter and
lemon
~ **tártaro** mayonnaise with
chopped gherkins, chives,
capers, olives
~ **verde** olive-oil and vinegar
with chopped spinach, parsley
and coriander leaves
com ~ with
sem ~ without
moqueca de peixe fish cooked in
an earthenware casserole with
coconut milk, palm-oil,
coriander leaves, ginger and
ground shrimps
morango strawberry
~ **silvestre** wild
morcela black pudding, blood
sausage

mortadela mortadella
(US Bologna sausage)
mostarda mustard
nabiça turnip greens
nabo turnip
nata(s) fresh cream
~ **batida(s)** whipped
(ao) natural plain, without
dressing, sauce, stuffing etc.
nêspera medlar, a small apple-
like fruit eaten when over-ripe
noz nut, walnut
~ **moscada** nutmeg
óleo oil
~ **de amendoim** peanut oil
omeleta omelette
~ **simples** plain
osso bone
ostras oysters
~ **recheadas** oystershells
stuffed with oysters, onions,
garlic, breadcrumbs, egg yolk,
lemon juice, spice and then
oven-browned
ouriço-do-mar sea-urchin
ovas fish roe
ovos eggs
~ **cozidos** hard-boiled
~ **escalfados** poached
~ **estrelados** fried, sunny side
up
~ **mexidos** scrambled
~ **moles** beaten egg yolks
cooked in syrup
~ **quentes** soft-boiled
~ **verdes** stuffed with hard-
boiled yolks mixed with onions
flavoured with vinegar and
deep-fried in olive-oil
paçoca 1) roast *carne de sol*
ground with cassava root and
served with sliced bananas
2) dessert made with roast
peanuts crushed with

sweetened cassavaroot meal

paio spicy cured pork fillet presented in a casing

~ **com ervilhas** simmered with peas and chopped onions

palmito palm heart

panado breaded

pão bread

~ **de centeio** rye

~ **de forma** white, for toast

pão-de-ló tea bread (US coffee cake)

pãozinho roll

papos de anjo baked egg yolks topped with syrup

pargo red porgy (fish)

passa (de uva) raisin, sultana

(bem) passado well done

(mal) passado medium

(muito mal) passado rare

pastel usually a type of pie

~ **de bacalhau** deep-fried croquette of dried cod and mashed potatoes flavoured with eggs and parsley

~ **de Belém/de nata** custard pie

~ **folhado** flaky pastry

~ **de massa tenra** soft crust-pastry pie filled with minced meat

~ **de Santa Clara** tartlet with almond-paste filling

~ **de Tentúgal** flaky pastry filled with beaten eggs cooked in syrup

pastelão de palmito e camarão shrimp and palm-heart pie

pato duck

~ **estufado** braised in white wine with onions, parsley and bay leaf

~ **ao tucupi** roasted, braised with carrots and *jambu* in cassava-root juice and served with fruit

pé de moleque peanut brittle

pé de porco pig's trotters (US feet)

peito breast

peixe fish

~**-espada** cutlass fish, scabbard fish

~**-galo** 1) moonfish 2) John Dory

~ **da horta** runner beans deep-fried in batter

pepino cucumber

pequeno almoço breakfast

pêra pear

perca perch

perceve barnacle

perdiz partridge

~ **à caçador(a)** simmered with carrots, onions, white wine, herbs and often tomatoes

~ **com molho de vilão** poached and served with a cold sauce of olive-oil, vinegar, onions, garlic and chopped parsley

perna leg

pernil ham

pêro variety of eating apple

peru turkey

pescada whiting

~ **cozida com todos** poached and served with boiled potatoes and runner beans

pescadinhas de rabo na boca plate of whitings fried whole

pêssego peach

pevide 1) pip (US seed) 2) salted pumpkin pip (US seed)

picado de carne minced meat

picante hot, spicy, highly seasoned

pimenta peppercorn

piment(ã)o sweet pepper

pinhão pine kernel

pinhoada pine-kernel brittle
piripiri tiny hot peppers (preserved in olive-oil)
polvo octopus
pombo pigeon
~ **estufado** braised with bacon, onions and white wine, served with fried bread
porco pork
posta slice of fish or meat
prato 1) plate 2) dish
~ **do dia** speciality of the day
preço price
prego small steak often served in a roll
presunto 1) cured ham 2) cooked (US boiled) ham (Brazil)
~ **cru** dried ham
pudim pudding
~ **de bacalhau** dried-cod loaf, served with tomato sauce
~ **flan** caramel custard
~ **à portuguesa** custard flavoured with brandy and raisins
puré puree
~ **de batata** mashed potatoes
queijada small cottage-cheese tart
~ **de Sintra** flavoured with cinnamon
queijinhos do céu marzipan balls rolled in sugar
queijo cheese
~ **de Azeitão** soft or hard and made with ewe's milk
~ **cabreiro** made with goat's milk
~ **cardiga** made with goat's and ewe's milk
~ **catupiri** small, white cream cheese
~ **flamengo** Dutch type of cheese
~ **da ilha** made in the Azores

and not unlike Cheddar
~ **de Minas** plain
~ **Prata** mild and yellow
~ **rabaçal** made with goat's milk
~ **requeijão** type of cottage cheese
~ **São Jorge** not unlike Cheddar
~ **da Serra** made with ewe's milk
quente hot
~ **e frio** chocolate-nut (US hot-fudge) sundae
quiabo okra (GB lady's finger)
quindim sweet made with eggs and grated coconut
rabanada slice of bread dipped into egg batter and sprinkled with sugar (US french toast)
rabanete radish
raia skate
rainha-cláudia greengage plum
recheado stuffed
recheio stuffing, forcemeat
refeição meal
~ **ligeira** snack
refogado onions fried in olive-oil (base of a stew)
repolho green cabbage
rins kidneys
rissol fritter with minced meat or fish
robalo sea-bass
rodela round slice
rojões à alentejana pork cubes fried with baby clams, diced potatoes and onions
rojões à moda do Minho pork cubes marinated in dry white wine with garlic and paprika, fried and mixed with boiled blood cubes
rolo de carne picada meatloaf

rolos de couve lombarda
savoy-cabbage leaves stuffed with minced or sausage meat

romã pomegranate

rosca ring-shaped white bread

ruivo red gurnard (fish)

sal salt

salada salad
~ **de fruta** fruit
~ **mista** mixed
~ **de pimentos assados** made with grilled sweet peppers
~ **russa** cooked, diced vegetables in mayonnaise

salgado 1), salty 2) salted

salmão salmon
~ **fumado** smoked

salmonete surmullet
~ **grelhado com molho de manteiga** grilled and served with melted butter, chopped parsley and lemon

salsa parsley

salsicha sausage

salva sage

sande, sanduíche sandwich

santola spider-crab
~ **ao natural** boiled in salted water with lemon
~ **recheada** stuffed with its own flesh, generally seasoned with mustard, curry powder, lemon and white wine

sarda mackerel

sardinha sardine

sável shad

seco 1) dry 2) dried

sêmola semolina

sericá alentejano cinnamon soufflé

serviço incluído service included

siri crab

sobremesa dessert

solha plaice

sonho type of doughnut

sopa soup
~ **de agriões** with watercress and potatoes
~ **de coentros** with coriander leaves, bread, poached eggs, olive-oil and garlic
~ **do dia** of the day
~ **de feijão** with kidney beans, cabbage, carrots and rice
~ **de hortaliça** with fresh vegetables
~ **juliana** with shredded vegetables
~ **de rabo de boi** oxtail
~ **de tomate à alentejana** with tomatoes, onions and poached eggs
~ **transmontana** with vegetables, ham, bacon and slices of bread

sorvete ice-cream
~ **com água** water-ice (US sherbet)

sururu type of cockle

suspiro meringue

tainha grey mullet (fish)

tâmara date

tangerina tangerine

tempero seasoning

tenro tender

tigelada dessert of eggs beaten with milk and cinnamon, baked in an earthenware bowl

toranja grapefruit

torrada toast

torrão de ovos marzipan sweet

torta swiss roll
~ **de Viana** filled with lemon curd

tosta mista toasted ham-and-cheese sandwich

toucinho bacon
~ **do céu** kind of marzipan
pudding
tornedó round cut of prime beef
tremoço salted lupine seed
tripas tripe (usually minced)
~ **à moda do Porto** cooked
with assorted pork products,
navy beans and pieces of
chicken; served with rice
trouxa de vitela veal olive (US
veal bird)
trouxas de ovos egg yolks
poached in sweetened water
and topped with syrup
trufa truffle
truta trout
tutano marrow
tutu à mineira puree of black
beans mixed with cassava-root

meal and served with cabbage
and fried bacon
uva grape
~ **moscatel** muscat
vaca beef
vagens runner beans (US green
beans)
variado assorted
vatapá fish and shrimp puree
flavoured with coconut milk
and palm-oil and served with a
peanut-and-cashew sauce
vieira scallop
vinagre vinegar
vitela veal
ximxim de galinha chicken
braised in palm-oil and served
with a sauce of ground shrimp,
sweet peppers, onions, peanuts
and ginger

Drink

adocicado slightly sweet
água water
~ **de coco** coconut milk
~-**pé** weak wine, made from a
base of watered-down wine
draff
~ **tónica** tonic
água mineral mineral water
~ **com gás/gaseificada** fizzy
(US carbonated)
~ **sem gás** still
aguardente spirit distilled from
vegetable matter or fruit
~ **bagaceira** spirit distilled
from grape husks
~ **de figo** spirit distilled from

figs
~ **de medronho** spirit distilled
from arbutus berries
~ **velha** well-aged brandy
Antiqua Portuguese grape
brandy, aged
aperitivo aperitif
batida long drink (US highball)
of rum, sugar and fruit juice,
usually lemon juice
batido milk-shake flavoured with
a scoop of ice-cream
bebida drink
~ **sem álcool/não alcoólica**
soft drink
~ **espirituosa** spirits

ca black coffee

orges Portuguese grape brandy, aged

ranco white

ucelas region north of Lisbon which produces the famous dry, straw-coloured *Bucelas* wine

acau cocoa

achaça white rum

afé coffee
~ **sem cafeína** caffeine-free
~ **duplo** large cup of coffee
~ **frio** iced coffee
~ **com leite** white coffee
~ **puro** genuine coffee

afezinho strong black coffee

aipirinha white rum served with lemon juice, ice cubes and a slice of lime or lemon

aldo de cana sugar-cane juice

aneca pint-size beer mug

arcavelos region west of Lisbon producing good fortified wines

arioca small weak coffee

água de) Castelo fizzy (US carbonated) mineral water

erveja 1) beer 2) lager
~ **em garrafa** bottled
~ **imperial** draught (US draft)
~ **preta** stout

há tea
~ **com leite** with milk
~ **com limão** with lemon
~ **de limão** made from an infusion of lemon peel
~ **maté** made from an infusion of the maté-tree leaf and usually served chilled with a slice of lemon

larete light red wine

Colares region to the north-west of Lisbon, producing good quality red and white wine; the reds have good colour and body and are rich in tanning; the whites have a strong aromatic flavour

conhaque cognac, French brandy
~ **espanhol** Spanish brandy

Constantino Portuguese brandy, aged

copo glass

Cuba livre rum and Coke

Dão some of the best wines of Portugal, normally drunk quite young, come from this region, in the south-east of Oporto; the reds are strong and of good flavour, the whites dry and fruity

doce sweet
meio- ~ medium-sweet (usually in reference to sparkling wine)

Douro the upper part of this valley, east of Oporto produces the renowned port wine (see *Porto*) and pleasant table wines

espumante 1) sparkling 2) sparkling wine

Favaios dessert wine similar to muscatel

fino draught (US draft) beer

fresco fresh, chilled

frio cold

galão white coffee served in a big glass

garoto white coffee served in a small cup

garrafa bottle
meia-~ half bottle

gasosa fizzy (US carbonated) soft drink

gelado iced

gelo ice, ice cubes
com ~ with ice
sem ~ without ice

genebra Dutch gin, usually produced under licence

gim gin

ginjinha spirit distilled from morello cherries

girafa draught (US draft) beer served in a fluted glass

guaraná soft drink flavoured with *guaraná,* a very sweet tropical fruit

jarro carafe

jeropiga locally made fortified wine (see also *vinho abafado*)

laranjada orangeade

leite milk

~ **com chocolate** chocolate drink

licor liqueur

limonada type of lemon squash (US lemon drink)

Madeira excellent red and white aperitif and dessert wines are produced on this island; *Sercial* is the driest, and this, with *Verdelho* (medium-dry), can be drunk as an aperitif; *Boal* (or *Bual*) is smoky and less sweet than the rich dark-amber *Malmsey* (or *Malvásia*), which is best served for dessert at room temperature

maduro mature (wine produced from ripe grapes, as opposed to "green wine"; see *Minho*)

(suco/sumo de) maracujá passion-fruit (juice)

Mateus rosé famous rosé wine from the district of Trás-os-Montes

mazagrã chilled black coffee served on the rocks with sugar and a slice of lemon

Minho area in the north-west of Portugal where the famous young *vinho verde,* or "green wine", is produced; it is made from unripened grapes; faintly sparkling and acid in taste, very refreshing and with low alcohol content; the whites are more popular than the reds, both should be drunk young and chilled

moscatel 1) muscat grape 2) muscatel, a rich, aromatic dessert wine

pinga 1) wine 2) crude white rum (Brazil)

(vinho do) Porto this famous fortified wine from the upper Douro valley, east of Oporto, is classified by *vintage* and *blend;* the *vintage* ports, only made in exceptional years (indicated on the label), are bottled at least two years after harvesting and stored to age for 10 to 20 years or more while the *blended* ports, a subtle mixture of the harvests of different years, are kept in barrels for a minimum of 5 years; there are two types of *blended* ports: the younger *Ruby* variety is full-coloured, full-bodied, and the *Tawny* amber-coloured and delicate; moreover, less sweet, aromatic white ports are also available and are suitable as an aperitif

quente hot

região demarcada controlled and classified wine-producing area e.g. *Bucelas, Colares, Dão, Douro, Minho,* etc.

seco dry

extra-~ extra-dry

meio-~ medium-dry

Setubal region south of Lisbon noted for its famous dessert wines *(moscatel)* and some good red and rosé table wines

sidra cider

simples neat (US straight)

suco/sumo fruit or vegetable juice

taça long-stemmed glass, cup

tinto red

uísque whisky

vermute vermouth

vinho wine

~ **abafado** locally made forti-fied wine (see also *jeropiga*)

~ **adamado** sweet wine

~ **da casa** house or carafe wine

~ **espumante natural** sparkling wine produced in a similar fashion to French champagne and available in extra-dry, dry and medium-dry blends

~ **generoso** well-aged and forti-fied wine, high in alcohol content

~ **licoroso** naturally sweet wine, high in alcohol content e.g. *Moscatel de Setúbal*

~ **da Madeira** Madeira wine (see *Madeira*)

~ **do Porto** port wine (see *Porto*)

~ **da região** local wine

~ **verde** ''green wine'' (see *Minho*)

xerez sherry

Russian

Guide to pronunciation

Each Russian word in the following menu reader is followed by a simplified transliteration in our own alphabet to help you to recognize and pronounce the word. However, if you're even more interested in speaking the language, you'll want to obtain a copy of RUSSIAN FOR TRAVELLERS from your favourite bookshop. This Berlitz phrase book uses imitated pronunciation which is read as if it were English.

Letter	Approximate pronunciation	Symbol
Vowels		
а	between the **a** in c**a**t and the **ar** in c**ar**t	a
е	like **ye** in **ye**t	ye
ё	like **yo** in **yo**nder	yo
и	like **ee** in s**ee**	i
й	like **y** in ga**y** or bo**y**	y
о	like **o** in h**o**t	o
у	like **oo** in b**oo**t	u
ы	similar to **i** in h**i**t	i

э	like e in met	e
ю	like u in duke	yu
я	like ya in yard	ya

Consonants

б	like b in bit	b
в	like v in vine	v
г	like g in go	g
д	like d in do	d
ж	like s in pleasure	zh
з	like z in zoo	z
к	like k in kitten	k
л	like l in lose	l
м	like m in my	m
н	like n in not	n
п	like p in pot	p
р	like r in run	r
с	like s in see	s
т	like t in tip	t
ф	like f in face	f
х	like ch in Scottish loch	kh
ц	like ts in sits	ts
ч	like ch in chip	ch
ш	like sh in shut	sh
щ	like sh followed by ch	shch

Other letters

ь   gives a "soft" pronunciation to the preceding consonant. A similar effect can be produced by pronouncing y as in yet—but very, very short—after the consonant. In our transliteration we'll show this with an apostrophe (') after the soft consonant.

ъ   is sometimes used between two parts of a compound word when the second part begins with я, ю or е to show that the pronunciation of the word should incorporate a clear separation of the two parts.

(left margin) RUSSIAN

The alphabet

Here are the characters which comprise the Russian alphabet. The column at left shows the printed capital and small letters, while written letters are shown in the center column. At right you'll find the corresponding letters in our simplified transliteration.

А а	*А а*	a		Р р	*Р р*	r
Б б	*Б б*	b		С с	*С с*	s
В в	*В в*	v		Т т	*Т т*	t
Г г	*Г г*	g		У у	*У у*	u
Д д	*Д д*	d		Ф ф	*Ф ф*	f
Е е	*Е е*	ye		Х х	*Х х*	kh
Ё ё	*Ё ё*	yo		Ц ц	*Ц ц*	ts
Ж ж	*Ж ж*	zh		Ч ч	*Ч ч*	ch
З з	*З з*	z		Ш ш	*Ш ш*	sh
И и	*И и*	i		Щ щ	*Щ щ*	shch
Й й	*Й й*	y		Ъ ъ	*ъ*	(mute)
К к	*К к*	k		Ы ы	*ы*	i
Л л	*Л л*	l		Ь ь	*ь*	'
М м	*М м*	m		Э э	*Э э*	e
Н н	*Н н*	n		Ю ю	*Ю ю*	yu
О о	*О о*	o		Я я	*Я я*	ya
П п	*П п*	p				

Some useful expressions

Hungry

I'm hungry/I'm thirsty.	**Я голоден/ Я хочу пить.**	ya golodyen/ ya khochu pit'
Can you recommend a good restaurant?	**Не можете ли порекомендовать, хороший ресторан?**	nye mozhetye li poryekomyendovat' khoroshiy ryestoran
Are there any good, cheap restaurants around here?	**Нет ли хорошего и недорогого ресторана поблизости?**	nyet li khoroshego i nyedorogogo ryestorana poblizosti
I'd like to reserve a table for … people.	**Я хотел бы заказать столик на…**	ya khotyel bi zakazat' stolik na…
We'll come at… o'clock.	**Мы придём в…**	mi pridyom v…

Asking

Good evening. I'd like a table for … people.	**Добрый вечер. Будьте добры, столик на…**	dobriy vyechyer. bud'tye dobri stolik na…
Could we have a table…?	**Пожалуйста столик…**	pozhaluysta stolik…
in the corner	**в углу**	v uglu
by the window	**у окна**	u okna
outside	**снаружи**	snaruzhi
on the terrace	**на террасе**	na tyerrasye
May I please have the menu?	**Будьте добры, меню.**	bud'tye dobri myenyu
What's this?	**Что это такое?**	chto eto takoye
Do you have…?	**Есть ли у вас…?**	yest' li u vas
a set menu	**комплексные обеды**	komplyeksniye obyedi
local dishes	**местные блюда**	myestniye blyuda
a children's menu	**детское меню**	dyetskoye myenyu
Waiter/Waitress!	**Официант/ Официантка!**	ofitsiant/ofitsiantka
What do you recommend?	**Что вы посоветуете?**	chto vi posovyetuyetye
Could I have (a/an)…please?	**Принесите мне, пожалуйста…**	prinyesitye mne pozhaluysta
ashtray	**пепельницу**	pyepyel'nitsu
another chair	**ещё один стул**	yeshchyo odin stul

finger bowl	воды сполоснуть пальцы	vodi spolosnut' pal'tsi
fork	вилку	vilku
glass	стакан	stakan
knife	нож	nozh
napkin	салфетку	salfyetku
plate	тарелку	taryelku
serviette	салфетку	salfyetky
spoon	ложку	lozhku
toothpick	зубочистку	zubochistku

Ordering

I'd like a/an/some...	Принесите, пожалуйста...	prinyesitye pozhaluysta
aperitif	аперитив	apyeritiv
appetizer	закуску	zakusku
beer	пива	piva
bread	хлеба	khlyeba
butter	масла	masla
cheese	сыру	siru
chips	картофель «фри»	kartofyel' fri
coffee	кофе	kofye
dessert	третье	tryet'ye
fish	рыбу	ribu
french fries	картофель «фри»	kartofyel' fri
fruit	фруктов	fruktov
game	дичи	dichi
green salad	салат	salat
ice-cream	мороженого	morozhenogo
ketchup	томатный соус	tomatniy sous
lemon	лимон	limon
meat	мясо	myaso
mineral water	минеральной воды	minyeral'noy vodi
milk	молока	moloka
mustard	горчицы	gorchitsi
noodles	лапшу	lapshu
oil	растительного масла	rastityel'nogo masla
olive oil	прованского масла	provanskogo masla
pepper	перцу	pyertsu
potatoes	картошки	kartoshki
poultry	птицу	ptitsu
rice	рису	risu
rolls	булочек	bulochyek
saccharin	сахарин	sakharin
salad	салат	salat
salt	соли	soli

sandwich	**бутерброд**	butyerbrod
seasoning	**приправу**	pripravu
soup	**супу**	supu
sugar	**сахару**	sakharu
tea	**чаю**	chayu
vegetables	**овощей**	ovoshchyey
vinegar	**уксусу**	uksusu
(iced) water	**воды (со льдом)**	vodi (so l'dom)
wine	**вина**	vina

ПРИЯТНОГО АППЕТИТА!

(priyatnogo apyetita)

ENJOY YOUR MEAL!

---

baked (of fish)	**печёную**	pyechyonuyu
baked (of meat)	**жареное**	zharyenoye
baked in parchment	**запеченное**	zapyechyennoye
boiled	**варёное**	varyonoye
braised	**тушёное**	tushonoye
cured	**копчёное/солёное/ сушёное**	kopchyonoye/solyonoye/ sushonoye
fried (of fish)	**жареную**	zharyenuyu
fried (of meat)	**жареное**	zharyenoye
grilled (of fish)	**жареное на рашпере**	zharyenoye na rashpyerye
grilled (of meat)	**жареное на рашпере**	zharyenoye na rashpyerye
marinated	**маринованое**	marinovanoye
poached	**отварное**	otvarnoye
roasted	**жареное**	zharyenoye
sautéed	**зажаренное в малом количестве жира**	zazharyennoye v malom kolichyestvye zhira
smoked	**копчёный**	kopchyoniy
steamed	**паровой**	parovoy
stewed (of fish)	**тушёную**	tushonuyu
stewed (of meat)	**тушёное**	tushonoye
underdone (rare)	**слегка поджаренное**	slyegka podzharyennoye
medium	**средне прожаренное**	sryednye prozharyennoye
well-done	**хорошо прожаренное**	khorosho prozharyennoye

RUSSIAN

ЗА ВАШЕ ЗДОРОВЬЕ!

(za vashe zdorov'ye)

CHEERS!

| glass | стакан | stakan |
| bottle | бутылка | butilka |

red	красное	krasnoye
white	белое	byeloye
rosé	розовое	rozovoye

very dry	очень сухое	ochyen' sukhoye
dry	сухое	sukhoye
sweet	сладкое	sladkoye
light	лёгкое	lyogKoye
full-bodied	крепкое	kryepkoye
sparkling	шипучее	shipuchyeye

| neat (straight) | неразбавленное | nyerazbavlyennoye |
| on the rocks | со льдом | so l'dom |

The bill

I'd like to pay.	Счёт, пожалуйста.	schyot, pozhaluysta
We'd like to pay separately.	Мы будем платить порознь.	mi budyem platit' porozn'
You've made a mistake in this bill, I think.	Мне кажется, вы ошиблись в счёте.	mnye kazhetsya vi oshiblis' v schyotye
What's this amount for?	А это за что?	a eto za chto
Is service included?	Чаевые включены?	chayeviye vklyuchyeni
Is everything included?	Всё включено?	vsyo vklyuchyeno
Do you accept traveller's cheques?	Берёте ли вы дорожные чеки?	byeryotye li vi dorozhniye chyeki
Thank you. This is for you.	Спасибо, это вам.	spasibo eto vam
Keep the change.	Сдачу оставьте себе.	sdachu ostav'tye syebye
That was a very good meal.	Было очень вкусно.	bilo ochyen' vkusno
We enjoyed it, thank you.	Нам понравилось, спасибо.	nam ponravilos' spasibo

Complaints

| That's not what I ordered. I asked for … | Я не это заказывал. Я заказал… | ya nye eto zakazival ya zakazal |
| May I change this? | Дайте мне, пожалуйста, что-нибудь другое. | daytye mnye pozhaluysta chto nibud' drugoye |

RUSSIAN

The meat is…	**Мясо…**	myaso
overdone	**пережарено**	pyeryezharyeno
underdone	**недожарено**	nyedozharyeno
too rare	**сырое**	siroye
too tough	**жёсткое**	zhostkoye
This is too…	**Это слишком…**	eto slishkom
bitter/salty/sweet	**горько/солоно/сладко**	gor'ko/solono/sladko
The food is cold.	**Еда холодная.**	yeda kholodnaya
This isn't fresh.	**Это не свежее.**	eto nye svyezheye
What's taking you so long?	**Почему вы так долго не подаёте?**	pochyemu vi tak dolgo nye podayotye
Where are our drinks?	**А напитки?**	a napitki
This isn't clean.	**Это грязно.**	eto gryazno
Would you ask the head waiter to come over?	**Позовите, пожалуйста-мэтр д'отеля.**	pozovitye pozhaluysta metr dotyelya

Numbers

1	**один**	odin
2	**два**	dva
3	**три**	tri
4	**четыре**	chyetirye
5	**пять**	pyat'
6	**шесть**	shest'
7	**семь**	syem'
8	**восемь**	vosyem'
9	**девять**	dyevyat'
10	**десять**	dyesyat'
11	**одиннадцать**	odinnadtsat'
12	**двенадцать**	dvyenadtsat'
13	**тринадцать**	trinadtsat'
14	**четырнадцать**	chyetirnadtsat'
15	**пятнадцать**	pyatnadtsat'
16	**шестнадцать**	shestnadtsat'
17	**семнадцать**	syemnadtsat'
18	**восемнадцать**	vosyemnadtsat'
19	**девятнадцать**	dyevyatnadtsat'
20	**двадцать**	dvadtsat'

Food

See also the index of Russian main entries, in Roman characters, on pages 322–324

абрикосы *(abrikosi)* apricots

азу *(azu)* slivered beef braised with tomatoes, onions and gherkins (Tartar Republic)

айва *(ayva)* quince

ананас *(ananas)* pineapple

антоновка *(antonovka)* one of the best varieties of winter apples; very sour, strong aroma

антрекот *(antryekot)* rib steak

анчоусы *(anchousi)* anchovies
~ **в масле** *(v maslye)* in oil

арбуз *(arbuz)* watermelon

ассорти *(assorti)* assorted appetizers
~ **рыбное** *(ribnoye)* assorted fish appetizers
~ **мясное** *(myasnoye)* cold cuts

баба *(baba)* tall moulded cake with hole in centre
~ **ромовая** *(romovaya)* sponge cake steeped in rum

баклажанная икра *(baklazhannaya ikra)* "eggplant caviar"; purée of cooked aubergines (eggplants), onions, tomatoes, olive oil and lemon juice

баклажаны *(baklazhani)* aubergine (eggplant)
~ **фаршированные** *(farshirovanyie)* stuffed with meat, vegetables and/or rice
~ **тушёные в сметане** *(tushonyie v smyetanye)* stewed in sour cream

балык *(balik)* dried back of sturgeon or similar fish

банан *(banan)* banana

баранина *(baranina)* mutton
~ **жареная** *(zharyenaya)* fried
~ **отварная в томатном соусе с яблоками** *(otvarnaya v tomatnom sousye s yablokami)* casserole of mutton, tomatoes and apples
~ **тушёная** *(tushonaya)* braised
плов из ~ы *(plov iz ~i)* rice and mutton casserole
поджарка из ~ы *(podzharka iz ~i)* minced mutton fried with onions and braised with sour cream
рагу из ~ы *(ragu iz ~i)*

RUSSIAN

stew with vegetables

бастурма *(basturma)* marinated and grilled chunks of mutton or beef (Armenia, Georgia)

безе *(byezye)* meringue

бекас *(byekas)* snipe

белуга *(byeluga)* white sturgeon; largest type of sturgeon; caviar from this sturgeon is considered fine; generally a greyish fish

беляши *(byelyashi)* fried meat pasties

беф-строганов *(byef-stroganov)* beef Stroganoff: sautéed beef with mushrooms and onions in sour cream sauce

~ **с картофелем фри** *(s kartofyelyem fri)* with chips (US french fries)

бешбармак *(byeshbarmak)* "five fingers"; thinly sliced meat with noodles, served with a bowl of the meat broth (Kazakstan)

бисквит *(biskvit)* cake, biscuits (US cookies)

бифштекс *(bifshtyeks)* beefsteak

~ **натуральный** *(natural'niy)* grilled

~ **рубленый** *(rublyeniy)* beefburger

~ **с яйцом** *(s yaytsom)* grilled, topped with a fried egg

блинчики *(blinchiki)* thin, unleavened pancakes

~ **с вареньем** *(s varye-n'yem)* filled with jam

~ **с мясом** *(s myasom)* filled with minced meat

~ **со сметаной** *(so smye-tanoy)* filled with sour cream

~ **с творогом** *(s tvorogom)* filled with cottage cheese

блины *(blini)* yeast buckwheat pancakes

~ **с икрой** *(s ikroy)* with caviar

~ **со сметаной** *(so smye-tanoy)* served with sour cream

~ **с сёмгой** *(s syomgoy)* served with smoked salmon

блюдо *(blyudo)* dish, course

второе ~ *(vtoroye)* main course

первое ~ *(pyervoye)* first course

сладкое ~ *(sladkoye)* dessert

фирменное ~ *(firmyen-noye)* speciality of the restaurant

бобы *(bobi)* butter beans (US navy beans)

турецкие ~ *(turyetskiye)* kidney beans

бозбаш *(bozbash)* mutton soup with peas (Azerbaijan)

борщ *(borshch)* borscht; beetroot soup to which other vegetables and meat can be added, served with sour cream

~ **зелёный** *(zyelyoniy)* with pork, sorrel, eggs, seasoning

~ **киевский** *(kiyevskiy)*

with beef, mutton, vegetables and herbs

~ московский *(moskovskiy)* with beef, vegetables, tomato purée, bacon

~ полтавский *(poltavskiy)* with goose or chicken, vegetables, dill

~ флотский *(flotskiy)* with bacon or ham bones, vegetables, tomato purée

~ украинский *(ukrainskiy)* with beef, cabbage, potato, carrot, tomato, red and green pepper, herbs

ботвинья *(botvin'ya)* chilled soup made with *kvass*, beet greens, onions and fish

брынза *(brinza)* matured cheese made from ewe's milk

брюква *(bryukva)* rutabaga

бублики *(bubliki)* bagel; a hard, glazed doughnut-shaped roll topped with poppy seeds

буженина *(buzhenina)* boiled pork, sliced and served cold

булочка *(bulochka)* roll, bun

~ ванильная *(vanil'naya)* vanilla-flavoured

~ с изюмом *(s izyumom)* raisin bun

~ с маком *(s makom)* poppy-seed roll

~ с марципаном *(s martsipanom)* with marzipan

~ с повидлом *(s povidlom)* jam doughnut

~ сдобная *(sdobnaya)* butter roll

бульон *(bul'on)* broth, consommé

~ из говядины с макаронами *(iz govyadini s makaronami)* beef and noodle soup

~ куриный с гренками *(kuriniy s gryenkami)* chicken consommé with sippets (croutons)

~ с пирожком *(s pirozhkom)* served with meat pasties

~ с фрикадельками *(s frikadyel'kami)* with meat dumplings

бутерброд *(butyerbrod)* sandwich

~ с ветчиной *(s vyetchinoy)* ham

~ с икрой *(s ikroy)* caviar

~ с кильками *(s kil'kami)* Norwegian sardines

~ с колбасой *(s kolbasoy)* sausage

~ с маслом и сыром *(s maslom i sirom)* cheese and butter

~ с огурцами, помидорами и яйцом *(s ogurtsami, pomidorami i yaytsom)* cucumber, tomato and egg

~ с паштетом *(s pashtyetom)* liver pâté

~ с сардинами *(s sardinami)* sardine

~ с сельдью *(s syel'd'yu)* herring

~ с сёмгой *(s syomgoy)* salmon

~ со шпротами *(so shpro-*

RUSSIAN

tami) sprats, small herring

ваниль *(vanil')* vanilla

вареники *(varyeniki)* poached pasties, made out of flour and cottage cheese thickened with egg yolk

~ **с квашеной капустой и грибами** *(s kvashenoy kapustoy i gribami)* with sauerkraut and mushroom filling

~ **ленивые** *(lyenivyie)* "lazy"; no filling

~ **с мясом** *(s myasom)* with meat filling

~ **с творогом** *(s tvorogom)* with cottage cheese filling

~ **с ягодами** *(s yagodami)* with berry filling

варёный *(varyoniy)* boiled

варенье *(varyen'ye)* jam

~ **вишнёвое** *(vishnyovoye)* cherry

~ **малиновое** *(malinovoye)* raspberry

ватрушка *(vatruchka)* cottage-cheese tartlets

~ **с повидлом** *(s povidlom)* with jam topping

вафля *(vaflya)* waffle

вермишель *(vyermishel')* thin noodles

(на) вертел(е) *([na] vyertyel [ye])* cooked on a skewer

ветчина *(vyechina)* ham

~ **жареная с горчицей и луком** *(zharyenaya s gorchitsey i lukom)* fried with onions, served with mustard

~ **с хреном** *(s khryenom)* served cold with horseradish sauce

винегрет *(vinyegryet)* vegetable salad (of potato, beetroot, etc.) served with an oil and vinegar dressing

виноград *(vinograd)* grapes

вишня *(vishnya)* morello cherries

вобла *(vobla)* roach (a variety of freshwater sunfish)

~ **вяленая** *(vyalyenaya)* dried in the open air

~ **сушёная** *(sushonaya)* dried

второе (блюдо) *(vtoroye [blyudo])* main course with vegetables

вымя отварное *(vimya otvarnoye)* cow's udder, boiled and served with onions and tomato sauce

вяленый *(vyalyeniy)* dried in the open air

галушки *(galushki)* fluffy dumpling served with sour cream and onions (Ukraine)

гарнир *(garnir)* garnish

с ~ом *(s ~om)* garnished

глазировка *(glazirovka)* icing

говядина *(govyadina)* beef

~ **отварная с молочным соусом** *(otvarnaya s molochnim sousom)* boiled, served with a white sauce

~ **тушёная с кореньями** *(tushonaya s koryen'yami)* braised with aromatic vegetables

~ **тушёная со сметаной** *(tushonaya so smyetanoy)*

braised with sour cream

~ **тушёная с грибами** (*tushonaya s gribami*) braised with mushrooms

~ **тушёная с черносливом** (*tushonaya s chernoslivom*) braised with prunes

головизна (*golovizna*) heads of sturgeon and similar fish, used in making soup or gelatine

голубцы (*golubtsi*) stuffed cabbage roll

горошек (*goroshek*) peas

~ **зелёный** (*zyelyoniy*) green peas

горчица (*gorchitsa*) mustard

горячий (*goryachiy*) hot

грибы (*gribi*) mushrooms

~ **белые** (*byeliye*) boletus

~ **маринованные** (*marinovanniye*) marinated

~ **в сметане** (*v smyetanye*) sliced mushrooms fried with onions, served with sour cream

~ **солёные** (*solyoniye*) salted

~ **сушёные** (*sushoniye*) dried

грудинка (*grudinka*) brisket

~ **баранья** (*baran'ya*) of mutton

~ **свиная** (*svinaya*) of pork

груша (*grusha*) pear

гуляш (*gulyash*) goulash

гусь (*gus'*) goose

~ **жареный с яблоками** (*zharyeniy s yablokami*) stuffed with apples, roasted

десерт (*dyesyert*) dessert

дичь (*dich'*) game, venison

долма (*dolma*) grape leaves stuffed with minced mutton (Caucasia)

домашний (*domashniy*) home-made

домашняя птица (*domashnyaya ptitsa*) fowl

дрожжи (*drozhzhi*) yeast

дыня (*dinya*) melon

ежевика (*yezhevika*) blackberries

жареный (*zharyeniy*) fried, roasted

жаркое (*zharkoye*) casserole of beef with tomatoes, potatoes and carrots

~ **из свинины со сливами** (*iz svinini so slivami*) roast pork with plums

желе (*zhelye*) fruit jam

~ **лимонное** (*limonnoye*) lemon

~ **из чёрной и красной смородины** (*iz chyornoy i krasnoy smorodini*) black- and redcurrant

~ **яблочное** (*yablochnoye*) apple

жир (*zhir*) fat, lard

жирный (*zhirniy*) fat (adj)

завтрак (*zavtrak*) breakfast

закуски (*zakuski*) appetizers, often very abundant and varied, usually accompanied by vodka

~ **горячие** (*goryachiye*) hot

~ **мясные** (*myasniye*) meat

~ **рыбные** (*ribniye*) fish

~ **холодные** (*kholodniye*)

cold appetizers

заяц *(zayats)* hare

~ **тушёный в сметане** *(tushoniy v smyetanye)* jugged and braised in sour cream

~ **шпигованный** *(shpigovanniy)* jugged, larded and roasted

зразы *(zrazi)* beef rolls made of slices of beef stuffed with a mixture of breadcrumbs, mushrooms, parsley and dill

изюм *(izyum)* raisins

икра *(ikra)*

1) caviar (sturgeon or salmon roe); three varieties of sturgeon give caviar: *osetr*, *beluga*, which can weigh up to 2000 lbs. and gives a large-grained caviar, and *sevryuga*, yielding small-grained caviar

~ **зернистая** *(zyernistaya)* soft grained, fresh or lightly salted

~ **кетовая** *(kyetovaya)* red, prepared from eggs of *kyeta*, a Siberian salmon

~ **красная** *(krasnaya)* red, prepared from salmon eggs

~ **малосольная** *(malosol'-naya)* lightly salted

~ **паюсная** *(payusnaya)* coarsely grained, pressed, heavily salted

~ **чёрная** *(chyornaya)* black

2) "vegetable caviar"; mashed or puréed vegetables

~ **баклажанная** *(bakla-*

zhannaya) "eggplant caviar"; mashed aubergine (eggplant) stewed with onions and tomatoes

~ **грибная** *(gribnaya)* "mushroom caviar"; minced mushrooms stewed in tomato sauce, oil and seasoning

~ **кабачковая** *(kabachkovaya)* "vegetable-marrow (US zucchini) caviar"; mashed vegetable marrow (US zucchini) stewed with carrots, onions and tomatoes

имбирь *(imbir')* ginger

индейка *(indyeyka)* turkey

~ **жареная с яблоками** *(zharyenaya s yablokami)* stuffed with apples, roasted

~ **фаршированная белым хлебом и печёнкой** *(farshirovannaya byelim khlyebom i pyechyonkoy)* stuffed with a bread and kidney dressing

~ **по-болгарски** *(po-bolgarski)* turkey casserole with carrots, onions, tomatoes and wine

кабачки *(kabachki)* vegetable marrow (US zucchini)

~ **жареные** *(zharyeniye)* fried

~ **по-русски** *(po-russki)* stuffed with mushrooms and vegetable-marrow (US zucchini) pulp, served with sour cream and eggs

~ **в томатном соусе** *(v*

tomatnom sousye) fried and served with tomato sauce

какао с мороженым *(kakao s morozhenim)* chilled cocoa sauce poured over ice-cream

калач *(kalach)* padlock-shaped bread

камбала *(kambala)* flounder

~ **в белом соусе** *(v byelom sousye)* poached, served with a white sauce

~ **в томатном соусе** *(v tomatnom sousye)* poached, served in tomato sauce

капуста *(kapusta)* cabbage

~ **белокочанная** *(byelokochannaya)* white

~ **квашеная** *(kvashenaya)* sauerkraut

~ **красная** *(krasnaya)* red

~ **цветная** *(tsvyetnaya)* cauliflower

карп *(karp)* carp

~ **фаршированный по-украински** *(farshirovanniy po-ukrainski)* stuffed with a seasoned mixture of ham and carp

картофель *(kartofyel')* potatoes

~ **жареный** *(zhareniy)* sautéed in butter

~ **молодой** *(molodoy)* new

~ **в молоке** *(v molokye)* mashed

~ **в «мундире»** *(v mundirye)* boiled in their jackets

~ **отварной** *(otvarnoy)* boiled

~ **печёный** *(pyechyoniy)* baked

~ **сваренный на пару** *(svaryenniy na paru)* steamed

~ **в сметане** *(v smyetanye)* boiled and sautéed, served with sour cream

~ **тушёный со свежими грибами** *(tushoniy so svyezhimi gribami)* stewed with fresh mushrooms

~ **с сельдью** *(s syel'dyu)* served with herring

~ **«фри»** *(fri)* chips (US french fries)

~ **ное пюре** *(~noye pyurye)* mashed

каша *(kasha)* gruel, porridge

~ **гречневая с грибами и луком** *(gryechnyevaya s gribami i lukom)* buckwheat, cooked with mushrooms and onions

~ **гречневая с маслом/молоком** *(gryechnyevaya s maslom/molokom)* buckwheat, served with butter or milk

~ **манная** *(mannaya)* semolina (farina)

~ **перловая** *(pyerlovaya)* pearl barley

~ **пшённая** *(pshonnaja)* millet gruel

~ **рисовая с маслом/молоком** *(risovaya s maslom/molokom)* rice, served with butter or milk

кебаб *(kyebab)* kebab; chunks of mutton marinated in lemon juice, cooked on a skewer with onions, toma-

RUSSIAN

toes and other vegetables

люля ~ *(lyulya)* minced mutton patties, seasoned and cooked on a skewer

тава ~ *(tava)* mutton pies

кекс *(kyeks)* plum cake

кета *(kyeta)* Siberian salmon

клёцки *(klyotski)* dumplings, for soup

~ из курицы *(iz kuritsi)* dumplings made of minced chicken mixed with breadcrumbs soaked in milk or water

~ из печёнки *(iz pyechyonki)* liver minced with bacon and mixed with breadcrumbs

кильки *(kil'ki)* pilchard

~ маринованные *(marinovanniye)* marinated

кисель *(kisyel')* a sourish, thickened fruit-juice dessert

~ вишнёвый *(vichnyoviy)* cherry

~ клюквенный *(klyukvyenniy)* cranberry

~ смородиновый *(smorodinoviy)* redcurrant

~ яблочный *(yablotchniy)* apple

кисло-сладкий *(kislo-sladkiy)* bitter-sweet

кислый *(kisliy)* sour

клубника *(klubnika)* strawberry

клюква *(klyukva)* cranberry

коврижка *(kovrizhka)* honey cake

коктейль с фруктами *(koktyeyl' s fruktami)* fruit cocktail steeped in liqueur, sparkling wine or wine

колбаса *(kolbasa)* cold cuts, sausages

~ ветчинно-рубленная *(vyechinno-rublyennaya)* boiled fat pork sausage

~ докторская *(doktorskaya)* type of meatloaf

~ домашняя *(domashnyaya)* highly seasoned pork sausage

~ копчёная *(kopchyonaya)* smoked salami

~ ливерная *(livyernaya)* liver sausage

~ любительская *(lyubityel'skaya)* bologna

~ языковая *(yazikovaya)* sausage made from beef or pork tongue

компот *(kompot)* stewed fruit

~ из слив *(iz sliv)* prunes

~ из сушёных фруктов *(iz sushonikh fruktov)* mixed fruit, served in syrup

консервированный *(konsyervirovanniy)* tinned (US canned)

конфеты *(konfyeti)* sweets (US candy)

копчёный *(kopchyoniy)* smoked

корейка *(koryeyka)* smoked and salted spare ribs

кость *(kost')* bone

котлеты (рубленые) *(kotlyeti [rublyeniye])* fried pies or breaded meat in the shape of a meat pie

~ капустные *(kapustniye)*

filled with cabbage

~ **морковные** *(morkovniye)* filled with carrot

~ **пожарские** *(pozharskiye)* chicken pie

~ **по-киевски** *(po-kiyevski)* breaded breast of chicken filled with butter, Kiev style

~ **рыбные** *(ribniye)* fish pie

котлеты натуральные *(kotlyeti natural'niye)* chops, cutlets

~ **бараньи** *(baran'i)* mutton chops

~ **куриные** *(kuriniye)* breast of chicken

~ **отбивные** *(otbivniye)* lamb, mutton, pork chops, pounded

~ **свиные** *(sviniye)* pork chops

кофе-«Гляссе» *(kofye-glyasse)* iced coffee topped with ice-cream

краб *(krab)* crab

креветки *(kryevyetki)* shrimp

крем *(kryem)* a frothy, creamy dessert

~ **апельсиновый** *(apyel'sinoviy)* orange

~ **ванильный** *(vanil'niy)* vanilla

~ **кофейный** *(kofyeyniy)* mocha

~ **лимонный** *(limonniy)* lemon

~ **миндальный** *(mindal'niy)* almond

~ **ромовый** *(romoviy)* rum

~ **сливочный с ягодами**

(slivochniy s yagodami) berry

~ **шоколадный** *(shokoladniy)* chocolate

крендель *(kryendyel')* tea bread (US coffee cake) shaped in a figure "8"

кролик *(krolik)* rabbit

~ **тушёный с гарниром из овощей** *(tushoniy s garnirom iz ovoshchyej)* stewed, garnished with vegetables

крупа *(krupa)* grits, porridge

крыжовник *(krizhovnik)* gooseberries

кукуруза *(kukuruza)* maize (US corn)

кулебяка *(kulyebyaka)* loaf, may be made of meat, fish or vegetables

кулич *(kulich)* tall Easter cake containing raisins and often iced with marzipan

купаты *(kupati)* grilled, spicy sausage, served with hot sauce (Georgia)

курага *(kuraga)* dried apricots

курица *(kuritsa)* chicken

~ **жареная с грибами** *(zharyenaya s gribami)* chicken and mushroom casserole

~ **отварная с рисом** *(otvarnaya s risom)* boiled, served with rice

~ **тушёная под белым соусом** *(tushonaya pod byelim sousom)* braised, served with a white sauce

~ **фаршированная потро-**

хами *(farshirovannaya pot-rokhami)* stuffed with giblets

куропатка *(kuropatka)* partridge

~ **жареная с вареньем** *(zharyenaya s varyen'yem)* roasted, served with jam

кусок *(kusok)* piece, slice

лаваш *(lavash)* unleavened white bread

лавровый лист *(lavroviy list)* bay leaf

лагман *(lagman)* meat soup made with spaghetti (Central Asia)

лангет *(langyet)* rib steak

лапша *(lapsha)* noodles, noodle soup

лещ *(lyeshch)* bream

лимон *(limon)* lemon

лисички *(lisichki)* chanterelle mushrooms

лобио *(lobio)* kidney beans with walnut purée and herb dressing (Georgia)

лососина *(lososina)* salmon, lightly salted and pinkish in colour

лук *(luk)* onion

~ **зелёный** *(zyelyoniy)* chives

майонез *(mayonyez)* mayonnaise

мак *(mak)* poppy seeds

макароны *(makaroni)* macaroni

макрель *(makryel')* mackerel

малина *(malina)* raspberries

мандарин *(mandarin)* tangerine

маринованный *(marinovan-niy)* marinated

маслины *(maslini)* olives

масло *(maslo)* oil, butter

~ **оливковое** *(olivkovoye)* olive oil

~ **подсолнечное** *(podsolnyechnoye)* sunflower oil

мастава *(mastava)* rice soup with mutton and sour milk

мёд *(myod)* honey

медвежатина *(myedvyezhatina)* bear meat, usually marinated and stewed

меню *(myenyu)* menu

миндаль *(mindal')* almond

минога *(minoga)* lamprey eel

~ **маринованная** *(marinovannaya)* marinated

~ **жареная** *(zharyenaya)* fried

мозги *(mozgi)* brains

морковь *(morkov')* carrot

мороженое *(morozhenoye)* ice-cream

~ **ванильное** *(vanil'noye)* vanilla

~ **миндальное** *(mindal'-noye)* almond

~ **молочное** *(molochnoye)* ice, sherbet

~ **ореховое** *(oryekhovoye)* walnut

~ **сливочное** *(slivochnoye)* ice-cream, enriched

~ **фруктово-ягодное** *(fruktovo-yagodnoye)* fruit ice

~ **шоколадное** *(shokoladnoye)* chocolate

~ **«эскимо»** *(eskimo)* chocolate-coated ice-cream bar

мука *(muka)* flour

мусака *(musaka)* stew of aubergine (eggplant), tomatoes, green peppers, carrots, vegetable marrows (US zucchini) and garlic

муссе *(muss)* dessert made from beaten egg whites folded into a fruit purée or honey

~ клюквенный *(klyukvyennyj)* cranberry

~ медовый *(myedovyj)* honey

~ яблочный *(yablochnyj)* apple

~ ягодный *(yagodnyj)* berry

мясо *(myaso)* meat

~ варёное *(varyonoye)* boiled

~ жареное *(zharyenoye)* fried

~ жаренное на рашпере *(zharyennoye na rashpyerye)* grilled

~ на вертеле *(na vyertyelye)* spit-roasted

~ не прожаренное *(nye prozharyennoye)* underdone (US rare)

~ сильно прожаренное *(sil'no prozharyennoye)* well done

~ средне прожаренное *(sryednye prozharyennoye)* medium

~ тушёное *(tushonoye)* braised, stewed

~ фаршированное *(farshirovannoye)* stuffed

мясной сок *(myasnoy sok)* drippings

мята *(myata)* mint

~ перечная *(pyeryechnaya)* peppermint

~ зелёная *(zyelyonaya)* spearmint

навага *(navaga)* cod

налистники *(nalistniki)* fried cabbage leaves

~ с творогом *(s tvorogom)* stuffed with cottage cheese

~ с яблоками *(s yablokami)* stuffed with apples

~ с мясом *(s myasom)* stuffed with forcemeat

начинка *(nachinka)* filling, stuffing

обед *(obyed)* lunch

овдух *(ovdukh)* chilled meat and cucumber soup with yoghurt (Azerbaijan)

овощи *(ovoshchi)* vegetables

~ консервированные *(konsyervirovanniye)* tinned (US canned)

~ свежие *(svyezhie)* fresh

огурец *(oguryets)* cucumber

малосольный ~ *(malosol'niy)* lightly salted

маринованный ~ *(marinovanniy)* pickled

свежий ~ *(svyezhiy)* fresh

солёный ~ *(solyoniy)* salted

салат из свежих огурцов *(salat iz svyezhikh ogurtsov)* cucumber salad

окорок *(okorok)* ham

окрошка *(okroshka)* chilled soup made with *kvass*

~ **овощная** *(ovoshchnaya)* with cucumbers and other vegetables

окунь *(okun')* perch

оладьи *(olad'i)* yeast fritter
~ **с вареньем** *(s varyen'yem)* served with jam
~ **с мёдом** *(s myodom)* served with honey
~ **со сметаной** *(so smyetanoy)* served with sour cream

оленина *(olyenina)* venison

омлет *(omlyet)* omelet
~ **с зелёным луком** *(s zyelyonim lukom)* chive
~ **с картофелем** *(s kartofyelyem)* potato
~ **натуральный** *(natural'niy)* plain
~ **с яблоками** *(s yablokami)* apple

орех *(oryekh)* nut
~ **грецкий** *(gretskiy)* walnut
~ **лесной** *(lyesnoy)* hazelnut

осетрина *(osyetrina)* sturgeon
~ **на вертеле** *(na vyertyelye)* grilled on a spit
~ **заливная** *(zalivnaya)* in gelatine
~ **под маринадом** *(pod marinadom)* marinated
~ **паровая** *(parovaya)* steamed
~ **по-русски** *(po-russki)* poached with tomato sauce

and vegetables
~ **в томате** *(v tomatye)* in tomato sauce
~ **«фри»** *(fri)* fried

отварной *(otvarnoy)* poached

палтус *(paltus)* halibut
~ **жареный** *(zharyeniy)* fried

паровой *(parovoy)* steamed

пастила *(pastila)* fruit-flavoured sweets (US candy)

паштет *(pashtyet)* meat pie
~ **из домашней птицы** *(iz domashnyej ptitsi)* chicken
~ **из зайца** *(iz zaytsa)* hare
~ **из кролика** *(iz krolika)* rabbit
~ **из печёнки** *(iz pyechyonki)* chopped liver

пельмени *(pyel'myeni)* dough envelope (like ravioli), poached in broth, served with melted butter and sour cream or with vinegar
~ **с капустой** *(s kapustoy)* with a cabbage filling
~ **сибирские** *(sibirskiye)* with a meat filling

первое (блюдо) *(pyervoye [blyudo])* first course (soup)

перепел *(pyeryepel)* quail
~ **жаренный на решётке** *(zharyennyj na ryeshotkye)* grilled

перец *(pyeryets)* pepper
~ **горький** *(gor'kiy)* pimento
~ **сладкий болгарский** *(sladkiy bolgarskiy)* sweet green pepper

~ фаршированный овощами в томатном соусе *(farshirovanniy ovoshchami v tomatnom sousye)* green pepper stuffed with vegetables

персик *(pyersik)* peach

петрушка *(pyetrushka)* parsley

печёнка куриная *(pyechyonka kurinaya)* chicken livers

~ в сметанном соусе *(v smyetannom sousye)* in sour cream sauce

~ в соусе с мадерой *(v sousye s madyeroy)* in madeira-type wine

печёный *(pyechyonyj)* baked

печень *(pyechyen')* liver

~ варёная с гарниром *(varyonaya s garnirom)* boiled, garnished with vegetables

~ в сметане *(v smyetanye)* braised with sour cream

~ телячья жареная *(tyelyach'ya zharyenaya)* fried calf's liver

~ тресковая в масле *(tryeskovaya v maslye)* cod liver in oil

печенье *(pyechyen'ye)* biscuits (cookies)

пирог *(pirog)* pie, flan, tart

~ с капустой *(s kapustoy)* cabbage tart

~ рисовый с яйцами *(risoviy s yaytsami)* rice and egg pie

~ сибирский с рыбой *(sibirskiy s riboy)* fish and onion pie

~ сладкий с яблоками *(sladkiy s yablokami)* apple pie

пирожки *(pirozhki)* turnover

~ с капустой *(s kapustoy)* cabbage

~ с мясом *(s myasom)* meat

~ с повидлом *(s povidlom)* jam

~ с творогом *(s tvorogom)* cottage cheese

пирожное *(pirozhnoye)* a rich, cream pastry; often like a napoleon

пити *(piti)* mutton soup with beans, potatoes and sour prunes (Azerbaijan)

плавленый *(plavlyeniy)* melted

плов *(plov)* rice casserole

~ с бараниной *(s baraninoy)* with minced mutton

~ с грибами *(s gribami)* with mushrooms

~ с изюмом *(s izyumom)* with raisins

~ по-казахски *(po-kazakhski)* with minced mutton, onions, dried apricots, apples and carrots

~ по-узбекски *(po-uzbyekski)* with mutton, carrots, peppers, onions

пломбир *(plombir)* ice-cream, enriched

повидло *(povidlo)* jam

~ сливовое *(slivovoye)* plum

~ **яблочное** (*yablochnoye*) apple

полуфабрикаты (*polufabrikati*) instant food

половина (*polovina*) half

помидоры (*pomidori*) tomatoes

~ **свежие** (*svyezhiye*) fresh

~ **фаршированные мясом и рисом** (*farshirovanniye myasom i risom*) stuffed with meat and rice

салат из свежих ~ов (*salat iz svyezhikh ~ov*) tomato salad

пончики (*ponchiki*) fritter

поросёнок (*porosyonok*) sucking pig

~ **жареный** (*zharyeniy*) roast

~ **заливной** (*zalivnoy*) in gelatine

~ **с начинкой** (*s nachinkoy*) stuffed

порция (*portsiya*) ration

потроха (*potrokha*) giblets, offal (US variety meat)

почки (*pochki*) kidneys

~ **тушёные в луковом соусе** (*tushoniye v lukovom sousye*) braised in onion sauce

~ **тушёные с вином** (*tushoniye s vinom*) braised in wine sauce

провансаль (*provansal'*) garnish of sauerkraut and grated apples and other fruits

простокваша (*prostokvasha*) yoghurt

пряники (*pryaniki*) gingerbread

~ **медовые** (*myedoviye*) made with honey

~ **мятные** (*myatniye*) mint-flavoured

пряность (*pryanost'*) spice

пудинг (*puding*) casserole

~ **с изюмом** (*s izyumom*) rice casserole with raisins

~ **с мясом** (*s myasom*) potato and meat casserole

~ **ореховый** (*oryekhoviy*) nutmeat casserole

~ **рисовый** (*risoviy*) rice casserole

~ **творожный** (*tvorozhniy*) cottage-cheese casserole

рагу (*ragu*) stew

~ **из овощей** (*iz ovoshchyey*) vegetable stew, containing potatoes, carrots, turnips, onions and tomato purée

раки (*raki*) crayfish

~ **натуральные** (*natural'niye*) poached with carrots, onions and parsley

~ **в пиве** (*v pivye*) poached in beer

рассольник (*rassol'nik*) gherkin soup, containing other vegetables and meat (often giblets)

~ **с курицей** (*s kuritsyey*) chicken, carrots, potatoes, sour cream

~ **«Ленинградский»** (*lyeningradskiy*) rice, potatoes, tomatoes, carrots and sour cream

~ с почками *(s pochkami)* kidneys, sorrel, potatoes

~ с рыбой *(s riboy)* fish, rice and vegetables

расстегай *(rasstyegay)* fish pies

рашпер *(rashpyer)* grill

ревень *(ryeven')* rhubarb

редис, редиска *(ryedis, ryediska)* radishes

~ тёртый со сметаной *(tyortiy so smyetanoy)* grated, served with sour cream

репа *(ryepa)* turnip

рис *(ris)* rice

рожок *(rozhok)* horn-shaped bread

рокфор *(rokfor)* blue cheese, made from ewe's milk

рольмопс *(rol'mops)* marinated, rolled herring

ромштекс *(romshtyeks)* rump steak

ростбиф *(rostbif)* roast beef

рулет *(rulyet)* pasty stuffed with meat or other filling

рыба *(riba)* fish

~ заливная *(zalivnaya)* in gelatine

~ по-запорожски *(po-zaporozhski)* casserole of fish, carrots, parsley, onions, tomatoes

~ жареная *(zharyenaya)* fried

~ жаренная на вертеле/рашпере *(zharyenaya na vyertyelye/rashpyerye)* spit-roasted/grilled

~ копчёная *(kopchyonaya)* smoked, as an appetizer

~ маринованная *(marinovannaya)* marinated

~ отварная *(otvarnaya)* poached

~ прожаренная *(prozharyennaya)* deep-fried

~ паровая *(parovaya)* steamed

~ печёная *(pyechyonaya)* baked

~ тушёная *(tushonaya)* stewed

~ фаршированная *(farshirovannaya)* stuffed

рябчики *(ryabchiki)* hazel grouse

~ жареные с вареньем *(zharyeniye s varyen'yem)* broiled and served with jam

~ тушёные в сметане *(tushoniye v smyetanye)* braised in sour cream

ряженка *(ryazhenka)* milk, pasteurized in the oven and soured naturally

салат *(salat)* salad

~ из картофеля с творогом *(iz kartofyelya s tvorogom)* potatoes, cottage cheese, onion, eggs in sour cream

~ из крабов *(iz krabov)* crab

~ из креветок *(iz kryevyetok)* shrimp

~ из моркови и яблок *(iz morkovi i yablok)* grated sour apples and carrots, served in oil and vinegar

~ Московский *(Moskov-*

skiy) beef, potatoes, eggs, carrots, apples

~ из огурцов *(iz ogurtsov)* mayonnaise or sour cream, cucumber

~ из помидоров *(iz pomidorov)* tomato

~ из редиса *(iz ryedisa)* finely sliced radishes with sour cream and salt

~ русский зелёный *(russkiy zyelyoniy)* cabbage, spinach, lettuce, green pepper, onions and cucumbers served in oil and vinegar or sour cream

~ Провансаль *(provansal')* sauerkraut, apples, raisins, marinated plums and cherries

~ из свежей капусты *(iz svyezhyey kapusti)* cabbage, spring onions, apples, mixed with sugar and vegetable oil

~ из сельди *(iz syel'di)* herring, potatoes, apples, cucumbers, eggs

сало *(salo)* bacon fat

сарделька *(sardyel'ka)* frankfurter-type sausage

сардины *(sardini)* sardines

сахар *(sakhar)* sugar

~ рафинад *(rafinad)* refined

~ная пудра *(~naya pudra)* castor (US powdered)

~ный песок *(~niy pyesok)* granulated

сациви *(satsivi)* sauce with walnuts, onions and spices (Georgia)

свежий *(svyezhiy)* fresh

свёкла *(svyokla)* beetroot

~ в соусе с укропом *(v sousye s ukropom)* in dill sauce

~ в сметане *(v smyetanye)* in sour-cream sauce

свекольник *(svyekol'nik)* chilled soup based on beetroot, with eggs, cucumber, dill, parsley, served with sour cream

свинина *(svinina)* pork

~ жареная с грибным соусом *(zharyenaya s gribnim sousom)* braised in mushroom sauce

~ тушённая в пиве *(tushonnaya v pivye)* chops braised in beer

~ тушёная с яблоками *(tushonaya s yablokami)* braised and served with apple slices

севрюга *(syevryuga)* smaller type of sturgeon giving smaller and generally darker roe

сельдерей *(syel'dyeryey)* celery

сельдь *(syel'd')* herring

~ с гарниром *(s garnirom)* with a garnish of sliced onions, sliced hard-boiled eggs, salted cucumbers, salted mushrooms and beetroot strips

~ с луком *(s lukom)* with onions

~ маринованная *(marinovannaya)* marinated

~ натуральная с отвар-

ным картофелем *(natural'naya s otvarnim kartofyelyem)* with boiled potatoes

~ в сметане *(v smyetanye)* served with sour cream

~ солёная *(solyonaya)* pickled

сёмга *(syomga)* salmon

скумбрия *(skumbriya)* mackerel

сладкий *(sladkiy)* sweet

слива *(sliva)* plum

сливки *(slivki)* cream

сметана *(smyetana)* sour cream

смородина *(smorodina)* currant

~ красная *(krasnaya)* red

~ чёрная *(tchyornaya)* black

солёный *(solyoniy)* salted

соломка *(solomka)* salted or sugared biscuits (US crackers or cookies), may be 2 ft. long

соль *(sol')* salt

солянка *(solyanka)* soup of gherkins and capers

~ грибная *(gribnaya)* with cabbage, mushrooms, and chunks of meat or fish

~ по-грузински *(po-gruzinski)* stew of beef or mutton, tomatoes, cucumbers and wine (Georgia)

~ из курицы *(iz kuritsi)* chicken casserole with tomato purée, cucumbers and sour cream

~ мясная сборная *(myas-*

naya sbornaya) stew containing chunks of meat or kidneys, sausages, gherkins, olives

~ рыбная *(ribnaya)* fish chowder

сом *(som)* catfish

сосиски *(sosiski)* frankfurters

соус *(sous)* sauce

~ белый *(byeliy)* white bechamel

~ кисло-сладкий *(kislosladkiy)* sweet and sour; tomato, prunes, raisins, red wine

~ «Кубанский» *(kubanskiy)* sweet-and-sour tomato sauce

~ молочный *(molochniy)* white, bechamel

~ сметанный *(smyetanniy)* cream

~ томатный *(tomatniy)* tomato

~ Ткемали *(tkyemali)* plum and coriander

~ с хреном *(s khryenom)* horseradish

сочный *(sochniy)* juicy

стерлядь *(styerlyad')* sterlet, a small sturgeon

студень *(studen')* brawn (US headcheese)

~ говяжий *(govyazhiy)* beef

~ из головизны *(iz golovizni)* sturgeon head

~ рыбный *(ribniy)* fish

~ из свиных ножек *(iz svinikh nozhek)* pig's trotters (US pig's feet)

~ **телячий** (*tyelyachiy*) veal

судак (*sudak*) pike-perch

~ **заливной** (*zalivnoy*) in gelatine

~ **запечённый с шампиньонами в сметанном соусе** (*zapyechyonniy s champin'onami v smyetannom sousye*) baked with mushrooms in sour-cream sauce

~ **отварной в яичном соусе** (*otvarnoy v yaichnom sousye*) poached in egg sauce

~ **в томатном соусе** (*v tomatnom sousye*) in tomato sauce

сулгуни (*sulguni*) matured cheese, made from ewe's milk (Georgia)

суп (*sup*) soup

~ **грибной** (*gribnoy*) mushroom

~ **картофельный** (*kartofyel'niy*) potato

~ **крестьянский** (*kryest'yanskiy*) cabbage, potato, carrot, parsley, tomato and sour cream

~ **лапша с курицей** (*lapsha s kuritsyey*) chicken-noodle

~ **овощной** (*ovoshchnoy*) vegetable

~ **рыбный** (*ribniy*) fish

~ **из фасоли** (*iz fasoli*) butter beans (US navy beans)

~ **харчо** (*kharcho*) mutton

with vegetables (Georgia)

суп молочный (*sup molochniy*) milk-based soup

~ **с вермишелью** (*s vyermishel'yu*) with noodles

~ **перловый** (*pyerloviy*) with pearl barley

~ **рисовый** (*risoviy*) with rice

суп-пюре (*sup-pyurye*) cream soup, cream of ... soup

~ **из гороха** (*iz gorokha*) pea

~ **грибной** (*gribnoy*) mushroom

~ **из курицы** (*iz kuritsi*) chicken

~ **из моркови** (*iz morkovi*) carrot

~ **из помидоров** (*iz pomidorov*) tomato

суп сладкий (*sup sladkiy*) fruit soup served chilled or hot, containing noodles, rice or dumplings

~ **из вишен** (*iz vishen*) cherries, cinnamon, cream

~ **из кураги с рисом** (*iz kuragi s risom*) dried apricots, rice, cream

~ **из ревеня с манными клёцками** (*iz ryevyenya s mannimi klyotskami*) rhubarb, served with dumplings

~ **из чёрной смородины с творожными клёцками** (*iz chyornoy smorodini s tvorozhnimi klyotskami*) blackcurrants, served with cottage-cheese dumplings

~ **из яблок** (*iz yablok*)

apples, cinnamon, cream

суфле *(suflye)* soufflé; a savoury sauce into which beaten egg whites are folded; mixture is baked until browned and puffed up

сухарь *(sukhar')* rusks (US zwieback)

сухой *(sukhoy)* dry

сыворотка *(sivorotka)* buttermilk

сыр *(sir)* cheese

   голландский ~ *(gollandskiy)* imitation Dutch edam cheese, yellow, mild and firm

   швейцарский ~ *(chvyeytsarskiy)* imitation swiss cheese, like gruyère; pale yellow, nutty flavour, with small holes

сырники со сметаной *(sirniki so smyetanoy)* cottage-cheese fritters served with sour cream

сырой *(siroy)* raw, cured

творог *(tvorog)* cottage cheese

телятина *(tyelyatina)* veal

   ~ духовая с кабачками *(dukhovaya s kabachkami)* braised with vegetable marrow (US zucchini)

   ~ жаренная с грибами и помидорами *(zharyennaya s gribami i pomidorami)* fried with mushrooms and tomatoes

   ~ отварная с белым соусом *(otvarnaya s byelim sousom)* poached and served with white sauce

   ~ тушённая с черносливом *(tushonnaya s chyernoslivom)* braised in white wine and prunes

тёртый *(tyortiy)* grated

тесто *(tyesto)* dough, batter

   ~ бездрожжевое *(byezdrozhzhevoye)* unleavened

   ~ дрожжевое *(drozhzhevoye)* leavened

   ~ сдобное *(sdobnoe)* made with butter

   ~ слоёное *(sloyonoye)* puff pastry

тетерев *(tyetyeryev)* black grouse

тефтели *(tyeftyeli)* meatballs, fried then braised in seasoned broth, served in tomato sauce

тмин *(tmin)* cumin

торт *(tort)* creamy layer cake

толстый *(tolstiy)* thick

треска *(tryeska)* cod

   ~ в белом соусе *(v byelom sousye)* in white sauce

   ~ под маринадом *(pod marinadom)* marinated

   ~ со сметаной и помидорами *(so smyetanoy i pomidorami)* in sour cream with tomatoes

тунец *(tunyets)* tunny (US tuna fish)

тушёный *(tushoniy)* stewed, braised

тыква *(tikva)* pumpkin

угорь *(ugor')* eel

   копчёный ~ *(kopchyoniy)* smoked

RUSSIAN

угро *(ugro)* soup of beef, potato and sour milk (Kirgiz Republic)

ужин *(uzhin)* dinner

укроп *(ukrop)* dill

уксус *(uksus)* vinegar

утка *(utka)* duck

~ **дикая** *(dikaya)* wild

~ **жареная с вишнями** *(zharyenaya s vishnyami)* roasted, served with cherry sauce

~ **жареная с яблоками** *(zharyenaya s yablokami)* roasted with baked apples

~ **тушёная с грибами** *(tushonnaya s gribami)* braised with mushrooms

уха *(ukha)* soup of fresh-water fish

~ **рыбацкая** *(ribatskaya)* a chowder of smelt-like fish

фазан *(fazan)* pheasant

~ **по-грузински** *(po-gruzinski)* braised in orange juice and green tea with walnuts and raisins

~ **жаренный с луком и грибами** *(zharyenniy s lukom i gribami)* fried with onions and mushrooms

~ **с яблоками** *(s yablokami)* browned with bacon, braised in a sauce with blackcurrant jelly, garnished with baked apples

фарш *(farsh)* stuffing

фаршированный *(farshirovanniy)* stuffed

фасоль *(fasol')* beans

филе *(filyɛ)* fillet

форель *(foryel')* trout

форшмак *(forshmak)* mixture of herring and apples

фрикадельки *(frikadyel'ki)* meatballs

фрукт(ы) *(frukt[i])* fruit

~ **овый коктейль** *(∼oviy koktyeyl')* fruit cocktail steeped in liqueur, Russian champagne or wine

халва *(khalva)* a sugary-loaf confection; may be made in one of several varieties, e.g., with pistachios

хамраши *(khamrashi)* mutton soup, with butter (US navy) beans, noodles, chives and parsley

харчо *(kharcho)* mutton, onion, rice and tomato soup (Georgia)

хачапури *(khachapuri)* cheese tarts (Georgia)

хворост *(khvorost)* crisp and flaky deep-fried pastry

хлеб *(khlyeb)* bread

~ **белый** *(byeliy)* white

~ **бородинский** *(borodinskiy)* coriander-flavoured black bread (US pumpernickel)

~ **с изюмом** *(s izyumom)* raisin

~ **с маком** *(s makom)* poppyseed

~ **ржаной** *(rzhanoj)* black (pumpernickel)

~ **чёрный** *(tchyorniy)* black (pumpernickel)

холодец *(kholodyets)* brawn (US headcheese)

хрен *(khryen)* horseradish

цесарка *(tsesarka)* guinea fowl

цукат *(tsukat)* candied fruit

цыплята *(tsiplyata)* chicken

~ **жареные с картофелем** *(zharyeniye s kartofyelyem)* broiled with potatoes

~ **жареные со сметанным соусом** *(zharyeniye so smyetannim sousom)* roasted, served with a sour-cream sauce

~ **отварные с рисом** *(otvarniye s risom)* cooked with rice

~ **Табака** *(tabaka)* boned, pounded, flavoured with garlic and fried under a weight (Georgia)

чанахи *(chanakhi)* casserole of mutton, potatoes, tomatoes, aubergine (eggplant) and green beans (Georgia)

чахохбили *(chakhokhbili)* spicy chicken and tomato casserole (Georgia)

чебуреки *(chyeburyeki)* deep-fried meat pies (Tartar Republic)

черешня *(chyeryeshnya)* cherries

черника *(chyernika)* bilberries

чернослив *(chyernosliv)* prunes

чеснок *(chyesnok)* garlic

чечевица *(chyechyevitsa)* lentils

чихиртма из баранины *(chikhirtma iz baranini)* mutton and egg soup with saffron (Caucasia)

чурек *(churyek)* unleavened bread with sesame seeds (Georgia)

шафран *(shafran)* saffron

шашлык *(shashlik)* shashlik; chunks of meat grilled on a skewer; may be served in a hot tomato sauce (Caucasia)

~ **из баранины** *(iz baranini)* mutton

~ **из говядины** *(iz govyadini)* beef

шницель *(shnitsel')* cutlet

~ **из телятины в сметанном соусе** *(iz tyelyatini v smyetannom sousye)* veal cutlet served with sour cream

шоколад *(shokolad)* chocolate

шпигованный *(shpigovanniy)* larded

шпик *(shpik)* bacon

шпинат *(shpinat)* spinach

шпроты *(shproty)* sprats

шурпа *(shurpa)* mutton soup and tomatoes (Central Asia)

щавель *(shchavyel')* sorrel

щи *(shchi)* cabbage or sauerkraut soup to which other vegetables can be added; served with sour cream

~ **зелёные с яйцом и сметаной** *(zyelyoniye s yaytsom i smyetanoy)* spinach or sorrel soup

~ **с квашеной капустой и грибами** *(s kvashenoy kapustoy i gribami)* sauer-

RUSSIAN

kraut, vegetables, mushrooms

~ **крапивные** (*krapivniye*) nettle soup

~ **ленивые** (*lyeniviye*) "lazy soup"; cabbage cut into chunks

~ **невские** (*nyevskiye*) sauerkraut, sautéed meat added before serving

~ **со свежей капустой и рыбой** (*so svyezhey kapustoy i riboy*) sturgeon or pike perch, fresh cabbage, carrots, parsley

~ **суточные** (*sutochniye*) "24 hours"; sauerkraut, carrot, tomato; served the day after its preparation

щука (*shchyuka*) pike

~ **тушёная с хреном** (*tushyonaya s khryenom*) stewed with horseradish and sour cream

эскалоп (*eskalop*) cutlet

яблоки (*yabloki*) apples

~ **маринованные** (*marinovanniye*) marinated in vinegar

~ **мочёные** (*mochyoniye*) pickled in a mixture of water, *kvass*, honey and sugar

~ **печёные** (*pyechyoniye*) baked

~ **сушёные** (*sushoniye*) dried

язык (*yazik*) tongue

~ **заливной** (*zalivnoy*) in gelatine

~ **отварной под белым соусом** (*otvarnoy pod byelim sousom*) boiled and served with white sauce

~ **под соусом с изюмом** (*pod sousom s izyumom*) boiled and served with a sauce made from tongue stock and raisins

яичница (*yaichnitsa*) fried eggs

~ **взбитая** (*vzbitaya*) scrambled eggs

~ **глазунья** (*glazun'ya*) fried, sunny-side up

~ **с сельдью** (*s syel'd'yu*) fried herring with eggs

~ **с сыром** (*s sirom*) cheese and bacon omelet

яйни (*yayni*) soup of beef, tomato and potato

яйца (*yaytsa*) eggs

~ **вкрутую** (*vkrutuyu*) hard-boiled

~ **всмятку** (*vsmyatku*) soft-boiled

~ **с икрой** (*s ikroy*) hard-boiled eggs filled with soft caviar and garnished with lettuce

~ **крутые с хреном** (*krutiye s khryenom*) hard-boiled eggs with horseradish, mayonnaise and sour cream

~ **под майонезом** (*pod mayonyezom*) egg salad

~ **в мешочек** (*v myeshochyek*) medium-boiled

Drink

Азербайджан Azerbaijan; particularly noted for its cordial wine like *Shemakha* (**Шемаха**); its *Kiurdamir* (**Кюрдамир**) is a velvety wine having the exotic aftertaste of chocolate

Армения Armenia; produces mainly dessert wine like the well-known *Artashat* (**Арташат)**

Боржоми *(borzhomi)* mineral water from the famous Georgian spa of the same name

вино *(vino)* wine

~ **белое** *(byeloye)* white

~ **десертное** *(dyesyertnoye)* dessert

~ **красное** *(krasnoye)* red

~ **полусухое***(polusukhoye)* slightly sweet

~ **сладкое** *(sladkoye)* sweet

~ **столовое** *(stolovoye)* table

~ **сухое** *(sukhoye)* dry

вода *(voda)* water

~ **газированная** *(gazirovannaya)* soda water

~ **минеральная** *(minyeral'naya)* mineral water

водка *(vodka)* vodka

~ **Горилка** *(gorilka)* a Ukrainian peper-flavoured vodka

~ **Зубровка** *(zubrovka)* flavoured with wild buffalo-grass

~ **крепкая** *(kryepkaya)* strong

~ **Московская** *(moskovskaya)* ordinary

~ **перцовая** *(pyertsovaya)* pepper-flavoured

~ **рябиновая** *(ryabinovaya)* mountain-ashberry-flavoured

~ **Столичная** *(stolichnaya)* considered the best among non-flavoured vodkas

~ **Старка** *(starka)* aged, a brownish colour

Грузия Georgia; this republic's wines have always been renowned; produces slightly sweet wine of superior quality, e.g., *Khvanchkara* (**Хванчкара**), *Kindzmarauli* (**Киндзмараули**),

Odzhaleshi (**Оджалеши**), *Chkhaveri* (**Чхавери**), *Tvishi* (**Твиши**); *Salkhino* (**Салхино**) is a favourite coffee-coloured dessert wine

какао *(kakao)* cocoa

квас *(kvas)* kvass, unalcoholic rye beer, often home-made from stale dark bread steeped in hot water and allowed to ferment for a few hours; sugar, fruit or honey usually added as a sweetener

кефир *(kyefir)* sour milk

коктейль *(koktyeyl')* cocktail, usually much sweeter than western-type cocktails

~ **Десертный** *(dyesyertniy)* liqueur, sweet wine, sparkling wine

~ **Игристый** *(igristiy)* sparkling cocktail; made with soda water or champagne base

~ **Крепкий** *(kryepkiy)* strong cocktail; vodka or brandy with fruit juice

~ **Коньячный** *(kon'yachniy)* brandy base

~ **Лимонный** *(limonniy)* lemon liqueur and juice

коньяк *(kon'yak)* brandy; excellent brandies are produced in Armenia and Georgia; those from Azerbaidjan, Moldavia and the northern slopes of the Caucasus are also considered of superior quality; the finest brandies are produced by

Ararat in Armenia under such labels as **Юбилейный** (*Yubilejnij*), **Армения** (*Armenia*), **Ереван** (*Erevan*), as well as by **Самтрест** (*Samtrest*) in Georgia; the stars on the label indicate the number of years the brandy has been aged: 1-5 years for one star, 6-10 years for two, etc.; initials also indicate age and quality: **ОС**, very old; **ОВ**, well aged; **ВК**, of exceptional quality; **ОВВК**, well aged, of exceptional quality

кофе *(kofye)* coffee

~ **по-восточному/по-турецки** *(po-vostochnomu/po-turyetski)* Turkish-style; boiled with sugar; poured in a demi-tasse with grounds

~ **с молоком** *(s molokom)* with milk

~ **чёрный** *(chyorniy)* black

Красный Камень *(krasniy kamen')* rosé muscat wine (Crimea, Ukraine)

крюшон *(kryushon)* sparkling punch (champagne or soda water added before being served)

кумыс *(kumis)* fermented mare's milk

ликёр *(likyor)* liqueur

~ **клубничный** *(klubnichniy)* strawberry

~ **лимонный** *(limonniy)* lemon

~ **сливовый** *(slivoviy)* plum

лимонад (*limonad*) lemonade

мадера (*madyera*) imitation madeira wine; dessert wine

Массандра (*massandra*) a vineyard in Crimea famed for its muscat wine, e.g., **Красный Камень** (*Krasniy Kamen'*) and **Таврида** (*Tavrida*)

Молдавия Moldavia; this republic produces one third of the nation's wine though most of it is table wine

молоко (*moloko*) milk

~ **пастеризованное** (*pastyerizovannoye*) pasteurized

~ **сгущённое** (*sgushchyonnoye*) condensed

~ **топлёное** (*toplyonoye*) baked milk

морс (*mors*) fruit water; liquid remaining from cooked fruit

~ **клюквенный** (*klyukvyenniy*) cranberry

мускат (*muskat*) muscat wine, produced mainly in Crimea, Ukraine

наливка (*nalivka*) alcoholic beverage made from macerated fruit

напиток (*napitok*) drink

Нарзан (*narzan*) a mineral water from northern Caucasus

настойка (*nastoyka*) liqueur

портвейн (*portvyeyn*) imitation port wine

пиво (*pivo*) beer; best brands are «**Жигулёвское**» (*Zhigulyovskoye*), «**Рижское**» (*Rizhskoye*), «**Московское**» (*Moskovskoye*)

~ **светлое** (*svyetloye*) light

~ **тёмное** (*tyomnoye*) dark

пунш (*punsh*) punch

~ **молочный** (*molochniy*) milk, brandy or liqueur and sugar

~ **ягодный с шампанским** (*yagodniy s shampanskim*) berry syrup and sparkling wine

~ **яичный** (*yaichniy*) egg yolks, milk, brandy, sugar

ром (*rom*) rum

рислинг (*risling*) a dry white wine, imitation riesling

РСФСР Russian Soviet Federated Socialist Republic; representing over three quarters of the USSR's area, the **РСФСР** sprawls over the heartland of the Soviet Union, with Moscow also serving as its administrative capital; some wine is produced in this vast region though principally table wine like the wine of the Abrow-Durso and Anapa vineyards

сладкий (*sladkiy*) sweet

сок (*sok*) juice

~ **апельсиновый** (*apyel'sinoviy*) orange

~ **виноградный** (*vinogradniy*) grape

~ **вишнёвый** (*vishnyoviy*) cherry

~ **мандариновый** (*mandarinoviy*) tangerine

~ **сливовый** *(slivoviy)* plum

~ **томатный** *(tomatniy)* tomato

~ **фруктовый** *(fruktoviy)* fruit

~ **яблочный** *(yablochniy)* apple

Средняя Азия Central Asia; wine from this region has a high sugar content; some examples: *Shirini* (**Ширини**) from Tadjikistan and *Yasman Salik* (**Ясман Салик**) and *Ter Bash* (**Тер Баш**) from Turkmenistan

сухой *(sukhoy)* dry

токай *(tokay)* tokay wine, dessert wine

херес *(khyeryes)* imitation sherry

Цимлянское *(tsimlyanskoye)* sparkling rosé wine, imitation pink champagne; produced in the Don area

чай *(chay)* tea

~ **с вареньем** *(s varyen'yem)* served with jam

~ **с лимоном** *(s limonom)* with lemon

~ **с молоком** *(s molokom)* with milk

~ **с мёдом** *(s myodom)* served with honey

Чёрный Камень *(chyorniy kamyen')* red, sweet Crimean wine

Украина Ukraine; with Crimea, this republic furnishes nearly all of the country's sparkling wine, referred to as *Shampanskoye* (**Шампанское**); the Soviet product is often a good imitation of French champagne; *Shato-Ikyem* (**Шато-Икем**) and *Barsak* (**Барсак**) are also imitations of white Bordeaux wines; muscat wine is a speciality, particularly from the vineyards around Massandra, e.g., *Krasniy Kamen'* (**Красный Камень**) and *Tavrida* (**Таврида**); tokay wine is produced, especially around Ay-Danil and Magaratch; favourite dessert wines are *Portvyeyn Yuzhnobyeryezhniy* (**Портвейн Южнобережный**) and *Pino gri* (**Пино Гри**)

шампанское *(shampanskoye)* sparkling wine, imitation *champagne;* can be of fine quality; nearly all produced in the Ukraine, particularly Crimea

~ **полусладкое** *(polusladkoye)* slightly sweet (7 per cent sugar content)

~ **полусухое** *(polusukhoye)* slightly dry (5 per cent sugar content)

~ **сладкое** *(sladkoye)* sweet (10 per cent sugar content)

~ **сухое** *(sukhoye)* dry (less than 5 per cent sugar content)

Serbo-Croatian

Guide to pronunciation

Letter	Approximate pronunciation
Consonants	

b	like **b** in **b**rother
c	like **ts** in **ts**etse
č	like **ch** in **ch**urch
ć	like **ch** in **ch**eap (a little further forward in the mouth than **č**; called a "soft" **č**)
d	like **d** in **d**own
dž	like **j** in **J**une
dj	like **j** in **j**eep (a "soft" **dž**); also written **đ**
f	like **f** in **f**ather
g	like **g** in **g**o
h	like **h** in **h**ouse
j	like **y** in **y**oke
k	like **k** in **k**ey

l	like l in lip
lj	like l in failure
m	like m in mouth
n	like n in not
nj	like ni in onion
p	like p in put
r	like r in rope
s	like s in sister
š	like sh in ship
t	like t in top
v	like v in very
z	like z in zip
ž	like s in pleasure

Notice that the letter **r** can also act as a vowel as, for example, in the word **vrlo** or in the name of the island **Krk**; in this case, it should be pronounced rather like a Scottish **r**.

Vowels

a	like a in car
e	like e in get
i	like i in it
o	like o in hot
u	like oo in boom

The alphabet

Two different alphabets are used in Yugoslavia. Our Roman alphabet is in use in Slovenia and Croatia; elsewhere the Cyrillic alphabet (more or less like the Russian one) is dominant. Given below are the characters which the Cyrillic alphabet, as used in Yugoslavia, comprises. The column at left shows the printed capital and small letters while written letters are shown in the center column. At right the corresponding letters are shown in the Roman alphabet which we're using in this book.

Printed	Written	Roman
А а		a
Б б		b
Ц ц		c
Ч ч		č
Ћ ћ		ć
Д д		d
Џ џ		dž (cap. Dž)
Ђ ђ		dj or đ (cap. Dj or Đ)
Е е		e
Ф ф		f
Г г		g
Х х		h
И и		i
Ј ј		j
К к		k
Л л		l
Љ љ		lj (cap. Lj).
М м		m
Н н		n
Њ њ		nj (cap. Nj)
О о		o
П п		p
Р р		r
С с		s
Ш ш		š
Т т		t
У у		u
В в		v
З з		z
Ж ж		ž

Some useful expressions

Hungry

I'm hungry/I'm thirsty.	**Ja sam gladan** (*fem:* **gladna**)/ **Ja sam žedan** (*fem:* **žedna**)
Can you recommend a good restaurant?	**Možete li preporučiti neki dobar restoran?**
Are there any good, cheap restaurants around here?	**Ima li ovde neki dobar, jeftin restoran?**
I'd like to reserve a table for ... people.	**Želim da rezervišem jedan sto za ...**
We'll come at ... o'clock.	**Dolazimo u ... sati.**

Asking

Good evening. I'd like a table for ... people.	**Dobro veče. Želeo bih sto za ...**
Could we have a table...?	**Možemo li dobiti sto...?**
in the corner	**u uglu**
by the window	**pored prozora**
outside	**napolju**
on the terrace	**na terasi**
May I please have the menu?	**Molim vas jelovnik.**
What's this?	**Šta je ovo?**
Do you have...?	**Imate li...**
a set menu	**meni**
local dishes	**lokalne specijalitete**
a children's menu	**meni za decu**
Waiter/Waitress!	**Kelner/Kelnerica!**
What do you recommend?	**Šta mi preporučujete?**
Could I have (a/an)... please?	**Mogu li, molim Vas, dobiti..**
ashtray	**pepeljaru**
another chair	**još jednu stolicu**
finger bowl	**zdelicu vode za pranje prstiju**
fork	**viljušku**

(Croatian usage is shown in brackets.)

glass	**čašu**
knife	**nož**
napkin	**salvetu**
plate	**tanjir**
pepper mill	**mlin za biber**
serviette	**salvetu**
spoon	**kašiku (žlicu)**
toothpick	**čačkalicu**

Ordering

I'd like a/an/some…	**Molim Vas…**
aperitif	**aperitiv**
appetizer	**predjelo**
beer	**pivo**
bread	**hleb [kruh]**
butter	**puter**
cheese	**sir**
chips	**prženi krompir (čips)**
coffee	**kafu**
dessert	**dezert**
fish	**ribu**
french fries	**pom frit**
fruit	**voće**
game	**divljač**
ice-cream	**sladoled**
ketchup	**kečap**
lemon	**limun**
lettuce	**salatu**
meat	**meso**
mineral water	**mineralnu vodu**
milk	**mleko**
mustard	**senf [slačicu]**
noodles	**rezance**
oil	**ulje**
olive oil	**maslinovo ulje**
pepper	**biber**
potatoes	**krompir**
poultry	**živinsko meso**
rice	**pirinač [rižu]**
rolls	**kajzericu**
saccharin	**saharin**

salad	**salatu**
salt	**so**
sandwich	**sendvič**
seafood	**morske specijalitete**
seasoning	**začin**
soup	**supu [juhu]**
starter	**predjelo**
sugar	**šećer**
tea	**čaj**
vegetables	**povrće**
vinegar	**sirće [ocat]**
(iced) water	**vodu (sa ledom)**
wine	**vino**

PRIJATNO! [DOBAR TEK!]
ENJOY YOUR MEAL!

---

baked	**pečeno**
boiled	**kuvano**
braised	**dinstovano**
cured	**dimljeno**
fried	**prženo**
grilled	**na roštilju**
marinated	**marinirane**
poached	**kuvana (lešo)**
roasted	**pečeno**
sautéed	**zapečeno**
smoked	**dimljeno**
steamed	**kuvano u pari**
stewed	**krčkano**
underdone (rare)	**nedopečeno [polupečeno]**
medium	**srednje pečeno**
well-done	**dobro pečeno**

ŽIVELI!
CHEERS!

---

glass	**čaša**
bottle	**flaša**

red	**crno**
white	**belo**
rosé	**ružica**
very dry	**vrlo oporo**
dry	**oporo**
sweet	**slatko**
light	**lagano**
full-bodied	**gusto, jako vino**
sparkling	**penušavo**
neat (straight)	**čisto**
on the rocks	**sa ledom**

The bill

I'd like to pay.	**Račun, molim.**
We'd like to pay separately.	**Posebne račune, molim.**
You've made a mistake in this bill, I think.	**Da niste možda pogrešili?**
What's this amount for?	**Šta je ovo?**
Is service included?	**Da li je servis uključen?**
Is everything included?	**Da li je sve uključeno?**
Do you accept traveller's cheques?	**Da li primate putne čekove?**
Thank you. This is for you.	**Hvala, to je za Vas.**
Keep the change.	**Zadržite sitninu.**
That was a very good meal.	**Vrlo dobro smo jeli.**
We enjoyed it, thank you.	**Bilo nam je vrlo prijatno, hvala Vam.**

Complaints

That's not what I ordered. I asked for…	**To nisam poručio, ja sam poručio (fem: poručila)…**
May I change this?	**Mogu li ovo da promenim?**
The meat is…	**Meso je…**
overdone	**prepečeno**
underdone	**nedopečeno**
too rare	**suviše sirovo**
too tough	**suviše žilavo**

This is too…	Ovo je suviše…
bitter/salty/sweet	gorko/slano/slatko
The food is cold.	Hrana je hladna.
This isn't fresh.	Ovo nije sveže.
What's taking you so long?	Zašto još nije gotovo ?
Where are our drinks?	Gde su naša pića?
This isn't clean.	Ovo nije čisto.
Would you ask the head waiter to come over?	Hoćete zamoliti glavnog kelnera da dodje?

Numbers

1	jedan	11	jedanaest
2	dva	12	dvanaest
3	tri	13	trinaest
4	četiri	14	četrnaest
5	pet	15	petnaest
6	šest	16	šesnaest
7	sedam	17	sedamnaest
8	osam	18	osamnaest
9	devet	19	devetnaest
10	deset	20	dvadeset

SERBO-CROATIAN

Food

a la kart à la carte

ajvar salad composed of fried green pepper and aubergine (eggplant), minced together with vinegar and oil

ananas pineapple

aperitiv aperitif

artičoke artichoke

asparagus asparagus

bademi almonds

bakalar cod

baklava a flaky pastry with a nut filling, steeped in syrup

banana banana

barbun red mullet

baren boiled

  ~a govedina boiled beef served generally with horseradish or other sauce

  ~ krompir boiled potatoes

batak leg of fowl

  pileći ~ chicken leg

bečki šnicl (or **odrezak**) breaded veal cutlet

beli luk garlic

belo meso white meat (of fowl)

bešamel white sauce

biber black pepper

biftek beefsteak

blitva mangel

bonboni sweets (candy)

boranija sa jagnjetinom a stew of lamb and green beans

borovnica bilberries (US blueber-

ries)

boršč borscht; vegetable soup with meat and sour cream; may be served hot or chilled

bosanski lonac a stew of several kinds of vegetables and meat

brancin bass

brašno flour

breskva peach

brizle sweetbreads

brusnica cranberries

bubrezi kidneys

bubrežnjak tenderloin

  teleći ~ tenderloin of veal

buljon bouillon

bundeva pumpkin

burek a meat or cheese pastry

but leg, haunch

celer celery

cena price

cenovnik menu

cikla beetroot

cimet cinnamon

cipoli mullet

cvekla beetroot

cvibak rusks (US zwieback)

češnjak garlic

čokolada chocolate

  mlečna ~ milk chocolate bar

  ~ sa lešnikom chocolate bar with hazelnuts

  ~ sa pirinčem chocolate bar with rice

  ~ sa voćem chocolate bar with

fruit
~ za kuvanje cooking chocolate
čorba soup
   govedja ~ beef
   jagnjeća ~ lamb
   krompir ~ potato
   ~ od graha butter bean (US navy-bean)
   ~ od pečuraka mushroom
   ~ od povraća vegetable
   pileća ~ chicken
   riblja ~ fish
   teleća ~ veal
čvarci crackling
ćevapčići minced meat grilled in rolled pieces, served with minced raw onion
ćufte meatball
   ~ u paradajz sosu braised in tomato sauce
ćulbastija grilled steak taken from veal heel of round
ćuretina turkey
ćurka turkey
dalmatinski brodet fish chowder and rice
dalmatinski sir a firm cheese made from ewe's milk
datule dates
dezert dessert
dijetalno low calorie
dimljen smoked
   ~a šunka smoked ham
dinstovano braised
dinja melon
divljač game
doboš torta chocolate layer cake with caramel frosting
dobro pečeno well done
domaća šunka country ham
domaće homemade
   ~ kobasice homemade sausages
domaći specijaliteti local specialities

doručak breakfast
dud mulberries, blackberries
dunja quince
džigerica liver
   dinstovana ~ braised liver
   ~ na roštilju grilled liver
   teleća ~ calf's liver
djevrek doughnut-shaped roll covered with sesame seeds
djuveč pork chop, rice and vegetables all oven-baked
ekler eclair, cream puff
faširani šnicli breaded hamburger steaks
faširano meso minced meat
fazan pheasant
fažol butter (US navy) beans
feferoni pimentos
(sa) fidom (with) noodles
file fillet
   ~ minjon small tenderloin steak
fileki tripe
filovano stuffed
   filovane paprike stuffed peppers
flekice flat, small noodles
   ~ sa kupusom with fried cabbage
   ~ sa šunkom with sliced ham
friško fresh
garnirano with vegetable garnish
germa yeast
geršl barley
gibanica thin layers of pastry alternated with crumpled ewe's-milk cheese
girice pickerel (US wall-eyed pike)
gljive mushrooms
golub pigeon
gomoljica truffles
gorak bitter
gotova jela short-order dishes; ready-to-serve dishes
govedina beef
govedje pečenje roast beef

(na) gradele grilled, generally outdoors; usually refers to fish

grah dry beans

grašak peas

grepfrut grapefruit

grgeč perch

grilovano grilled

griz farina
  ~ na mleku farina pudding

grožđje grapes
  belo ~ green grapes
  suvo ~ raisins

grožđjice raisins

grudi breast
  filovane ~ stuffed
  nadevene ~ stuffed
  pileće ~ breast of chicken

gulaš goulash; a spicy meat stew
  govedji ~ beef
  sekelji ~ chunks of pork and veal braised with sauerkraut, chopped pimentos and onions
  teleći ~ veal

guščija džigerica goose-liver

hajdučki ćevap spit-roasted chunks of beef served with a hot sauce

halva a sugary loaf confection made with honey and nuts

haringa herring

hladna predjela cold appetizers

hleb bread
  beli ~ white bread
  crni ~ black bread (US pumpernickel)
  polubeli ~ bread made with unblanched flour
  ~ sa kimon rye bread with caraway seeds

hobotnica octopus

hrana food

ikra roe

iverak halibut

jabuka apple

pita od ~ apple pie

jabuke u šlafroku apple fritters

jagnjeća sarma lamb's liver, heart and tripe braised with onion and rice and baked in lamb's lights (Serbia and Macedonia)

jagnjeće grudi breast of lamb

jagnjeće pečenje roast lamb

jagnjeći kotlet lamb chop

jagnjetina lamb

jagode strawberries

jaja eggs
  filovana ~ devilled
  meko kuvana ~ soft boiled
  ~ na oko fried, sunny-side up
  poširana ~ poached
  pržena ~ fried
  punjena ~ stuffed
  tvrdo kuvana ~ hard-boiled
  ~ u majonezu egg salad

jaje egg

jarebica partridge

jastog lobster

jegulja eel

jelo course, dish
  glavno ~ main course
  ~ na žaru grilled food

jelovnik menu

jesetra sturgeon

jetra liver

jezik tongue
  ~ u sosu tongue in gravy

jogurt yoghurt

juha soup (see also **čorba**)

junetina beef

kačamak Indian-corn porridge (US cornmeal mush)

kačkavalj a tasty hard cheese from sheep's milk; mild if young, slightly sharp if aged

kajgana scrambled eggs

kajmak 1) skin of boiled milk; 2) dairy product made from the skin of boiled milk

kajsije apricots
kajzerica roll
kalamara squid
  rizoto od ~ rice and squid casserole
kalja mutton braised with cabbage
kamenice a type of oyster
kandirano voće candied fruit
kapama lamb braised with onion and scallions
karamel caramel
karfiol cauliflower
kari curry
kasato Neapolitan ice-cream (US spumoni)
kavijar caviar
kečap ketchup
keks biscuits (US cookies)
keleraba kohlrabi
kelj kale
kesten pire chestnut purée
  ~ **sa šlagom** with whipped cream
kesteni chestnuts
kifla crescent roll
kiflice crescent-shaped biscuits (US cookies), often made with nuts
kijevski kotlet boned breast of chicken stuffed with butter, breaded, then deep fried; Kiev style
kim caraway
kisela čorba meat and vegetable soup, flavoured with lemon juice
kisela pavlaka sour cream
kisela štrudla a rolled flaky pastry with a poppy-seed filling; strudel
kisele paprike pickled peppers
kiseli krastavac gherkin
kiseli kupus sauerkraut
(sa) kiselim mlekom (with) sour milk
kiselo mleko sour milk
kiselo testo a rolled flaky pastry with a poppy-seed filling; strudel
kiseo sour
kitir popcorn
knedle dumplings
  ~ **od šljiva** plum dumplings
  ~ **u supi** noodles
kobasice sausages
  domaće ~ homade sausages
  kranjske ~ sausages, similar to frankfurters though richer
koh cracked-wheat groats or Indian-corn porridge (US cornmeal mush) with hazelnuts
kokice popcorn
kokosov orah coconut
kolač cake
  suvi ~i biscuits (US cookies)
kolenica knuckle
  svinjska ~ pig's knuckle
kompot stewed fruit
  mešani ~ stewed fruit
  ~ **od jabuka** stewed apples
  ~ **od krušaka** stewed pears
  ~ **od šljiva** stewed plums
konzerva tin (US can)
konzervirana hrana tinned (US canned) food
konzome broth
kornfleks corn flakes
kost bone
kotlet cutlet
kozlac tarragon
krastavac cucumber
  kiseli ~ gherkin
krastovnik watercress
kravlji sir any cheese made of cow's milk
krem pudding
  ~ **čorba** creamed soup
  ~ **od čokolade** chocolate pud-

ding
~ **pita** napoleon
~ **torta** napoleon
krezle veal sweetbreads
krmenadle pork chop
krofne doughnuts
kroketi croquettes
krompir potatoes
  baren ~ boiled
  kuvani ~ boiled
  ~ **pire** mashed
  restovani ~ fried, hashed-brown
krto lean
krtola potatoes
kruh bread
kruška pear
krvavice black pudding, blood sausage
kuglof a moulded cake with a hole in the centre, usually made with raisins and almonds
kukuruz Indian corn (US corn)
  kuvani ~ boiled
  ~ **no brašno** Indian-corn meal (US cornmeal)
  pečeni ~ roasted
kumin caraway
kunić rabbit
kupine blackberries
kupus cabbage
  ~ **sa ovčetinom** mutton braised with cabbage
kuruza Indian-corn bread (US corn-bread)
kuvana govedina boiled beef
  ~ **sa renom** with horseradish
kuvana šunka boiled ham
kuvani krompir boiled potatoes
kuvano boiled
  ~ **meso** boiled meat
kvasac yeast
ladetina aspic
lagan light
  ~**a hrana** snack

leće lentils
led ice
  sa ~**om** with ice
lenja pita apple tart, pie
leskovačka mućkalica well-seasoned pork braised with onions and tomatoes
lešnik hazelnuts
lešo poached (of fish)
lignji squid
limun lemon
list sole (plaice)
lokum Turkish delight
(bosanski) lonac a stew of several kinds of vegetables and meat
lorber laurel
losos salmon
lubenica watermelon
luk onion
ljute paprike pimentos
ljuto hot, spicy
mahune green beans
majčina dušica thyme
majonez mayonnaise
makaroni macaroni
  ~ **sa mesom** with meat
  ~ **sa sirom** and cheese
maline raspberries
mandarine tangerine
marcipan marzipan
marelice apricots
margarin margarine
marinirano marinated
marmelada jam
maslac butter
masline olives
maslinovo ulje olive oil
masni sir a creamy, rich cheese
masno fatty, oily
mast lard
med honey
meni menu
merlan whiting
mešan(o) mixed, assorted

mešana salata mixed salad
mešani sladoled mixed ice-cream
mešano meso assorted meats
  ~ na žaru mixed grilled meat
meza snack, generally with a drink
mileram sour cream
minjoni small cakes (similar to American cupcakes) with cream filling and icing on top
mirodjija capers
mladi sir fresh, unripened cheese
mladica river trout
mleko milk
  kiselo ~ sour milk
mlinci a type of crispbread (US wheat cracker); matzo
modri patlidžan aubergine (egg-plant)
morski specijaliteti seafood specialities
mozak brains
mrkva carrots
mućkalica grilled pork
musaka layers of minced meat and either sliced potatoes or aubergine (eggplant), with a topping of eggs and sour milk; oven browned
mušule mussels
nadev stuffing
  ~en stuffed
  ~ene grudi stuffed breast
nar pomegranate
narandža orange
naravni plain
  ~ odrezak plain steak
naresci cold cuts
nedopečeno rare
  ~ meso underdone (US rare) meat
noklice dumplings, noodles
nudle noodles
obložen with vegetables
ocat vinegar

odrezak steak
  bečki ~ breaded veal cutlet
ogrozl gooseberries
okruglice meat dumplings
omlet omelet
  naravni ~ plain
  ~ sa sirom cheese
  ~ sa šunkom ham
orasi nuts, walnuts
ostrige oysters
ovčetina mutton
ovčiji sir sheep's milk cheese
palačinke pancakes
  ~ sa džemom with jam
  ~ sa orasima with chopped nuts
  ~ sa prelivom od jaja with egg brandy
palenta Indian-corn porridge (US corn-meal mush)
papar black pepper
papren peppery, hot

paprika green pepper
  aleva ~ paprika
paprikaš stew
  govedji ~ beef
  pileći ~ stewed chicken
  teleći ~ veal
paradajz tomato
  ~salata tomato salad
  ~sos tomato sauce
parfe parfait; a chilled dessert made of layers of fruit, ice-cream, and whipped cream
pariski šnicl (or **odrezak**) veal cutlet dipped in egg and flour, sautéed
parizer veal sausage
parmezan Parmesan cheese
pasirano creamed
pastrmka trout
pasulj butter beans (US navy beans)
  ~ prebranac (chilled) bean stew

~ sa rebrima with smoked spare ribs

paški sir fat and fairly sharp cheese

pašteta pâté

~ od džigerice liver pâté

patišpanj sponge cake

patka duck

patlidžan aubergine (eggplant)

pavlaka cream

kisela ~ sour cream

pečena piletina roast chicken

pečene paprike grilled peppers, prepared as a salad with oil and seasoning

pečenica roast joint

pečeno roasted

pečenje roast

jagnjeće ~ lamb

prasеće ~ sucking pig

svinjsko ~ pork

teleće ~ veal joint

pečurke mushrooms

pekmez jam

perkelt chopped veal, pork or lamb braised with onion; sour cream added

peršun parsley

pešmelba peach melba; peaches poached in syrup and topped with ice-cream and raspberry jam

pihtije aspic

pijani šaran carp poached in white wine

piktije cold meats in aspic

pilav lamb and rice

pileći paprikaš stewed chicken

piletina chicken

pečena ~ roast chicken

pire purée

~ od jabuka apple sauce

~ od krompira mashed potatoes

pirinač rice

piškota sponge finger (US ladyfinger)

pita a rolled flaky pastry with a filling

~ od sira with cheese filling

plavi patlidžan aubergine (eggplant)

plećka shoulder

pljeskavica hamburger steak served with raw onion

podvarak pork chops or turkey garnished with sauerkraut

pofezne bread soaked in milk and egg, fried (US french toast)

pogača type of round, flat bread, may be unleavened

pogačice pasty, plain or filled with cheese or meat

~ od čvaraka sort of biscuit made with crackling

pohovani šnicli breaded pork or veal chops

pohovano breaded

pom frit chips (US french fries)

pomorandža orange

porcija portion

poriluk leek

potaž vegetable soup

povrće vegetables

prasеće pečenje roast sucking pig

prasetina sucking pig

praška šunka pressed ham

praziluk leek

prebranac butter beans (US navy beans) with onion

predjelo appetizer

hladno ~ cold appetizer

toplo ~ warm appetizer

prepelica quail

prepržen hleb toast

proja Indian-corn bread (US corn-bread)

prokelj or **prokula** brussels sprouts

prošarana slanina bacon with

strips of meat

prstaci a kind of shellfish

pršut Dalmatian cured ham

pršuta cured beef or pork

prženi krompir fried potatoes

prženo fried

pržolica grilled beefsteak

puding custard cream (US pudding)

punč torta frosted sponge cake sprinkled with rum

punjene stuffed

  ~ paprike green peppers stuffed with minced meat and rice; cooked in tomato sauce

  ~ tikvice marrow (US zucchini) stuffed with minced meat and rice; cooked in tomato sauce

pura (**palenta** or **kačamak**) Indian corn porridge (US cornmeal mush)

puran turkey

puter butter

puževi snails

račići prawns, shrimp

ragu stew

  ~ supa thick meat soup

rajčica tomatoes

rakovi crabs

  morski ~ saltwater crawfish

  rečni ~ freshwater crayfish

ramstek rump steak

rashladjeno chilled

ratluk Turkish delight

raviole ravioli; dough envelopes

ražanj skewer

ražnjići chunks of veal or pork grilled on a skewer

rebra ribs

  ~ sa kiselim kupusom spare ribs with sauerkraut

  suva ~ smoked spare ribs

ren horseradish

(sa) renom (with) horseradish

repa turnip

restovani krompir fried, hashed-brown potatoes

rezanci noodles

riba fish

  morska ~ saltwater fish

  rečna ~ freshwater fish

  sveža ~ fish, kept in the restaurant's aquarium

ribanac sauerkraut

ribić veal heel of round

  teleći ~ stew made of veal heel of round

ribizle red currants

riblji rizoto fish and rice casserole

ričet barley groats boiled with beans

ringlovi greengages

rizi bizi spring pea and rice casserole

rizoto casserole of rice, meat and vegetables

riža rice

rolat roll-shaped cake

roštilj grill

  meso sa ~a grilled meat

  pržiti meso na ~u grilled meat

  ~ radi grilled meat specialities

rotkvica radish

rozbratna rib-eye steak

ručak lunch

ruska salata Russian salad; diced vegetables with mayonnaise

saft sauce, gravy

salama salami

  Gavrilovićeva ~ the best known, very rich

salamura brine

salata salad

  krastavac ~ cucumber

  mešana ~ mixed salad

  ~ od boranije green-bean

  ~ od cvekle beetroot

  ~ od kiselog kupusa sauerkraut

~ **od krompira** potato
~ **od kupusa** cole slaw, with a vinegar and oil dressing
~ **od pečenih paprika** fried green peppers
paradajz ~ tomato
srpska ~ tomato, green pepper and onion
šopska ~ tomato salad with onions, pimentos and grated white chesse
zelena ~ green salad
sanpiero John Dory
sardela anchovies
sardine sardines
sarma cabbage leaves stuffed with minced meat and rice
sarmice u zelju minced meat and rice rolled in grape leaves and served with fresh curds
sataraš lamb braised with green peppers, onions, eggs and tomatoes
seckano diced, chopped
sekelji gulaš chunks of pork and veal braised with sauerkraut, chopped pimentos and onions
sendvič sandwich
~ **sa sirom** cheese
~ **sa šunkom** ham
senf mustard
servis service
~ **uključen** (or **uračunat**) service included
sipa cuttlefish
sir cheese
kravlji ~ from cow's milk
mladi ~ fresh
ovčiji ~ from sheep's milk
posni ~ fat-free
somborski ~ mild cheese made from cow's mild, smooth texture
srpski ~ a crumbly white cheese

topljeni ~ a semi-hard, mild cheese
travnički ~ rich and fairly salty cheese made from sheep's milk
~ **za mazanje** cheese spread
Zdenka ~ mild, semi-hard cheese, very rich and fat
sirće vinegar
sirup syrup
sitni luk chives
skampi scampi, prawns, shrimp
skorup skin of boiled milk
skuše mackerel
slačica mustard
sladoled ice-cream
mešani ~ assorted
~ **od čokolade** chocolate
~ **od jagoda** strawberry
~ **od limuna** lemon
~ **vanilije** vanilla
voćni ~ tuttifrutti
slan salted
slanina bacon
prošarana ~ with strips of meat
slatki kupus cabbage
slatkiši sweets (US candy)
smokve figs
smudj pike-perch
so(l) salt
sočan juicy
soft sauce, gravy
som sheatfish; a large catfish
somborski sir mild cheese made from cow's milk, smooth texture
somun round, flat bread
sos sauce
spanać spinach
srce heart
srdele pilchard
srednje pečeno medium rare
sremske kobasice rich, paprika sausage
srneće meso venison

srpski sir a crumbly, white cheese
strugano grated
sufle soufflé
supa bouillon (see **čorba**)
sutlijaš a kind of rice pudding
suv dry (smoked)
  ~a pita sa orasima flaky leaves of pastry alternating with walnut filling
  ~a rebra smoked spare ribs
  ~e šljive prunes
  ~i vrat smoked shoulder of pork
  ~o meso smoked meat
svež fresh
svinjetina pork
svinjska glava brawn (US headcheese)
svinjske kobasice pork sausage
svinjske kolenice pig's knuckles
svinjski kare roast shoulder of pork
svinjski kotlet pork chop
svinjsko pečenje roast pork
šam beaten egg white and sugar
šampita whipped cream pie
šamrolna whipped cream roll
šaran carp
  pečeni ~ baked
šargarepa carrots
šatobrijan tenderloin steak
šaum beaten egg white and sugar
šećer sugar
  ~ u kocki lump
  ~ u kristalu granulated
  ~ u prahu castor (US powdered)
šipak rose hip
škembići tripe
školjke shellfish
škrapina red mullet
šlag whipped cream
šne nokle small mounds of meringue served on a custard base
šnicl(a) cutlet

bečki ~ breaded veal cutlet
natur ~ beef, veal or pork cutlet, pan-fried
pariski ~ veal cutlet dipped in egg and flour, sautéed
pohovani ~i breaded pork or veal chops
špageti spaghetti
  ~ sa mesom with meat sauce
  ~ sa sirom with cheese
špargle or **šparoge** asparagus
špikivano larded
špinat spinach
štrudla paper-thin layers of pastry filled with fruit, strudel
  ~ od jabuka filled with apple slices, nuts, raisins
štruklji breaded cheese dumplings
štuka pike
šufnudle potato dumplings
šumske jagode wild strawberries
šunka ham
  dimljena ~ smoked
  domaća ~ country
  praška ~ pressed
švargla sausage of pork offal
tanjir plate
taške type of fritter, with jam or meat
teleća džigerica calf's liver
teleće pečenje roasted veal joint
teleći ajmokac veal stew
teleći paprikaš veal stew
teleći ribić stew made of veal heel of round
teletina veal
testo dough
tikva marrow (US zucchini)
topfn a kind of cottage cheese, very mild and fat-free
topla predjela warm appetizers
topljeni sir a semi-hard, mild cheese
torta cake

krem ~ napoleon
  ~ **od čokolade** chocolate cake
  punč ~ frosted sponge cake
  sprinkled with rum
  vočna ~ fruit cake
trapist a firm, mild ewe's milk
  cheese
travnički sir rich and fairly salty
  cheese made from sheep's milk
trešnja cherries
tripe tripe
tufahije baked apples filled with
  nuts and syrup
tulumbe fritters served with syrup
tunjevina (or **tunjina**) tunny (US
  tuna)
turšija pickled sweet peppers
ulje oil
  maslinovo ~ olive oil
umak dripping
urmašice a rich dessert steeped
  in syrup
urme dates
uštipci fritters
užina snack (during the morning)
vafle waffle
varivo cooked vegetables
večera dinner
vegetarijansko jelo vegetarian
  food
vekna loaf
vešalica grilled veal cutlet
viršle frankfurters

višnje Morello cherries
voće fruit
  južno ~ citrus fruit
  kandirano ~ candied fruit
voćna salata fruit cocktail
vrgnji mushrooms
vrhnje cream
  kiselo ~ sour cream
začin spice
zakuska refreshment, snack
Zdenka sir mild, semi-hard cheese,
  very rich and fat
zečetina hare
zejtin oil
zelenje vegetables
zeljanica tart made of layers of
  pastry and spinach
zelje cabbage
zemička roll, bun
zubatac dentex (fish)
žablji bataci frog's legs
(na) žaru meso grilled meat
žele jelly, aspic
želudac tripe
žganjci Indian-corn porridge (US
  cornmeal mush)
žito 1) wheat 2) cracked wheat
  mixed with sugar, nuts, cinnamon and other spices
živina fowl
živinsko meso fowl
žumance egg yolk
žutenica chicory (US endive)

SERBO-CROATIAN

Drink

ajer konjak egg brandy
ajs kafe iced coffee
Bakarska vodica a sparkling white
  wine (Croatia)
belo vino white wine
bevanda wine diluted with water

Blatina red wine (Herzegovina)
boza refreshing non-alcoholic
  drink made of Indian-corn meal
  (US cornmeal), water, yeast,
  sugar
brendi brandy

Burgundac a red wine (Dalmatia and Kosovo)

Crna Gora Montenegro; this region in the southwest produces mostly red table wine, e.g., *Vranac, Plavka*

crno vino red wine

Crno župsko vino a dry red wine (Serbia)

Cviček a light, red wine (Slovenia)

čaj tea
   narodni ~ fruit tea
   Ruski ~ Russian tea
   ~ **sa limunom** with lemon
   ~ **sa mlekom** with milk

čisto neat (US straight)

Dalmacija Dalmatia; the rugged, Adriatic coastal region, whose most notable red wine is *Plavac* with a full-bodied flavour and pleasant bouquet; the area's slightly dry red wines are also well known, e.g., *Dingač* and *Postup*

dezertno vino dessert wine

Dingač one of the best Yugoslavian full-bodied red wines (Dalmatia)

Džervin Muskat-Hamburg a red dessert wine (Macedonia)

džin gin
   ~ **i tonik** gin and tonic

flaša bottle

Fruškogorski biser a sparkling wine, medium dry (Serbia)

Graševina dry white wine (Croatia)

Grk white, golden yellow wine with a fine bouquet (Dalmatia)

grog mulled brandy diluted with water

Grom full-bodied, dry red wine (Serbia)

Hercegovina Herzegovina produces a red table wine, *Blatina*, and a white one, *Žilavka*

hladno cold
   ~ **piće** cold drink

Hrvatska Croatia is one of the most important wine-producing regions; white wine is produced of varying character, from light, slightly acid wine like *Graševina,* to rich, full-bodied types like *Muskat otonel;* some red wine is also produced

Istra Istria, the northern peninsula just south of Slovenia, is best known for its red wine like *Merlot* and *Tokaj,* though some white, like *Malvazija* is produced there too

jabukovača apple cider

Kabernet full-bodied red wine (Slovenia, Serbia)

kafa coffee
   bela ~ white coffee
   espresso ~ expresso coffee
   turska ~ strong, Turkish style

kajsijevača apricot brandy

kakao cocoa

Kavadarka dry red wine (Macedonia)

kisela voda mineral water

klekovača plum brandy mixed with berries

Knjaz Miloš name of a popular mineral water

koka kola cola drink

kokta a soft drink made from cola

koktel cocktail

komovica grape brandy

konjak brandy, cognac

Kosovo southwest part of Serbia, principally red wine is produced, like *Burgundac*

Kosovski božur full-bodied red wine (Kosovo)

Kratošija a dry red wine (Macedonia)

kuvano vino mulled wine with water and sugar added

led ice

liker liquor, brandy

limunada lemonade

lozovača grape brandy

Ljutomer a slightly sweet white wine (Slovenia)

Makedonija Macedonia, the southernmost region, produces principally red table wine, e.g., *Kavadarka, Kratošija; Džervin muskat hamburg* is a red dessert wine from the area.

Malvazija slightly sweet white wine (Slovenia, Croatia)

Mapa a dry rosé wine (Serbia, Macedonia)

Maraskino maraschino cherry liqueur

Martini vermouth

mastika an aniseed liqueur

Milijon a Yugoslav sparkling wine (Serbia)

mineralna voda mineral water

mleko milk
  hladno ~ cold milk

Muškat otonel a white dessert wine (Croatia)

Opolo rosé wine from the islands (Dalmatia)

oporo dry

oranžada orangeade

otvoreno vino open wine

pelinkovac absinth liqueur

penušavo sparkling

pića drinks
  alkoholna ~ alcoholic drinks
  bezalkoholna ~ soft drinks
  žestoka ~ spirits

pivo beer
  crno ~ dark beer

dijetalno ~ low-calorie beer
specijalno ~ extra strong beer
svetlo ~ light beer

plavac full-bodied red wine from Dalmatia

Plemenka a dry white wine (Serbia)

poluslatko vino slightly sweet wine

Postup red wine (Dalmatia)

Pošip dry white wine (Dalmatia)

prepečenica plum brandy

prirodno vino natural wine

Prokupac rosé wine (Serbia)

Prošek a famous dessert wine (Dalmatia)

punč rum punch

rakija plum brandy; hard liquor

rashladjeno chilled

rizling riesling, a dry white wine

Rubinova ružica a dry rosé wine (Serbia)

rum rum

ružica rosé wine

Semijon dry white wine from various regions

Silvanec white wine (Vojvodina)

Slovenija Slovenia; the country's northernmost vineyards are considered among the best of Yugoslavia; they go from the Adriatic to the east across to the River Drava valley at the Hungarian border; principally white wine is produced, e.g., *Cviček, Ljutomer, Malvazija*

Smederevsko a white wine from Serbia

soda (voda) soda (water)

sok juice
  ~ **od ananas** pineapple
  ~ **od borovnice** bilberry (US blueberry)
  ~ **paradajza** tomato
  ~ **prirodni** ~ natural juice

SERBO-CROATIAN

voćni ~ fruit juice

Srbija Serbia has the most extensive vineyards and produces almost half the nation's wine; most of the wine is white though there is some red like *Grom, Kabernet, Prokupac* and *Župa;* the latter wine along with *Župsko crno* can vary considerably in taste from bitter to agreeably fruity; some noted white wines are the *Fruškogorska, Smederevska* and *Vršačka*

stono vino open wine

šampanjac sparkling wine

šljivovica plum brandy

   domaća ~ local plum brandy

špricer wine mixed with soda water

šumadijski čaj see *vruća rakija*

šveps tonic water

tonik voter tonic water

Traminac a dry white wine (Slovenia)

travarica a kind of brandy made from herbs

Tri srca type of mineral water

vermut vermouth

   svetli ~ light

   tamni ~ dark

veštačko vino fruit wine to which sugar has been added to increase its alcoholic content

vino wine

belo ~ white

crno ~ red

dezerto ~ dessert wine

domaće ~ local wine

oporo ~ dry wine

prirodno ~ natural wine, i.e., to which no sugar has been added

sto(l)no ~ table wine

veštačko ~ fruit wine to which sugar has been added to increase its alcoholic content

vinska karta wine list

vinjak brandy

viski whisky

   ~ **sa sodom** whisky and soda

voćni sok fruit juice

voda water

   mineralna ~ mineral water

   soda ~ soda water

Vojvodina the region north of Belgrade where principally white wine is produced, e.g., *Banatski* and *Fruškogorski rizling*

votka vodka

Vranac a full-bodied, dry red wine (Montenegro)

Vršačko belo vino a light white wine from the Vršac region of Vojvodina

vruća rakija mulled brandy sweetened with sugar

Vugava a red wine from the island of Vis (Dalmatia)

Žilavka a dry white wine

Spanish

Guide to pronunciation

Letter	Approximate pronunciation
Consonants	
ch, f, k, l, m, n, p, t, y	as in English
b	generally as in English but sometimes more like **v**
c	1) before **e** and **i**, like **th** in **thin** 2) otherwise, like **k** in **kit**
d	1) generally as in **dog**, although less decisive 2) between vowels and at the end of a word, like **th** in **this**
g	1) before **e** and **i**, like **ch** in Scottish lo**ch** 2) otherwise, like **g** in **go**
h	always silent
j	like **ch** in Scottish lo**ch**
ll	like **lli** in million
ñ	like **ni** in onion
qu	like **k** in **kit**

r	more strongly trilled (like a Scottish **r**), especially at the beginning of a word
rr	strongly trilled
s	always like the **s** in si**t**, often with a slight lisp
v	tends to be like **b** in **b**ad, but less tense; within a word, more like English **v**
z	like **th** in **th**in

Vowels

a	like **a** in c**a**r, but fairly short
e	1) sometimes like **a** in l**a**te 2) less often, like **e** in g**e**t
i	like **ee** in f**ee**t
o	1) sometimes fairly like **o** in r**o**pe 2) sometimes like **o** in g**o**t
u	like **oo** in l**oo**t
y	only a vowel when alone or at the end of a word; like **ee** in f**ee**t

Note

1) In forming diphthongs, **a**, **e** and **o** are strong vowels, and **i** and **u** are weak vowels. This means that in diphthongs the strong vowels are pronounced more strongly than the weak ones. If two weak vowels form a diphthong, the second one is pronounced more strongly.

2) In words ending with a consonant (except **n** and **s**), the last syllable is stressed.

3) In words ending with a vowel (and in those ending with **n** and **s**), the next to the last syllable is stressed.

4) Words not stressed in accordance with these rules have an acute accent (') over the vowel of the stressed syllable.

SPANISH

Some useful expressions

Hungry

I'm hungry/I'm thirsty.	**Tengo hambre/Tengo sed.**
Can you recommend a good restaurant?	**¿Puede recomendarme un buen restaurante?**
Are there any good, cheap restaurants around here?	**¿Hay algún restaurante bueno y barato cerca de aquí?**
I'd like to reserve a table for ... people.	**Quiero reservar una mesa para ...**
We'll come at ... o'clock.	**Vendremos a las ...**

Asking

Good evening. I'd like a table for ... people.	**Buenas tardes, quisiera una mesa para ...**
Could we have a table...?	**¿Nos puede dar una mesa...?**
in the corner	**en el rincón**
by the window	**al lado de la ventana**
outside	**fuera**
on the terrace	**en el patio**
May I please have the menu?	**¿Puedo ver la carta, por favor?**
What's this?	**¿Qué es esto?**
Do you have...?	**¿Tienen...?**
a set menu	**platos combinados**
local dishes	**especialidades locales**
a children's menu	**un menú para niños**
Waiter/Waitress!	**¡Camarero/Señorita!**
What do you recommend?	**¿Qué me aconseja?**
Could I have (a/an)... please?	**¿Puede darme..., por favor?**
ashtray	**un cenicero**
another chair	**otra silla**
finger bowl	**un enjuagatorio [un lavadedos]**
fork	**un tenedor**
glass	**un vaso**

(Latin American usage is shown in brackets)

SPANISH

knife	**un cuchillo**
napkin	**una servilleta**
plate	**un plato**
serviette	**una servilleta**
spoon	**una cuchara**
toothpick	**un palillo**

Ordering

I'd like a/an/some...	**Quisiera...**
aperitif	**un aperitivo**
appetizer	**unas tapas [unos saladitos]**
beer	**una cerveza**
bread	**pan**
butter	**mantequilla [manteca]**
cheese	**queso**
chips	**patatas fritas [papas fritas]**
coffee	**un café**
dessert	**un postre**
fish	**pescado**
french fries	**patatas fritas [papas fritas]**
fruit	**frutas**
game	**carne de caza**
ice-cream	**un helado**
ketchup	**salsa de tomate**
lemon	**limón**
lettuce	**lechuga**
meat	**carne**
mineral water	**agua mineral**
milk	**leche**
mustard	**mostaza**
noodles	**tallarines**
oil	**aceite**
olive oil	**aceite de oliva**
pepper	**pimienta**
potatoes	**patatas [papas]**
poultry	**aves**
rice	**arroz**
rolls	**panecillos [pancitos]**
saccharin	**sacarina**
salad	**una ensalada**
salt	**sal**

sandwich	**un bocadillo [un sandwich/un emparedado]**
seafood	**mariscos**
seasoning	**condimentos**
soup	**una sopa**
starter	**unas tapas [unos saladitos]**
sugar	**azúcar**
tea	**un té**
vegetables	**legumbres**
vinegar	**vinagre**
(iced) water	**agua (helada)**
wine	**vino**

¡QUE APROVECHE!
ENJOY YOUR MEAL!

---

baked	**al horno**
baked in parchment	**cocido envuelto**
boiled	**hervido**
braised	**estofado**
cured	**en salazón**
fried	**frito**
grilled	**a la parrilla**
marinated	**en escabeche**
poached	**hervido**
roasted	**asado**
sautéed	**salteado [sofreído/sofrito]**
smoked	**ahumado**
steamed	**cocido al vapor**
stewed	**estofado**
underdone (rare)	**poco hecho**
medium	**regular**
well-done	**muy hecho**

¡SALUD!
CHEERS!

---

glass	**un vaso**
bottle	**una botella**

SPANISH

red	tinto
white	blanco
rosé	clarete [rosado, rosé]
very dry	muy seco
dry	seco
sweet	dulce
light	liviano
full-bodied	de cuerpo
sparkling	espumoso
neat (straight)	solo
on the rocks	con hielo

The bill

I'd like to pay.	Quisiera pagar.
We'd like to pay separately.	Quisiéramos pagar separadamente.
You've made a mistake in this bill, I think.	Me parece que se ha equivocado en esta cuenta.
What's this amount for?	¿A qué corresponde esta cantidad?
Is service included?	¿Está el servicio incluido?
Is everything included?	¿Está todo incluido?
Do you accept traveller's cheques?	¿Acepta cheques de viajero?
Thank you. This is for you.	Gracias, esto es para usted.
Keep the change.	Quédese con el cambio.
That was a very good meal.	Ha sido una comida excelente.
We enjoyed it, thank you.	Nos ha gustado, gracias.

Complaints

That's not what I ordered.	Esto no es lo que he pedido.
I asked for...	He pedido...
May I change this?	¿Puede cambiarme esto?

The meat is...	La carne está...
overdone	demasiado hecha
underdone	poco hecha
too rare	demasiado cruda
too tough	demasiado dura
This is too...	Esto está demasiado...
bitter/salty/sweet	amargo/salado/dulce
The food is cold.	La comida está fría.
This isn't fresh.	Esto no está fresco.
What's taking you so long?	¿Por qué se demora tanto?
Where are our drinks?	¿Dónde están nuestras bebidas?
This isn't clean.	Esto no está limpio.
Would you ask the head waiter to come over?	¿Quiere decirle al jefe que venga?

Numbers

1	uno	11	once
2	dos	12	doce
3	tres	13	trece
4	cuatro	14	catorce
5	cinco	15	quince
6	seis	16	dieciséis
7	siete	17	diecisiete
8	ocho	18	dieciocho
9	nueve	19	diecinueve
10	diez	20	veinte

SPANISH

Food

Please note that **ch, ll,** and **ñ** are treated as separate letters in Spanish alphabetical order.

a caballo steak topped with two eggs
acedera sorrel
aceite oil
aceituna olive
achicoria endive (US chicory)
(al) adobo marinated
aguacate avocado (pear)
ahumado smoked
ajiaceite garlic mayonnaise
ajiaco bogotano chicken soup with potatoes
(al) ajillo cooked in garlic and oil
ajo garlic
al, a la in the style of, with
albahaca basil
albaricoque apricot
albóndiga spiced meat- or fishball
alcachofa artichoke
alcaparra caper
aliñado seasoned
alioli garlic mayonnaise
almeja clam, cockle
almejas a la marinera cooked in hot, pimento sauce
almendra almond
  ~ garrapiñada sugared almond
almíbar syrup
almuerzo lunch
alubia bean

anchoa anchovy
anguila eel
angula baby eel
anticucho beef heart grilled on a skewer with green peppers
apio celery
a punto medium (done)
arenque hérring
  ~ en escabeche marinated, pickled herring
arepa flapjack made of maize (corn)
arroz rice
  ~ blanco boiled, steamed
  ~ escarlata with tomatoes and prawns
  ~ a la española with chicken liver, pork, tomatoes, fish stock
  ~ con leche rice pudding
  ~ primavera with spring vegetables
  ~ a la valenciana with vegetables, chicken, shellfish (and sometimes eel)
asado roast
  ~ antiguo a la venezolana mechado roast beef stuffed with capers
asturias a strong, fermented cheese with a sharp flavour

atún tunny (US tuna)
avellana hazelnut
azafrán saffron
azúcar sugar
bacalao cod
~ **a la vizcaína** with green peppers, potatoes, tomato sauce
barbo barbel (fish)
batata sweet potato, yam
becada woodcock
berberecho cockle
berenjena aubergine (US eggplant)
berraza parsnip
berro cress
berza cabbage
besugo sea bream
bien hecho well-done
biftec, bistec beef steak
bizcocho sponge cake, sponge finger (US ladyfinger)
~ **borracho** cake steeped in rum (or wine) and syrup
bizcotela glazed biscuit (US cookie)
blando soft
bocadillo 1) sandwich 2) sweet (Colombia)
bollito, bollo roll, bun
bonito a kind of tunny (US tuna)
boquerón 1) anchovy 2) whitebait
(en) brocheta (on a) skewer
budín blancmange, custard
buey ox
buñuelo 1) doughnut 2) fritter with ham, mussels and prawns (sometimes flavoured with brandy)
burgos a popular soft, creamy cheese named after the Spanish province of its origin
butifarra spiced sausage
caballa fish of the mackerel family
cabeza de ternera calf's head

cabra goat
cabrales blue-veined goat's-milk cheese
cabrito kid
cacahuete peanut
cachelos diced potatoes boiled with cabbage, paprika, garlic, bacon, *chorizo* sausage
calabacín vegetable marrow, courgette (US zucchini)
calabaza pumpkin
calamar squid
calamares a la romana squids fried in batter
caldereta de cabrito kid stew (often cooked in red wine)
caldillo de congrio conger-eel soup with tomatoes and potatoes
caldo consommé
~ **gallego** meat and vegetable broth
callos tripe (often served in pimento sauce)
~ **a la madrileña** in piquant sauce with *chorizo* sausage and tomatoes
camarón shrimp
canela cinnamon
cangrejo de mar crab
cangrejo de río crayfish
cantarela chanterelle mushroom
caracol snail
carbonada criolla baked pumpkin stuffed with diced beef
carne meat
~ **asada al horno** roast meat
~ **molida** minced beef
~ **a la parrilla** charcoal-grilled steak
~ **picada** minced beef
carnero mutton
carpa carp
casero home made

castaña chestnut

castañola sea perch

(a la) catalana with onions, parsley, tomatoes and herbs

caza game

(a la) cazadora with mushrooms, spring onions, herbs in wine

cazuela de cordero lamb stew with vegetables

cebolla onion

cebolleta chive

cebrero blue-veined cheese of creamy texture with a pale, yellow rind; sharp taste

cena dinner, supper

centolla spider-crab, served cold

cerdo pork

cereza cherry

ceviche fish marinated in lemon and lime juice

cigala Dublin Bay prawn

cincho a hard cheese made from sheep's milk

ciruela plum

~ pasa prune

cocido 1) cooked, boiled 2) stew of beef with ham, fowl, chick peas, potatoes and vegetables (the broth is eaten first)

cochifrito de cordero highly seasoned stew of lamb or kid

codorniz quail

col cabbage

~ de Bruselas brussels sprout

coliflor cauliflower

comida meal

compota stewed fruit

conejo rabbit

confitura jam

congrio conger eel

consomé al jerez chicken broth with sherry

copa nuria egg-yolk and egg-white, whipped and served with jam

corazón de alcachofa artichoke heart

corazonada heart stewed in sauce

cordero lamb

~ recental spring lamb

cortadillo small pancake with lemon

corzo deer

costilla chop

crema 1) cream or mousse

~ batida whipped cream

~ española dessert of milk, eggs, fruit jelly

~ nieve frothy egg-yolk, sugar, rum (or wine)

crema 2) soup

criadillas (de toro) glands (of bull)

(a la) criolla with green peppers, spices and tomatoes

croqueta croquette, fish or meat dumpling

crudo raw

cubierto cover charge

cuenta bill (US check)

curanto dish consisting of seafood, vegetables and suck(l)ing pig, all cooked in an earthen well, lined with charcoal

chabacano apricot

chalote shallot

champiñón mushroom

chancho adobado pork braised with sweet potatoes, orange and lemon juice

chanfaina goat's liver and kidney stew, served in a thick sauce

chanquete whitebait

chile chili pepper

chiles en nogada green peppers stuffed with whipped cream and nut sauce

chimichurri hot parsley sauce

chipirón small squid

chopa a kind of sea bream

chorizo pork sausage, highly seasoned with garlic and paprika

chuleta cutlet

chupe de mariscos scallops served with a creamy sauce and gratinéed with cheese

churro sugared tubular fritter

damasco variety of apricot

dátil date

desayuno breakfast

dorada gilt-head

dulce sweet

~ de naranja marmalade

durazno peach

embuchado stuffed with meat

embutido spicy sausage

empanada pie or tart with meat or fish filling

~ de horno dough filled with minced meat, similar to ravioli

empanadilla small patty stuffed with seasoned meat or fish

empanado breaded

emperador swordfish

encurtido pickle

enchilada a maizeflour (US cornmeal) pancake *(tortilla)* stuffed and usually served with vegetable garnish and sauce

~ roja sausage-filled maizeflour pancake dipped into a red sweet-pepper sauce

~ verde maizeflour pancake stuffed with meat or fowl and braised in a green-tomato sauce

endibia chicory (US endive)

eneldo dill

ensalada salad

~ común green

~ de frutas fruit salad

~ (a la) primavera spring

~ valenciana with green peppers, lettuce and oranges

ensaladilla rusa diced cold vegetables with mayonnaise

entremés appetizer, hors-d'oeuvre

erizo de mar sea urchin

(en) escabeche marinated, pickled

~ de gallina chicken marinated in vinegar

escarcho red gurnard (fish)

escarola endive (US chicory)

espalda shoulder

(a la) española with tomatoes

espárrago asparagus

especia spice

especialidad de la casa chef's speciality

espinaca spinach

esqueixada mixed fish salad

(al) estilo de in the style of

estofado stew(ed)

estragón tarragon

fabada (asturiana) stew of pork, beans, bacon and sausage

faisán pheasant

fiambres cold meat (US cold cuts)

fideo thin noodle

filete steak

~ de lomo fillet steak (US tenderloin)

~ de res beef steak

~ de lenguado empanado breaded fillet of sole

(a la) flamenca with onions, peas, green peppers, tomatoes and spiced sausage

flan caramel mould, custard

frambuesa raspberry

(a la) francesa sautéed in butter

fresa strawberry

~ de bosque wild

fresco fresh, chilled

fresón large strawberry

fricandó veal bird, thin slice of meat rolled in bacon and braised

frijol bean

frijoles refritos fried mashed beans

frío cold

frito 1) fried 2) fry

~ **de patata** deep-fried potato croquette

fritura fry

~ **mixta** meat, fish or vegetables deep-fried in batter

fruta fruit

~ **escarchada** crystallized (US candied) fruit

galleta salted or sweet biscuit (US cracker or cookie)

~ **de nata** cream biscuit (US sandwich cookie)

gallina hen

~ **de Guinea** guinea fowl

gallo cockerel

gamba shrimp

~ **grande** prawn

gambas con mayonesa shrimp cocktail

ganso goose

garbanzo chick pea

gazpacho seasoned broth made of raw onions, garlic, tomatoes, cucumber and green pepper; served chilled

(a la) gitanilla with garlic

gordo fatty, rich (of food)

granada pomegranate

grande large

(al) gratín gratinéed

gratinado gratinéed

grelo turnip greens

grosella currant

~ **espinosa** gooseberry

~ **negra** blackcurrant

~ **roja** redcurrant

guacamole a purée of avocado and spices used as a dip, in a salad, for a *tortilla* filling or as a garnish

guarnición garnish, trimming

guayaba guava (fruit)

guinda sour cherry

guindilla chili pepper

guisado stew(ed)

guisante green pea

haba broad bean

habichuela verde French bean (US green bean)

hamburguesa hamburger

hayaca central maizeflour (US cornmeal) pancake, usually with a minced-meat filling

helado ice-cream, ice

hervido 1) boiled 2) stew of beef and vegetables (Latin America)

hielo ice

hierba herb

hierbas finas finely chopped mixture of herbs

hígado liver

higo fig

hinojo fennel

hongo mushroom

(al) horno baked

hortaliza greens

hueso bone

huevo egg

~ **cocido** boiled

~ **duro** hard-boiled

~ **escalfado** poached

~ **a la española** stuffed with tomatoes and served with cheese sauce

~ **a la flamenca** baked with asparagus, peas, peppers, onions, tomatoes and sausage

~ **frito** fried

~ **al nido** egg-yolk placed into small, soft roll, fried, then covered with egg-white

~ **pasado por agua** soft-boiled

~ **revuelto** scrambled

~ **con tocino** bacon and egg

humita boiled maize (US corn) with tomatoes, green peppers, onions and cheese

(a la) inglesa 1) underdone (of meat) 2) boiled 3) served with boiled vegetables

jabalí wild boar

jalea jelly

jamón ham

~ **cocido** boiled (often referred to as *jamón de York*)

~ **en dulce** boiled and served cold

~ **gallego** smoked and cut thinly

~ **serrano** cured and cut thinly

(a la) jardinera with carrots, peas and other vegetables

jengibre ginger

(al) jerez braised in sherry

judía bean

~ **verde** French bean (US green bean)

jugo gravy, meat juice

en su ~ in its own juice

juliana with shredded vegetables

jurel variety of mackerel

lacón shoulder of pork

~ **curado** salted pork

lamprea lamprey

langosta spiny lobster

langostino Norway lobster, Dublin Bay prawn

laurel bay leaf

lechón suck(l)ing pig

lechuga lettuce

legumbre vegetable

lengua tongue

lenguado sole, flounder

~ **frito** fried fillet of sole on bed of vegetables

lenteja lentil

liebre hare

~ **estofada** jugged hare

lima 1) lime   2) sweet lime (Latin America)

limón lemon

lista de platos menu

lista de vinos wine list

lobarro a variety of bass

lombarda red cabbage

lomo loin

longaniza long, highly seasoned sausage

lonja slice of meat

lubina bass

macarrones macaroni

(a la) madrileña with *chorizo* sausage, tomatoes and paprika

magras al estilo de Aragón cured ham in tomato sauce

maíz maize (US corn)

(a la) mallorquina usually refers to highly seasoned fish and shellfish

manchego hard cheese from La Mancha, made from sheep's milk, white or golden-yellow in colour

maní peanut

mantecado 1) small butter cake 2) custard ice-cream

mantequilla butter

manzana apple

~ **en dulce** in honey

(a la) marinera usually with mussels, onions, tomatoes, herbs and wine

marisco seafood

matambre rolled beef stuffed with vegetables

mayonesa mayonnaise

mazapán marzipan, almond paste

mejillón mussel

mejorana marjoram

melaza treacle, molasses

melocotón peach

membrillo quince

menestra boiled green vegetable soup

~ **de pollo** chicken and vegetable soup

menta mint

menú menu

~ **del día** set menu

~ **turístico** tourist menu

menudillos giblets

merengue meringue

merienda snack

merluza hake

mermelada jam

mezclado mixed

miel honey

(a la) milanesa with cheese, generally baked

minuta menu

mixto mixed

mole poblano chicken served with a sauce of chili peppers, spices and chocolate

molusco mollusc (snail, mussel, clam)

molleja sweetbread

mora mulberry

morcilla black pudding (US blood sausage)

morilla morel mushroom

moros y cristianos rice and black beans with diced ham, garlic, green peppers and herbs

mostaza mustard

mújol mullet

nabo turnip

naranja orange

nata cream

~ **batida** whipped cream

natillas custard

~ **al limón** lemon cream

níspola medlar (fruit)

nopalito young cactus leaf served with salad dressing

nuez nut

~ **moscada** nutmeg

olla stew

~ **gitana** vegetable stew

~ **podrida** stew made of vegetables, meat, fowl and ham

ostra oyster

oveja ewe

pabellón criollo beef in tomato sauce garnished with beans, rice and bananas

paella consists basically of saffron rice with assorted seafood and sometimes meat

~ **alicantina** with green peppers, onions, tomatoes, artichokes and fish

~ **catalana** with sausages, pork, squid, tomatoes, red sweet peppers and peas

~ **marinera** with fish, shellfish and meat

~ **(a la) valenciana** with chicken, shrimps, peas, tomatoes, mussels and garlic

palmito palm heart

palta avocado (pear)

pan bread

panecillo roll

papa potato

papas a la huancaína with cheese and green peppers

(a la) parrilla grilled

parrillada mixta mixed grill

pasado done, cooked

bien ~ well-done

poco ~ underdone (US rare)

pastas noodles, macaroni, spaghetti

pastel cake, pie

~ **de choclo** maize with minced beef, chicken, raisins and olives

pastelillo small tart

pata trotter (US foot)

patatas potatoes
~ **fritas** fried; usually chips (US french fries)
~ **(a la) leonesa** with onions
~ **nuevas** new
pato duck, duckling
pavo turkey
pechuga breast (of fowl)
pepinillo gherkin (US pickle)
pepino cucumber
(en) pepitoria stewed with onions, green peppers and tomatoes
pera pear
perca perch
percebe barnacle (shellfish)
perdiz partridge
~ **en escabeche** cooked in oil with vinegar, onions, parsley, carrots and green pepper; served cold
~ **estofada** stewed and served with a white-wine sauce
perejil parsley
perifollo chervil
perilla a firm, bland cheese
pescadilla whiting
pescado fish
pez espada swordfish
picadillo minced meat, hash
picado minced
picante sharp, spicy, highly seasoned
picatoste deep-fried slice of bread
pichoncillo young pigeon (US squab)
pierna leg
pimentón chili pepper
pimienta pepper
pimiento sweet pepper
~ **morrón** red (sweet) pepper
pincho moruno grilled meat (often kidneys) on a skewer, sometimes served with spicy sauces
pintada guinea fowl

piña pineapple
pisto diced and sautéed vegetables: mainly aubergines, green peppers and tomatoes; served cold
(a la) plancha grilled on a girdle
plátano banana
plato plate, dish, portion
~ **típico de la región** regional speciality
pollito spring chicken
pollo chicken
~ **pibil** simmered in fruit juice and spices
polvorón hazelnut biscuit (US cookie)
pomelo grapefruit
porción portion
porotos granados shelled beans served with pumpkin and maize (US corn)
postre dessert, sweet
potaje vegetable soup
puchero stew
puerro leek
pulpo octopus
punta de espárrago asparagus tip
punto de nieve dessert of whipped cream with beaten egg-whites
puré de patatas mashed potatoes
queso cheese
quisquilla shrimp
rábano radish
~ **picante** horse-radish
raja slice or portion
rallado grated
rape angler fish
ravioles ravioli
raya skate, ray
rebanada slice
rebozado breaded or fried in batter
recargo extra charge
rehogada sautéed

relleno stuffed
remolacha beetroot
repollo cabbage
requesón a fresh-curd cheese
riñón kidney
róbalo haddock
rodaballo turbot, flounder
(a la) romana dipped in batter and fried
romero rosemary
roncal cheese made from sheep's milk; close grained and hard in texture with a few small holes; piquant flavour
ropa vieja cooked, left-over meat and vegetables, covered with tomatoes and green peppers
rosbif roast beef
rosquilla doughnut
rubio red mullet
ruibarbo rhubarb
sal salt
salado salted, salty
salchicha small pork sausage for frying
salchichón salami
salmón salmon
salmonete red mullet
salsa sauce
  ~ **blanca** white
  ~ **española** brown sauce with herbs, spices and wine
  ~ **mayordoma** butter and parsley
  ~ **picante** hot pepper
  ~ **romana** bacon or ham, egg, cream (sometimes flavoured with nutmeg)
  ~ **tártara** tartar
  ~ **verde** parsley
salsifi salsify
salteado sauté(ed)
salvia sage
san simón a firm, bland cheese

resembling *perilla*; shiny yellow rind
sandía watermelon
sardina sardine, pilchard
sémola semolina
sencillo plain
sepia cuttlefish
servicio service
  ~ **(no) incluido** (not) included
sesos brains
seta mushroom
sobrasada salami
solomillo fillet steak (US tenderloin)
sopa soup
  ~ **(de) cola de buey** oxtail
  ~ **sevillana** a highly spiced fish soup
suave soft
suflé soufflé
suizo bun
surtido assorted
taco wheat or maizeflour (US cornmeal) pancake usually with a meat filling and garnished with a spicy sauce
tajada slice
tallarín noodle
tamal a pastry dough of coarsely ground maizeflour with meat or fruit filling, steamed in maizehusks (US corn husks)
tapa appetizer, snack
tarta cake, tart
  ~ **helada** ice-cream tart
ternera veal
tocino bacon
  ~ **de cielo** 1) caramel mould 2) custard-filled cake
tomate tomato
tomillo thyme
tordo thrush
toronja variety of grapefruit
tortilla 1) omelet   2) a type of

pancake made with maizeflour (US cornmeal)

~ **de chorizo** with pieces of a spicy sausage

~ **a la española** with onions, potatoes and seasoning

~ **a la francesa** plain

~ **gallega** potatoes with ham, red sweet peppers and peas

~ **a la jardinera** with mixed, diced vegetables

~ **al ron** rum

tortita waffle

tortuga turtle

tostada toast

tripas tripe

trucha trout

~ **frita a la asturiana** floured and fried in butter, garnished with lemon

trufa truffle

turrón nougat

ulloa a soft cheese from Galicia, rather like a mature camembert

uva grape

~ **pasa** raisin

vaca salada corned beef

vainilla vanilla

(a la) valenciana with rice, toma-

toes and garlic

variado varied, assorted

varios sundries

venado venison

venera scallop, coquille St. Jacques

verdura greens

vieira scallop

villalón a cheese from sheep's milk

vinagre vinegar

vinagreta a piquant vinegar dressing (vinaigrette) to accompany salads

(a la) ~ marinated in oil and vinegar or lemon juice with mixed herbs

(a la) vizcaína with green peppers, tomatoes, garlic and paprika

yema egg-yolk

yemas a dessert of whipped egg-yolks and sugar

zanahoria carrot

zarzamora blackberry

zarzuela savoury stew of assorted fish and shellfish

~ **de mariscos** seafood stew

~ **de pescado** selection of fish served with a highly seasoned sauce

~ **de verduras** vegetable stew

SPANISH

Drink

abocado sherry made from a blend of sweet and dry wines

agua water

aguardiente spirits

Alicante this region to the south

of Valencia produces a large quantity of red table wine and some good rosé, particularly from Yecla

Amontillado medium-dry sherry,

light amber in colour, with a nutty flavour

Andalucía a drink of dry sherry and orange juice

Angélica a Basque herb liqueur similar to yellow Chartreuse

anís aniseed liqueur

Anís del Mono a Calatonian aniseed liqueur

anís seco aniseed brandy

anisado an aniseed-based soft drink which may be slightly alcoholic

batido milk shake

bebida drink

Bobadilla Gran Reserva a wine-distilled brandy

botella bottle

  media ~ half bottle

café coffee

  ~ cortado small cup of strong coffee with a dash of milk or cream

  ~ descafeinado coffeine-free

  ~ exprés espresso

  ~ granizado iced (white)

  ~ con leche white

  ~ negro/solo black

Calisay a quinine-flavoured liqueur

Carlos I a wine-distilled brandy

Cataluña Catalonia; this region southwest of Barcelona is known for its *xampañ*, bearing little resemblance to the famed French sparkling wine

Cazalla an aniseed liqueur

cerveza beer

  ~ de barril draught (US draft)

  ~ dorada light

  ~ negra dark

cola de mono a blend of coffee, milk, rum and *pisco*

coñac 1) French Cognac 2) term

applied to any Spanish wine-distilled brandy

Cordoníu a brand-name of Catalonian sparkling wine locally referred to as *xampañ* (champagne)

cosecha harvest; indicates the vintage of wine

crema de cacao cocoa liqueur, crème de cacao

Cuarenta y Tres an egg liqueur

Cuba libre rum and Coke

champán, champaña 1) French Champagne 2) term applied to any Spanish sparkling wine

chicha de manzana apple brandy

Chinchón an aniseed liqueur

chocolate chocolate drink

  ~ con leche hot chocolate with milk

Dulce dessert wine

Fino dry sherry wine, very pale and straw-coloured

Fundador a wine-distilled brandy

Galicia this Atlantic coastal region has good table wines

gaseosa fizzy (US carbonated) water

ginebra gin

gran vino term found on Chilean wine labels to indicate a wine of exceptional quality

granadina pomegranate syrup mixed with wine or brandy

horchata de almendra (or **de chufa**) drink made from ground almonds (or Jerusalem artichoke)

Jerez 1) sherry 2) the Spanish region near the Portuguese border, internationally renowned for its *Jerez*

jugo fruit juice

leche milk

limonada lemonade, lemon

squash

Málaga 1) dessert wine 2) the region in the south of Spain, is particularly noted for its dessert wine

Manzanilla dry sherry, very pale and straw-coloured

margarita *tequila* with lime juice

Montilla a dessert wine from near Cordoba, often drunk as an aperitif

Moscatel fruity dessert wine

naranjada orangeade

Oloroso sweet, dark sherry, drunk as dessert wine, resembles brown cream sherry

Oporto port (wine)

pisco grape brandy

ponche crema egg-nog liquor

Priorato the region south of Barcelona produces good quality red and white wine but also a dessert wine, usually called *Priorato* but renamed *Tarragona* when it is exported

refresco a soft drink

reservado term found on Chilean wine labels to indicate a wine of exceptional quality

Rioja the northern region near the French border is considered to produce Spain's best wines—especially red; some of the finest Rioja wines resemble good Bordeaux wines

ron rum

sangría a mixture of red wine, ice, orange, lemon, brandy and sugar

sangrita *tequila* with tomato, orange and lime juices

sidra cider

sol y sombra a blend of wine-distilled brandy and aniseed liqueur

sorbete (iced) fruit drink

té tea

tequila brandy made from agave (US aloe)

tinto 1) red wine 2) black coffee with sugar (Colombia)

Tío Pepe a brand-name sherry

Triple Seco an orange liqueur

Valdepeñas the region south of Madrid is an important wine-producing area

vermú vermouth

Veterano Osborne a wine-distilled brandy

vino wine

~ **blanco** white

~ **clarete** rosé

~ **común** table wine

~ **dulce** dessert

~ **espumoso** sparkling

~ **de mesa** table wine

~ **del país** local wine

~ **rosado** rosé

~ **seco** dry

~ **suave** sweet

~ **tinto** red

xampañ Catalonian sparkling wine

Yerba mate South American holly tea

zumo juice

Swedish

Guide to pronunciation

Letter	Approximate pronunciation
Consonants	

b, c, d, f, h, l, m, n, p, v, w, x	as in English
ch	at the beginning of words borrowed from French, like **sh** in **sh**ut
g	1) before stressed **i, e, y, ä, ö** and sometimes after **l** or **r**, like **y** in **y**et 2) before **e** and **i** in many words of French origin, like **sh** in **sh**ut 3) elsewhere, generally like **g** in **g**o
j, dj, gj, lj	like **y** in **y**et
k	1) before stressed **i, e, y, ä, ö**, generally like **ch** in Scottish lo**ch**, but pronounced in the front of the mouth 2) elsewhere, like **k** in **k**it
kj	like **ch** in Scottish lo**ch**, but pronounced in the front of the mouth

qu	like **k** in **k**it followed by **v** in **v**at
r	slightly rolled near the front of the mouth
s	1) in the ending **-sion** like **sh** in **sh**ut 2) elsewhere, like **s** in **s**o 3) the groups **sch, skj, stj** are pronounced like **sh** in **sh**ut
sk	1) before stressed **e, i, y, ä, ö**, like **sh** in **sh**ut 2) elsewhere, like **sk** in **sk**ip
t	1) **ti** in the ending **-tion** is pronounced like **sh** in **sh**ut or like **ch** in **ch**at 2) elsewhere, like **t** in **t**op
tj	like **ch** in Scottish lo**ch**; but pronounced in the front of the mouth; sometimes with a **t** sound at the beginning
z	like **s** in **s**o

Notice that in the groups **rd, rl, rn, rs** and **rt**, the letter **r** is generally not pronounced but influences the pronunciation of the **d, l, n, s** or **t** which is then pronounced with the end of the tongue, *not* on the upper front teeth, but behind the gums of the upper teeth.

Vowels

A vowel is generally long in stressed syllables when it's the final letter or followed by only one consonant. If followed by two or more consonants or in unstressed syllables, the vowel is generally short.

a	1) when long, like **a** in c**a**r 2) when short, something like the **u** in c**u**t
e	1) when long, like **ay** in s**ay**, but a *pure* vowel, not a diphthong 2) in the stressed prefix **er-**, like **a** in m**a**n, but longer 3) when short, like **e** in g**e**t 4) when unstressed, like **a** in **a**bout
ej	like **a** in m**a**te
i	1) when long, like **ee** in b**ee** 2) when short, between **ee** in m**ee**t and **i** in h**i**t
o	1) when long, often like **oo** in s**oo**n, but with the lips more tightly rounded and with a puff of breath at the end 2) the same sound can be short 3) when long, it's also sometimes pronounced like **oa** in m**oa**n 4) when short, sometimes like **o** in h**o**t
u	1) when long, like Swedish **y**, but with the tongue a little lower in the mouth and with a puff of breath at the end

	2) when short, a little more like the **u** of p**u**t; a very difficult sound
y	pronounce the **ee** of b**ee** and then round your lips without moving your tongue; the sound can be long or short
å	1) when long, like **aw** in r**aw,** but with the tongue a little higher in the mouth 2) when short, like **o** in h**o**t
ä	1) when followed by **r**, like **a** in m**a**n; either long or short 2) elsewhere, like **e** in g**e**t; either long or short
ö	like **u** in f**u**r; either long or short; when followed by **r**, it's pronounced with the mouth a little more open

Note

The principal stress is generally on the *first* syllable of a word unless it comes from Latin or French.

Some useful expressions

Hungry

I'm hungry/I'm thirsty.	**Jag är hungrig/Jag är törstig.**
Can you recommend a good restaurant?	**Kan Ni rekommendera en bra restaurang?**
Are there any good, cheap restaurants around here?	**Finns det några bra och billiga restauranger i närheten?**
I'd like to reserve a table for ... people.	**Jag skulle vilja beställa ett bord för ...**
We'll come at ... o'clock.	**Vi kommer kl. ...**

Asking

Good evening. I'd like a table for ... people.	**God afton, jag skulle vilja ha ett bord för ...**
Could we have a table...?	**Kan vi få ett...?**
in the corner	**hörnbord**
by the window	**fönsterbord**
outside	**bord utomhus**
on the terrace	**bord på terrassen**

May I please have the menu?	**Kan jag få se på matsedeln?**
What's this?	**Vad är detta?**
Do you have…?	**Har Ni…?**
a set menu	**en "dagens meny"**
local dishes	**specialiteter från trakten**
a children's menu	**en barnmatsedel**
Waiter/Waitress!	**Hovmästaren/Fröken!**
What do you recommend?	**Vad föreslår Ni?**
Could I have (a/an)… please?	**Kan jag få…**
ashtray	**en askkopp**
another chair	**en stol till**
finger bowl	**en sköljkopp**
fork	**en gaffel**
glass	**ett glas**
knife	**en kniv**
napkin	**en servett**
plate	**en tallrik**
pepper mill	**en pepparkvarn**
serviette	**en servett**
spoon	**en sked**
toothpick	**en tandpetare**

Ordering

I'd like a/an/some…	**Jag skulle vilja ha…**
aperitif	**en aperitif**
appetizer	**en förrätt**
beer	**en öl**
bread	**bröd**
butter	**smör**
cheese	**ost**
chips	**pommes frites**
coffee	**kaffe**
dessert	**en efterrätt**
fish	**fisk**
french fries	**pommes frites**
fruit	**frukt**
game	**vilt**
ice-cream	**glass**

lemon	**citron**
lettuce	**grönsallad**
meat	**kött**
mineral water	**mineralvatten**
milk	**mjölk**
mustard	**senap**
noodles	**nudlar**
oil	**olja**
olive oil	**olivolja**
pepper	**peppar**
potatoes	**potatis**
poultry	**fågel**
rice	**ris**
rolls	**kuvertbröd**
saccharin	**sackarin**
salad	**en sallad**
salt	**salt**
sandwich	**en smörgås**
seafood	**skaldjur**
seasoning	**kryddor**
soup	**en soppa**
starter	**en förrätt**
sugar	**socker**
tea	**te**
vegetables	**grönsaker**
vinegar	**vinäger**
(iced) water	**(is)vatten**
wine	**vin**

SMAKLIG MÅLTID!
ENJOY YOUR MEAL!

---

baked	**ugnsbakad**
baked in parchment	**ugnsbakad i smörgåspapper**
boiled	**kokt**
braised	**bräserad**
cured	**saltad**
fried	**stekt**
grilled	**grillad**
marinated	**marinerad**

poached	pocherad
poached (of eggs)	förlorat
roasted	ugnstekt
sautéed	brynt
smoked	rökt
steamed	ångkokt
stewed	kokt på svag värme
underdone (rare)	blodig
medium	lagom
well-done	välstekt

SKÅL!
CHEERS!

glass	glas
bottle	flaska
red	rött
white	vitt
rosé	rosé
very dry	mycket torrt
dry	torrt
sweet	sött
light	lätt
full-bodied	fylligt
sparkling	mousserande
neat (straight)	ren
on the rocks	med isbitar

The bill

I'd like to pay.	Kan jag få notan, tack?
We'd like to pay separately.	Vi vill betala var och en för sig.
You've made a mistake in this bill, I think.	Jag tror Ni har gjort ett litet fel på notan.
What's this amount for?	Vad står den här summan för?
Is service included?	Är dricksen inräknad?
Is everything included?	Är allt inräknat?

Do you accept traveller's cheques?	**Tar Ni emot resecheker?**
Thank you. This is for you.	**Tack så mycket, det här är för Er.**
Keep the change.	**Behåll växeln.**
That was a very good meal.	**Det var mycket gott.**
We enjoyed it, thank you.	**Vi tyckte mycket om det.**

Complaints

That's not what I ordered.	**Jag har inte beställt det här.**
I asked for...	**Jag bad om...**
May I change this?	**Kan jag få byta ut det här?**
The meat is...	**Köttet är...**
overdone	**för hårt stekt**
underdone	**inte tillräckligt stekt**
too rare	**för rått**
too tough	**för segt**
This is too...	**Det här är alltför...**
bitter/salty/sweet	**beskt/salt/sött**
The food is cold	**Maten är kall.**
This isn't fresh.	**Det här är inte färskt.**
What's taking you so long?	**Varför tar det så lång tid?**
Where are our drinks?	**Vad händer med vår beställning?**
This isn't clean.	**Det här är inte rent.**
Would you ask the head waiter to come over?	**Kan Ni be hovmästaren komma hit?**

Numbers

1	en, ett		11	elva
2	två		12	tolv
3	tre		13	tretton
4	fyra		14	fjorton
5	fem		15	femton
6	sex		16	sexton
7	sju		17	sjutton
8	åtta		18	arton
9	nio		19	nitton
10	tio		20	tjugo

SWEDISH

Food

Please note that Swedish alphabetical order is **a-z, å, ä, ö.**

abborre perch
aladåb aspic
ananas pineapple
and wild duck
anka duck
ansjovis marinated sprats
apelsin orange
aprikos apricot
aromsmör herb butter
bakad baked
bakelse pastry, fancy cake
banan banana
barnmatsedel children's menu
betjäningsavgift service charge
biff beef steak
   ~ à la Lindström minced beef mixed with pickled beetroot, capers and onions. shaped into patties and fried
   ~ Rydberg fried diced beef and potatoes, served with a light mustard sauce
bit piece
björnbär blackberry
bladspenat spinach
blandad mixed, assorted
blini buckwheat pancake
blodpudding black pudding (US blood sausage)
blomkål cauliflower

blåbär bilberry (US blueberry)
bondbönor broad beans
bruna bönor baked brown beans flavoured with vinegar and syrup
brylépudding caramel blanc-mange (US caramel custard)
brynt browned
brysselkål brussels sprout
bräckkorv smoked pork sausage
bräckt sautéed, fried
bräserad braised
bröd bread
   ~ och smör bread and butter
bröst breast (of fowl)
buljong consommé
bär berry
böckling smoked herring
böna bean
camembert soft, runny cheese with pungent flavour
champinjon button mushroom
choklad chocolate
citron lemon
dagens rätt dish of the day
dietmat diet food
dill dill
   ~ kött stewed lamb or veal served with a sour-sweet dill sauce

dricks tip
duva pigeon (US squab)
efterrätt dessert
enbär juniper berry
endiv chicory (US endive)
enrisrökt smoked over juniper embers
entrecote sirloin steak, rib-eye steak
falukorv lightly smoked pork sausage
fasan pheasant
fastlagsbulle bun filled with almond paste and cream, eaten during Lent
fattiga riddare French toast; bread dipped in batter and fried, served with sugar and jam
femöring med ägg small steak topped with fried egg and served with onions
filbunke junket
filé fillet (US tenderloin)
~ **Oscar** fillets of veal served with bearnaise sauce (vinegar, egg-yolks, butter, shallots and tarragon), asparagus tips and lobster
filmjölk sour milk, type of thin junket
fisk fish
~ **bullar** codfish-balls
~ **färs** loaf, mousse
~ **gratäng** baked casserole
~ **pinnar** sticks
flamberad flamed (with liquor)
flundra flounder
fläsk pork
~ **med löksås** slices of thick bacon served with onion sauce
~ **filé** fillet (US tenderloin)
~ **karré** loin
~ **korv** boiled sausage
~ **kotlett** chop
~ **lägg** boiled, pickled knuckle
~ **pannkaka** pancake with diced bacon
~ **stek** roast
forell trout
franskbröd white bread
frasvåffla warm (crisp) waffle
frikadell boiled veal meat ball
friterad deep-fried
~ **camembert** deep-fried pieces of *camembert* served with Arctic cloudberry jam
fromage mousse, blancmange
frukost breakfast
~ **flingor** dry breakfast cereal, cornflakes
frukt fruit
frusen grädde frozen whipped cream
fylld stuffed, filled
fyllning stuffing, forcemeat
fågel fowl, game bird
får mutton
~ **i kål** Irish stew; mutton (more usually lamb) and cabbage stew
fänkål fennel
färsk fresh, new
färska räkor unshelled fresh shrimps
färskrökt lax slightly smoked salmon
förrätt starter, first course
gelé jelly, aspic
getost a soft, rather sweet whey cheese made from goat's milk
glace au four sponge cake filled with ice-cream, covered with meringue, quickly browned in oven and served flaming (US baked Alaska)
glass ice-cream
~ **tårta** ice-cream cake

grapefrukt grapefruit
gratinerad oven-browned
gratäng (au) gratin
gravad lax (gravlax) fresh salmon cured with sugar, sea salt, pepper and dill; served with mustard sauce
gravad strömming marinated Baltic herring
grillad grilled, broiled
grillkorv grilled sausage
gris pork
~ **fötter** pigs' trotters (US pigs' feet)
~ **hals** scrag
grodlår frogs' legs
grytstek pot roast
grädde cream
gräddfil sour cream
gräddmjölk light cream (half and half)
gräddtårta sponge layer cake with cream and jam filling
gräslök chive
grönkål kale
grönpeppar green peppercorn
grönsak vegetable
grönsakssoppa vegetable soup
grönsallad lettuce
gröt porridge
gurka cucumber, gherkin
gås goose
~ **lever** 1) goose liver 2) goose-liver pâté
gädda pike
gäddfärsbullar pike dumplings
gös pike-perch (US walleyed pike)
hackad minced, chopped
~ **biff med lök** hamburger steak with fried onions
hallon raspberry
halstrad grilled over open fire

haricots verts French beans (US green beans)
harstek roast hare
hasselbackspotatis sliced potatoes covered with melted butter, then roasted
hasselnöt hazelnut
havregryn oats
havregrynsgröt oatmeal (porridge)
havskräfta seawater crayfish, Dublin Bay prawn
helgeflundra halibut
helstekt roasted whole
hemlagad home-made
herrgårdsost hard cheese with a mild to slightly strong flavour
hjortron Arctic cloudberry
honung honey
hovdessert meringue with whipped cream and chocolate sauce
hummer lobster
husmanskost home cooking, plain food
hälleflundra halibut
hälsokost organic health food
hökarpanna kidney stew with bacon, potatoes and onions, braised in beer
höna boiling fowl
höns med ris och curry boiled chicken, curry sauce and rice
ingefära ginger
inkokt boiled and served cold
inlagd marinated in vinegar, sugar and spices
is ice
~ **glass** water ice (US sherbet)
~ **kyld** iced
islandssill Iceland herring
isterband coarse, very tasty pork sausage
Janssons frestelse layers of sliced

potatoes, onions and marinated
sprats, baked with cream
jordgubbe strawberry
jordgubbstårta sponge cake with
whipped cream and strawberries
jordnöt peanut
jordärtskocka Jerusalem artichoke
jordärtskockspuré purée of Jerusalem artichoke
julbord buffet of Christmas
specialities
julskinka baked ham
jultallrik plate of specialities
taken from the *julbord*
jägarschnitzel veal cutlet with
mushrooms
järpe hazelhen
kaka cake, biscuit (US cookie)
kalkon turkey
kall cold
kallskuret cold meat (US cold
cuts)
kalops beef stew flavoured with
bay leaves
kalorifattig low calorie
kalv veal, calf
  ~ **bräss** sweetbread
  ~ **filé** fillet (US tenderloin)
  ~ **frikassé** stew
  ~ **järpe** meatball made of
minced veal
  ~ **kotlett** chop
  ~ **lever** liver
  ~ **njure** kidney
  ~ **schnitzel** cutlet
  ~ **stek** roast
  ~ **sylta** potted veal
  ~ **tunga** tongue
kanel cinnamon
  ~ **bulle** cinnamon roll
kanin rabbit
kantarell chanterelle mushroom
kapris caper

karljohanssvamp boletus mushroom
kassler lightly smoked loin of
pork
kastanj chestnut
kastanjepuré chestnut purée
katrinplommon prune
kaviar caviar
  röd ~ cod's roe (red, salted)
  svart ~ black caviar, roe from
lumpfish
keso a type of cottage cheese
kex biscuit (US cookie)
knyte filled puff pastry (US turnover)
knäckebröd crisp bread (US hardtack)
kokad boiled, cooked
kokos grated coconut
  ~ **kaka** coconut macaroon
kokt boiled, cooked
kolasås caramel sauce
kolja haddock
kompott stewed fruit
korv sausage
krabba crab
krasse cress
kronärtskocka artichoke
kronärtskocksbotten artichoke
bottom
kroppkakor potato dumplings
stuffed with minced bacon and
onions, served with melted butter
krusbär gooseberry
krusbärspaj gooseberry tart/pie
krydda spice
kryddnejlika clove
kryddost hard semi-fat cheese
with cumin seeds
kryddpeppar allspice
kryddsmör herb butter
kräftor freshwater crayfish boiled
with salt and dill, served cold

(Swedish speciality available only during August and September)

kräm 1) cream, custard 2) stewed fruit or syrup thickened with potato flour

kummin cumin

kuvertavgift cover charge

kuvertbröd French roll

kyckling chicken
~**bröst** breast
~**lever** liver
~**lår** leg

kål cabbage
~**dolmar** cabbage leaves stuffed with minced meat and rice
~**pudding** layers of cabbage leaves and minced meat
~**rot** turnip

käx biscuit (US cookie)

körsbär cherry

körvel chervil

kött meat
~**bullar** meat balls

köttfärs minced meat
~**limpa** meat loaf
~**sås** meat sauce for spaghetti

lagerblad bay leaf

lake burbot (freshwater fish)

lamm lamb
~**bog** shoulder
~**bringa** brisket
~**kotlett** chop
~**sadel** saddle
~**stek** roast

landgång a long, open sandwich with different garnishes

lapskojs lobscouse; casserole of potatoes, meat and vegetables

lax salmon
~**pudding** layers of flaked salmon, potatoes, onions and eggs, baked

laxöring salmon trout

legymsallad blanched vegetables, served in a mayonnaise sauce

lever liver
~**korv** sausage
~**pastej** paste

limpa rye bread; loaf

lingon lingonberry, small cranberry
~**sylt** lingonberry jam

lutfisk specially treated, poached stockfish, served with white sauce (Christmas speciality)

låda casserole

lättstekt underdone (US rare)

löjrom vendace roe often served on toast with onions and sour cream

lök onion

lövbiff thinly sliced beef

majonnäs mayonnaise

majs maize (US corn)
~**kolv** corn on the cob

makaroner macaroni

makrill mackerel

mandel almond
~**biskvi** almond biscuit (US cookie)

marinerad marinated

marmelad marmalade

marsipan marzipan, almond paste

maräng meringue

marängsviss meringue with whipped cream and chocolate sauce

matjessill marinated herring fillets, served with sour cream and chives

matsedel bill of fare

mejram marjoram

meny menu, bill of fare

mesost whey cheese

messmör soft whey cheese

middag dinner

mixed grill pieces of meat, onions, tomatoes and green peppers grilled on a skewer

mjukost soft white cheese

morkulla woodcock

morot (pl morötter) carrot

mullbär mulberry

munk doughnut

murkelstuvning creamed morel mushrooms

murkelsås morel mushroom sauce

murkla morel mushroom

muskot nutmeg

mussla mussel, clam

märg marrow
~ **ben** marrow bone

njure kidney

nota bill (US check)

nypon rose-hip
~ **soppa** rose-hip soup (dessert)

nässelsoppa nettle soup

oliv olive

olja oil

orre black grouse

ost cheese
~ **bricka** cheese board
~ **gratinerad** oven-browned, with cheese topping
~ **kaka** kind of curd cake served with jam
~ **stänger** cheese straws

ostron oyster

oxbringa brisket of beef

oxfilé fillet of beef (US tenderloin)

oxjärpe meatball of minced beef

oxkött beef

oxrulad beef olive; slice of beef rolled and braised in gravy

oxstek roast beef

oxsvanssoppa oxtail soup

oxtunga beef tongue

paj pie, tart

palsternacka parsnip

panerad breaded

pannbiff hamburger steak with fried onions

pannkaka pancake

paprika (grön) (green) pepper

parisare minced beef with capers, beetroot and onions served on toast, topped with a fried egg

pastej pie, patty, pâté

peppar pepper
~ **kaka** ginger biscuit (US ginger snap)
~ **rot** horseradish
~ **rotskött** boiled beef with horseradish sauce

persika peach

persilja parsley

persiljesmör parsley butter

piggvar turbot

pilgrimsmussla scallop, coquille St. Jacques

pirog Russian pasty; stuffed pasty (caviar, cheese, fish or vegetables)

plankstek a thin steak served on a wooden platter (US plank steak)

plommon plum
~ **späckad fläskkarré** roast loin of pork flavoured with prunes

plättar small, thin pancakes

pommes frites chips (US French fries)

potatis potato
färsk ~ new potatoes
~ **mos** mashed potatoes

pressgurka marinated sliced, fresh cucumber

pressylta brawn (US head cheese)

prinsesstårta sponge cake with vanilla custard and whipped cream, covered with green almond paste

prinskorv cocktail sausage, small frankfurter

pudding mould, baked casserole

purjolök leek

pyttipanna kind of bubble and squeak; fried pieces of meat, sausage, onions and potatoes, served with an egg-yolk or a fried egg and pickled beetroot

päron pear

pölsa hash made of boiled pork and barley

rabarber rhubarb

raggmunk med fläsk potato pancake with bacon

rapphöna partridge

ren reindeer
~ **sadel** saddle
~ **skav** in thin slices
~ **stek** roast

revbensspjäll spare-rib

rimmad, rimsaltad slightly salted

ris rice

risgrynsgröt rice pudding served with milk and cinnamon

riven, rivna grated

rom roe

rosmarin rosemary

rostat bröd toast

rostbiff roast beef

rotmos mashed turnips

russin raisin

rysk kaviar caviar

rå raw
~ **biff** steak tartare: finely chopped raw beef with egg-yolks, capers, onions, pickled beetroot and seasoning

rådjur venison

rådjurssadel saddle of venison

rådjursstek roast venison

råkost uncooked shredded vegetables

rån small wafer

rårörda lingon lingonberry (small cranberry) jam preserved with-out cooking

rädisa radish

räka shrimp

räkcocktail shrimp cocktail

rättika black radish

rödbeta beetroot

rödbetssallad beetroot salad

röding char (fish)

rödkål red cabbage

rödspätta plaice

rökt smoked

rönnbär rowanberry (mountain ashberry)

rönnbärsgelé rowanberry jelly

rött (pl **röda**) **vinbär** redcurrant

saffran saffron

saffransbröd sweet saffron loaf or rolls

sallad salad

salta biten salted boiled beef

saltad salted

saltgurka salt-pickled gherkin

sardell anchovy
~ **smör** anchovy butter

sardin sardine

schalottenlök shallot

schweizerost Swiss cheese

schweizerschnitzel cordon bleu; veal scallop stuffed with ham and cheese

selleri celery
~ **rot** celery root

senap mustard

serveringsavgift service charge

sik whitefish
~ **löja** vendace (small whitefish)
~ **rom** whitefish roe

sill herring
~ **bricka** board of assorted herring
~ **bullar** herring dumplings
~ **gratäng** baked casserole of herring, onions and potatoes

~**sallad** herring salad with pickled beetroot and gherkins, apples, boiled potatoes, onions and whipped cream

~ **tallrik** portion of assorted herring

sirap treacle, molasses

sjömansbiff beef casserole with carrots, onions and potatoes, braised in beer

sjötunga sole

sjötungsfilé fillet of sole

skaldjur shellfish

skarpsås mayonnaise enriched with mustard and herbs

skinka ham

skinklåda ham-and-egg casserole

skinkomelett ham omelet

skiva slice

sky dripping, gravy

sköldpaddssoppa turtle soup

slottsstek pot roast flavoured with brandy, molasses and marinated sprats

slätvar brill

smultron wild strawberry

småfranska French roll

småkaka fancy biscuit (US fancy cookie)

småvarmt small hot dishes (on *smörgåsbord*)

smör butter

smörgås open sandwich

~ **bord** a buffet offering a wide variety of appetizers, hot and cold meats, smoked and pickled fish, cheese, salads, relishes, vegetables and desserts

sniglar snails

snöripa ptarmigan

socker sugar

~ **kaka** sponge cake

~ **ärter** sugar peas

solöga marinated sprats, onions,

capers, pickled beetroot and raw egg-yolk

soppa soup

sotare grilled Baltic herring

sparris asparagus

~ **knopp** asparagus tip

spenat spinach

spettekaka tall, cone-shaped cake made on a spit

spicken sill salted herring

spritärter green peas

spädgris suck(l)ing pig

stekt fried, roasted

~ **(salt) sill** fried (salt) herring

stenbitssoppa lumpfish soup

strömming fresh Baltic herring

strömmingsflundra fried double fillets of Baltic herring stuffed with dill or parsley

strömmingslåda baked casserole of Baltic herring and potatoes

stuvad cooked in white sauce, creamed

~ **spenat** creamed spinach

sufflé soufflé

supé (late) supper

sur sour

~ **kål** sauerkraut

~ **stek** marinated roast beef

~ **strömming** specially processed, cured and fermented Baltic herring

svamp mushroom

~ **stuvning** creamed mushrooms

~ **sås** mushroom sauce

svart (pl **svarta**) **vinbär** blackcurrant

svartsoppa soup made of goose blood

svartvinbärsgelé blackcurrant jelly

sveciaost hard cheese with pungent flavour

SWEDISH

sylt jam
syltad 1) preserved (fruit)
2) pickled (vegetables)
syltlök pickled pearl onion
sås sauce, dressing, gravy
söt sweet
T-benstek T-bone steak
timjan thyme
tjäder wood-grouse, capercaillie
tomat tomato
tonfisk tunny (US tuna)
torkad frukt dried fruit
torr dry
torsk cod
~ rom cod's roe
tranbär cranberry
tryffel truffle
tunga tongue
tunnbröd unleavened barley
bread
tårta cake
ugnsbakad baked
ugnspannkaka kind of batter
pudding
ugnstekt roasted
vaktel quail
valnöt walnut
vanilj vanilla
~ glass vanilla ice-cream
~ sås vanilla custard sauce
varm warm
~ rätt hot dish, main dish
vattenmelon watermelon
vaxbönor butter beans (US wax
beans)
vilt game
vinbär currant (black, red or
white)
vindruva grape
vinlista wine list
vintersallad salad of grated carrots,
apples and cabbage
vinäger vinegar
vinägrettsås vinegar-and-oil

dressing
vispgrädde whipped cream
vitkål cabbage
vitling whiting
vitlök garlic
våffla waffle
välling soup made of cereal,
gruel
välstekt well-done
västerbottenost pungent, hard
cheese, strong when mature
västkustsallad seafood salad
Wallenbergare steak made of
minced veal, egg-yolks and
cream
wienerbröd Danish pastry
wienerkorv wiener, frankfurter
wienerschnitzel breaded veal
cutlet
ål eel
inkokt ~ jellied
ägg egg
förlorat ~ poached
hårdkokt ~ hard-boiled
kokt ~ boiled
löskokt ~ soft-boiled
stekt ~ fried
~ röra scrambled
~ stanning baked egg custard
äggplanta aubergine (US eggplant)
älg elk
~ filé fillet (US tenderloin)
~ stek roast
äppelkaka apple charlotte, apple
pudding
äppelmos apple sauce
äpple apple
ärter peas
~ och fläsk yellow pea soup
with diced pork
ättika white vinegar
ättiksgurka pickled gherkin
(US pickle)

akvavit aquavit, spirits distilled from potatoes or grain, often flavoured with aromatic seeds and spices

alkoholfri(tt) non-alcoholic

apelsinjuice orange juice

apelsinsaft orange squash (US orange drink)

brännvin aquavit
1) **Absolut rent brännvin (Renat)** unflavoured
2) **Bäska droppar** bitter and flavoured with a leaf of worm-wood
3) **Herrgårds Aquavit** flavoured with herbs and slightly sweet
4) **O. P. Anderson Aquavit** flavoured with aniseed, caraway and fennel seeds
5) **Skåne Akvavit** less spicy than *O. P. Anderson*
6) **Svart-Vinbärs-Brännvin** flavoured with blackcurrants

choklad chocolate drink
kall ~ cold
varm ~ hot

exportöl beer with high alcoholic content

fatöl draught (US draft) beer

folköl light beer

fruktjuice fruit juice

glögg similar to mulled wine, served with raisins and almonds

grädde cream

Grönstedts French cognac bottled in Sweden

husets vin open wine

härtappning imported wine bottled in Sweden

julmust a foamy, malted drink served at Christmas

julöl beer specially brewed at Christmas

kaffe coffee
~ **med grädde och socker** with cream and sugar
~ **utan grädde och socker** black
koffeinfri(tt) ~ caffeine-free

Kaptenlöjtnant liqueur and brandy

karaffvin wine served in a carafe

Klosterlikör herb liqueur

konjak brandy, cognac

kärnmjölk buttermilk

likör liqueur

lingondricka cranberry drink

läskedryck soft drink, lemonade
~ **med kolsyra** fizzy (US carbonated)
~ **utan kolsyra** flat (US non-carbonated)

lättmjölk skim milk

lättöl beer with low alcoholic content

mjölk milk
kall ~ cold
varm ~ hot

portvin port (wine)

punsch a yellow liqueur on a base of arrack (spirit distilled from rice and sugar) served hot with pea soup or ice-cold as an after-dinner drink with coffee

rom rum

saft squash (US fruit drink)

slottstappning produced and bottled at the château

snaps glass of aquavit

SWEDISH

sodavatten soda water
spritdrycker spirits
starksprit spirits
starköl beer with high alcoholic
  content
te tea
  ~ **med citron** with lemon
  ~ **med mjölk** with milk
  ~ **med socker** with sugar
vatten water
  is~ iced
  mineral~ mineral
vin wine

mousserande ~ sparkling
röd~ red
stark~ fortified
sött ~ sweet
torrt ~ dry
vitt ~ white
vindrinkar wine cobblers, long
  drinks on a wine base
äppelmust apple juice
öl beer
  ljust ~ light
  mörkt ~ dark
örtte infusion of herbs

American

Food

Some peculiarly American culinary terms explained to the British

à la mode a scoop of vanilla ice-cream on a tart, pie or cake

angel food cake cake made of egg-whites and sugar

apple pan dowdy sliced apples with a crumbly topping of brown sugar and butter, moistened with treacle and syrup; oven-baked

bagel bread ring

baked Alaska Norwegian omelet, omelet surprise

barbecue 1) spicy meat sauce 2) outdoor meal with meat from the grill
~ **sauce** spicy tomato sauce

barbecued grilled on open flame

biscuit similar to scone

Bismarck jam doughnut

black-eyed pea see cowpea

borsch(t) beetroot soup, often served chilled with sour cream

Boston baked beans dish of haricot beans in tomato sauce

Boston cream pie sponge filled with cream and topped with rich chocolate

braunschweiger a kind of liver sausage, pâté

brownie small square cake made with chocolate and nuts

brunch a meal between breakfast

time and midday

Brunswick stew spicy stew, originally of squirrel; now made with poultry, lima beans, sweet corn and okra (Virginia)

bun soft bread roll

(Kentucky) burgoo spicy stew with beef, pork, veal, lamb, poultry and vegetables

butter pecan ice-cream ice-cream with pecan nuts

Caesar salad romaine lettuce, anchovies and croutons with a tangy cheese and garlic dressing

Canadian bacon smoked bacon cut in thick slices

candy sweets or confectionery

check bill

chef's salad cheese, chicken or other cold meats, lettuce and tomatoes

Chesapeake Bay crab soup savoury crab soup

chicken à la King cooked diced chicken, fried mushrooms, shreds of red pimento in a well-seasoned white sauce

chiffon cake sponge cake

chitlins, chitlins, chitterlings pork tripe

chocolate pudding thick, creamy sweet made with milk, chocolate and cornflour

chowder thick, spicy stew or soup of seafood; stock usually made with bacon and vegetables
    Manhattan clam ~ clams in tomato-flavoured stock
    New England clam ~ clams in a soup containing milk

cioppino a kind of fish stew with crab, lobster, fish, clams, vegetables and spices (San Francisco)

cobbler stewed fruit topped with dough or batter and baked until crusty; served warm with ice-cream, cream or a sweet sauce

coffee cake any plain cake which is served with coffee

cookies biscuits

corn sweet corn, maize
    ~ on the cob ears of sweet corn

country captain baked chicken with tomatoes, almonds, raisins and spices (Georgia)

cowpea pealike seeds from a tropical plant grown in southern United States

creole creole style; usually highly seasoned, with tomatoes and green peppers; creole dishes are often served with rice

cupcake small, round, iced cake, often in a paper-case

Danish pastry name given to a whole range of pastries served at breakfast time

donut doughnut

Dutch apple pie apple tart with a crumbly topping of butter and brown sugar

eggplant aubergine

eggs Benedict poached eggs and ham or Canadian bacon on an English muffin topped with hollandaise sauce

English muffin crumpet

flapjacks fluffy pancakes

French dressing tomato-flavoured mayonnaise

french fries chips

frosting icing

fry used as a noun, it often refers to the frying of fish

green goddess dressing mayonnaise of herbs, sour cream, anchovies, vinegar, chives, parsley, tarragon (San Francisco)

griddle cakes fluffy pancakes

grits sweet corn gruel

gumbo soup or stew thickened with okra pods, containing vegetables, meat or seafood

Hangtown fry scrambled eggs with bacon and oysters (San Francisco)

hardtack hard bread made of flour and water

Harvard beets beetroot in a vinegar, sugar and clove sauce

hash 1) chopped or minced meat 2) chopped corned beef mixed with potatoes and fried

hero long bread roll filled with cold cuts, cheese, lettuce, tomato and onions

hoagy see hero

hominy grits sweet corn gruel

huckleberries bilberries, whortleberries

hushpuppy fritter made with sweet-corn flour and onions

Italian dressing salad sauce with oil, vinegar and seasoning

Italian sandwich see hero

jambalaya rice cooked with shrimps, ham, vegetables and spices (New Orleans)

Jell-O a brand of fruit-flavoured gelatin

jelly donut jam doughnut

key lime pie tart of limes and cream (Florida)

ladyfingers sponge fingers

lemon pudding lemon whip

Long Island duck of high quality, very appreciated in the United States

long john long, iced breakfast roll

lox smoked salmon

matzo unleavened bread

minute steak small, thin steak

muffin a quick bread baked in a cup-shaped pan

navy bean white-seeded kidney bean

open-faced sandwich open sandwich

oyster plant salsify

parfait alternate layers of fruit or sauce and ice-cream in a tall dessert glass

patty small, flat cake of minced food

peanut brittle slabs of peanuts in toffee

peanut butter cookie peanut biscuits

pecan pie rich tart with pecan nuts

pickles usually refers only to pickled gherkins

pig in a blanket 1) frankfurter sausage wrapped with dough and baked 2) small sausage wrapped in a pancake; served for breakfast with syrup

pot roast beef stewed with onions, carrots and potatoes

potato chips potato crisps

potato pancakes potato griddle cakes

powdered sugar icing sugar

rice creole rice with green peppers and pimentos

Rock Cornish hen a small crossbred domestic fowl used especially for broiling

Rocky Mountain oysters mutton glands, sliced and fried

round steak silverside, chump

AMERICAN

end of loin

Russian dressing mayonnaise and chili sauce

sherbet sorbet

shoofly pie honey and treacle tart with a crumbly topping of brown sugar, spices, flour and butter

shortcake a rich scone

sloppy Joe stewed minced beef in a spicy tomato-flavoured sauce; served on a bread roll

snickerdoodles cinnamon biscuits

soda ice-cream, syrup and a jigger of soda, served in a tall glass

sour dough dough of fermented flour, water and sugar

Southern fried chicken chicken soaked in milk, then in an egg and milk paste; fried in hot oil until crispy

squash vegetable marrow

strawberry shortcake a rich scone garnished with strawberries in their syrup, topped with ice-cream and/or whipped cream

streusel crumbly cake topping made of butter and brown sugar

submarine sandwich see hero

swiss steak slices of beef braised with onions and tomatoes

taffy toffee

~ **apple** toffee apple

tamale dough made from sweet-corn flour, filled with minced beef and spices; often served in a seasoned tomato sauce

Thousand Island dressing salad sauce of mayonnaise, cream, chili sauce and onions

veal birds veal olives

Virginia ham a lean, hickory-smoked ham with dark red meat

Waldorf salad diced apples, walnuts and celery in a mayonnaise sauce

wholeweat wholemeal

zucchini baby marrows, courgettes

zwieback rusks

Drink

Bacardi cocktail drink with rum, sugar, grenadine and lime juice

bitters 1) herb-based aperitif 2) tonic made from bitter herbs and roots or angostura bark; added to drinks

black cow root beer with vanilla ice-cream

Boston coffee coffee with a

double helping of cream

bourbon whisky disilled mainly from sweet corn

daiquiri rum with sugar and lime juice

double shot a measure for spirits; is equal to a double whisky, gin, etc.

gin fizz gin, lemon juice and soda

water

grasshopper creme de menthe with creme de cacao

highball any spirits diluted with water or with a fizzy drink

Manhattan bourbon, sweet vermouth, glacé cherries and angostura

old-fashioned whisky, angostura, sugar and glacé cherries

pink lady drink made from gin, apple brandy, lemon juice, grenadine and egg whites

root beer a sweetened, sparkling soft drink flavoured with herbs or roots

rye whisky distilled mainly from rye

screwdriver vodka and orange juice

shot a measure for spirits; is equal to a single whisky, gin, etc.

sloe gin fizz liqueur of sloes with lemon juice, sugar and soda

stinger creme de menthe with a base of spirits

Tom Collins gin, lemon juice, sugar, seltzer water and glacé cherries

whiskey sour whisky, lemon juice, sugar and glacé cherries

British

Food

Some peculiarly British culinary terms explained to Americans

Abernethy biscuit caraway-seed cookie

Alma tea cake cookie made on a griddle

angels on horseback skewered oysters wrapped in bacon

apple snow apple purée mixed with beaten egg white; served with/on custard

Arbroath smokies smoked haddock (Scotland)

Bakewell tart an almond cake with a filling of raspberry preserves

Banbury cake a currant tart

bannock a flat, round, unleavened oat biscuit made on a griddle

barmbrack cake containing raisins and other dried fruit

bath bun raisin bun with sugar topping

Bath Oliver a type of cracker

beef olives thin slices of beef wrapped around a well-flavored bread stuffing

biscuits cookies, crackers

bramble jam blackberry preserves

bramble pudding blackberry

compote; sliced apples usually added

brandy snaps brandy-ginger snaps

brochan oatmeal (Scotland)

brown bread may be wholewheat or rye bread

brown pudding a boiled pudding flavored with dried fruit, ground almonds and spices

bubble and squeak a mixture of boiled cabbage and potatoes, fried until crispy

bun always sweet, much like a sweet roll; flavored with dried fruit, coconut and/or raspberry preserves

cabinet pudding a combination of custard, candied fruit, preserves and ladyfingers

Caerphilly a mild, white Welsh cheese

cake cookie, sweet roll

canapé Diane chicken livers wrapped in bacon, broiled and served on toast

canary pudding lemon pudding

castle puddings individual sponge cakes, served with a jam sauce

cheese biscuit cheese cracker

Chelsea bun sweet roll with dried fruit, glazed with honey

Cheshire cheese one of the best-known English cheeses; there are three types: the yellowish-white and reddish varieties are soft-textured and mild, the blue variety has a characteristically tangy flavor

chicory endive

chips french fries

Christmas pudding combination of flour, suet and dried fruit, steamed and served warm with brandy butter or custard

cock-a-leekie soup chicken and leek soup

Colchester oysters considered England's best

corn grain

Cornish pasty a turnover with meat-and-vegetable filling

Cornish split sweet roll, halved and filled with preserves and cream

cottage pie a casserole of chopped meat and onions topped with a layer of mashed potatoes

courgette zucchini

Cox's orange pippin an eating apple

crisps potato chips

crubeens, cruibíns pig's feet (Ireland)

crumpet English muffin

Cumberland rum butter butter blended with brown sugar, nutmeg and rum

Cumberland sauce a sweet sauce of wine and redcurrant jelly, with orange and lemon peel and juice; often served with game

Cumberland sausage a large pork sausage

currant a small seedless raisin

demerara sugar brown sugar

Derby cheese a tangy white cheese

Derby sage Derby cheese flavored with sage

devilled kidneys halved kidneys, seasoned with mustard, pepper and chutney; broiled

devils on horseback prunes wrapped in bacon, fried; served on toast

Devonshire cream a thick, heavy cream

digestive biscuit a type of cookie

double Gloucester a cheese which is similar to Cheddar, though sharper in taste

Dover sole the favorite sole of England

drop scone biscuit made on a griddle

Dublin Bay prawn a variety of large shrimp

Dundee cake cake containing almonds, cherries, dried fruit and lemon peel

Dunlop cheese a cheese similar to Cheddar

Easter biscuit currant cookie, sometimes with spices

eggs mimosa halved, hard-boiled egg whites stuffed with crumbled egg yolk

endive chicory

essence extract

Eve's pudding baked apple slices topped with a sponge batter

Exeter stew a stew of chopped beef, onions, carrots and herbs

faggots fried, spiced balls of chopped meat, usually containing pig's liver

Finnan haddock/haddie smoked haddock (Scotland)

fish and chips fried fish with french fries

fish cake fish croquette

flan pie

flapjack oatmeal pancake

fry generally means fried variety meats of a specified animal (pig's fry)

gammon hind leg of smoked pork

Genoa cake cake with raisins, lemon peel, cherries and almonds

ginger biscuit ginger snap

girdle/griddle scone biscuit made on a griddle

haggis sheep's stomach stuffed with oatmeal, onions and chopped sheep's liver, lights and heart; boiled (Scotland)

ice-cream cornet ice-cream cone

Irish stew a stew of lamb's neck, potatoes, onions and beer

jam doughnut jelly doughnut, Bismarck

jam roll jelly roll

jelly can mean fruit-flavored gelatin

kale/kail brose kale and oatmeal soup

kedgeree hot mixture of flaked smoked haddock, rice and eggs; usually served for breakfast

Lancashire cheese fresh, mild cheese; very tangy if allowed to ripen

Lancashire hot pot a casserole of lamb, sliced kidneys, potatoes and onions combined in layers

Leicester cheese a fairly mild, orange-coloured cheese

lemon curd a lemon spread

maize corn

marrow squash

Melton Mowbray pie well-seasoned chopped pork in a pie shell; eaten cold

muffin a small cake

mulligatawny soup a highly spiced curried soup from India made with carrots, onions, celery and apples; served with rice and strips of cooked chicken

oatcake oat cracker

BRITISH

parkin a cake made of oatmeal, ginger and molasses

pasty usually a turnover filled with meat

patty tart

pease pudding a baked purée of split peas

peppermint creams peppermint patties

pickerel a young pike

pickles usually means pickled vegetables

pig's trotters pig's feet

porridge oatmeal

prawn large shrimp

pudding dessert; can also be a boiled or baked dish with suet

queen of puddings a baked pudding topped with jam and meringue

rissole chopped meat, fish or vegetables mixed with potato, eggs, breadcrumbs and fried

rock bun/cake raisin roll

roly-poly pudding a rolled suet cake; steamed

rum butter butter mixed with brown sugar, rum and nutmeg

salad cream mayonnaise

sausage and mash sausages and mashed potatoes

scampi large shrimp

scone a kind of biscuit

Scotch broth a soup of chopped beef or lamb, barley and diced vegetables

Scotch egg hard-boiled egg rolled in sausage meat and breadcrumbs; fried

Scotch girdle scone biscuit made on the griddle

Scotch woodcock scrambled eggs flavored with anchovy paste and seasonings; served on toast

seedcake caraway-seed roll

shepherd's pie a casserole of chopped meat, diced onions in a thick gravy covered with mashed potatoes and oven-browned

Shrewsbury cakes lemon-flavored cookies

sillabub, syllabub a whipped mixture of sweet wine, cream and eggs

silverside (of beef) top round steak

Simnel cake a layer cake containing dried fruit, cherries, orange and lemon peel, spices and almond paste

singin' hinny a sweet roll cooked on the griddle, halved and buttered

soda bread a quick bread, similar to sourdough bread

sorbet sherbet

soused herring marinated herring

sponge fingers ladyfingers

spotted Dick white suet pudding with raisins and currants

starter appetizer

steak and kidney pie beef and kidney stew covered with a crust

Stilton cheese one of the best English cheeses, blue-veined and sharp; there is also a white Stilton

suet pudding a rich pudding made of suet, flour, bread crumbs, sugar and milk; served with a sweet sauce

summer pudding fruit-and-bread pudding

sweets candy

tea cake sweet roll

tinned canned

BRITISH

toad in the hole sausages baked in batter
treacle molasses
trifle sponge cake flavored with sherry or brandy, fruit or preserves and almonds, topped with custard or cream
tunny tuna
Victoria sandwich layer cake filled with preserves
Welsh rabbit/rarebit a well-seasoned, creamy cheese mixture served hot over toast
Wensleydale cheese a creamy, crumbly cheese that comes in two main varieties: one tangy, the other mild
wholemeal wholewheat
York ham one of the best hams of England; served thinly sliced
Yorkshire pudding similar to a popover; the traditional accompaniment to roast beef

Drink

ale a strong, slightly sweet beer fermented at a high temperature
appleade apple juice, often carbonated
Athol Brose a drink of honey, oatmeal, water and whisky (Scotland)
Babycham (brand-name) a sparkling non-alcoholic drink
barley wine a beer with a high alcohol content
beer
   bitter ~ has a high hops content; usually draft; amber
   brown ~ fairly weak and sweet
   mild ~ weakest draft beer, slightly sweet
black and tan combines stout and bitter beer
black velvet combines stout and champagne
British wines wine made in Britain with imported grapes

cider apple drink with low alcohol content
   ~ cup cider, spices, sugar and ice
cups various summer drinks containing alcohol diluted with water
double a double shot
gin and It a cocktail of gin and sweet Italian vermouth ("It")
ginger beer a sparkling, slightly alcoholic beverage flavored with ginger
half short for "half a pint" in reference to beer
Irish mist a whisky and honey liqueur
neat straight
Pimm's a brand-name alcoholic beverage
   ~ No. 1 gin based
   ~ No. 2 whisky based
   ~ No. 3 rum based
   ~ No. 4 brandy based

porter similar to bock beer

shandy equal portions of beer and lemonade

short a short drink; undiluted liquor

squash fruit-flavored beverage

stout a bock beer with a high hops content; Guinness is the best-known brand

BRITISH

Greek index

This index will help you to find your way about the Greek list of food and drink, pages 113–127

Russian index

This index will help you to find your way about the Russian list of food and drink, pages 221–246

Tipping guide

The figures below are shown either as a percentage of the bill or in local currency. They indicate a suggested tip for the service described. Even where service is included, additional gratuities are expected by some employees; it's also customary to round off a bill or payment, and leave the small change.

Obviously, tipping is an individual matter, and the correct amount to leave varies enormously with category of restaurant, size of city and so on. The sums we suggest represent normal tips for average middle-grade establishments in big cities.

Austria

Service charge, bill	10–15% included
Waiter	optional
Cloakroom attendant	5–10 shillings
Lavatory attendant	5 shillings

Belgium

Service charge, bill	15% included
Waiter	optional
Cloakroom attendant	50 francs
Lavatory attendant	10 francs

Canada

Service charge, bill	–
Waiter	15%
Cloakroom attendant	$1
Lavatory attendant	50 cents

Finland

Service charge, bill	14–15% included
Waiter	optional
Cloakroom attendant	3–5 marks
Lavatory attendant	charges posted or 2.50 marks

France

Service charge, bill	12–15% generally included
Waiter	optional
Cloakroom attendant	3–5 francs
Lavatory attendant	2 francs

Germany

Service charge, bill	15% generally included
Waiter	optional
Cloakroom attendant	1–2 marks
Lavatory attendant	50 pfennigs–1 mark

Great Britain

Service charge, bill	15% generally included
Waiter	10–15% (if not included)
Cloakroom attendant	20 pence
Lavatory attendant	20 pence

Greece

Service charge, bill	15% included
Waiter	optional
Cloakroom attendant	20 drachmas
Lavatory attendant	20 drachmas

Netherlands
Service charge, bill	included
Waiter	optional
Cloakroom attendant	1–2 florins
Lavatory attendant	50 cents

Ireland
Service charge, bill	generally included
Waiter	optional
Cloakroom attendant	20 pence
Lavatory attendant	20 pence

Italy
Service charge, bill	12–15% included
Waiter	10%
Cloakroom attendant	500 lire
Lavatory attendant	300 lire

Norway
Service charge, bill	10–15% included
Waiter	optional
Cloakroom attendant	charges posted or 3–5 kroner
Lavatory attendant	charges posted or 3 kroner

Poland
Service charge, bill	10% included
Waiter	optional
Cloakroom attendant	charges posted or 5 zlotys
Lavatory attendant	5 zlotys

Portugal

Service charge, bill	15% included
Waiter	optional
Cloakroom attendant	20–30 escudos
Lavatory attendant	20 escudos

Spain

Service charge, bill	15% generally included
Waiter	10%
Cloakroom attendant	25–50 pesetas
Lavatory attendant	25–50 pesetas

Sweden

Service charge, bill	13½% included
Waiter	optional
Cloakroom attendant	charges posted or 3.50 kronor
Lavatory attendant	3 kronor

Switzerland

Service charge, bill	15% included
Waiter	optional
Cloakroom attendant	1 franc
Lavatory attendant	50 centimes

USA

Service charge, bill	–
Waiter	15–20%
Cloakroom attendant	50 cents–$1
Lavatory attendant	50 cents

USSR

Service charge, bill	10–15% included
Waiter	optional
Cloakroom attendant	50 kopecks
Lavatory attendant	30–50 kopecks

Yugoslavia

Service charge, bill	10% included
Waiter	5–10%
Cloakroom attendant	$0.25*
Lavatory attendant	$0.25*

REFERENCE SECTION

* Considering Yugoslavia's rampant inflation, any listing of values in dinars is soon out-dated. We have suggested some amounts in dollar terms for you to convert according to the latest exchange rate.

Metric conversion tables

All countries of continental Europe employ the metric system throughout. While the English-speaking world is increasingly changing over to this mode of measurement, traditional weights and measures continue to be used to varying degrees. The charts on the following pages provide a quick means of converting from one system to the other for everyday purposes.

In these charts, the figure in the centre column stands for both metric and Anglo-American measurements. For example, in the chart below, 1 centimetre = 0.40 inches, and 1 inch = 2.54 centimetres.

REFERENCE SECTION

Length		
Centimetres (cm.)		Inches (in.)
2.54	**1**	0.40
5.08	**2**	0.80
7.62	**3**	1.20
10.16	**4**	1.60
12.70	**5**	2.00
15.24	**6**	2.40
17.78	**7**	2.80
20.32	**8**	3.20
22.86	**9**	3.50
25.40	**10**	3.90
38.10	**15**	6.00
50.80	**20**	7.90
63.50	**25**	10.00
254.00	**100**	39.40

Length (continued)		
Metres (m.)		**Feet (ft.)**
0.30	**1**	3.28
0.61	**2**	6.56
0.91	**3**	9.84
1.22	**4**	13.12
1.52	**5**	16.40
1.83	**6**	19.69
2.13	**7**	22.97
2.44	**8**	26.25
2.74	**9**	29.53
3.05	**10**	32.81
4.57	**15**	49.21
6.10	**20**	65.62
7.62	**25**	82.02
30.48	**100**	328.08

Kilometres (km.)		Miles (mi.)
1.61	**1**	0.62
3.22	**2**	1.24
4.83	**3**	1.86
6.44	**4**	2.49
8.05	**5**	3.11
9.65	**6**	3.73
11.26	**7**	4.35
12.88	**8**	4.97
14.48	**9**	5.59
16.09	**10**	6.21
24.14	**15**	9.32
32.18	**20**	12.43
40.23	**25**	15.54
160.90	**100**	62.14

Weight		
Grams (g.)		Ounces (oz.)
28.35	1	0.035
56.70	2	0.070
85.05	3	0.105
113.40	4	0.140
141.75	5	0.175
170.10	6	0.210
198.45	7	0.245
226.80	8	0.280
255.15	9	0.315
283.50	10	0.350
425.25	15	0.525
567.00	20	0.700
708.75	25	0.875
2,835.00	100	3.500

Kilograms (kg.)		Avoirdupois pounds (lb.)
0.45	1	2.205
0.91	2	4.409
1.36	3	6.614
1.81	4	8.818
2.27	5	11.023
2.72	6	13.227
3.17	7	15.432
3.62	8	17.636
4.08	9	19.841
4.53	10	22.045
6.80	15	33.068
9.06	20	44.090
11.33	25	55.113
45.30	100	220.450

Area		
Square centimetres (cm²)		**Square inches (in²)**
6.45	**1**	0.15
12.90	**2**	0.31
19.36	**3**	0.46
25.81	**4**	0.62
32.26	**5**	0.77
38.71	**6**	0.93
45.16	**7**	1.08
51.62	**8**	1.24
58.07	**9**	1.39
64.52	**10**	1.55
96.78	**15**	2.32
129.04	**20**	3.10
161.30	**25**	3.87
645.20	**100**	15.49

Square metres (m²)		**Square feet (ft²)**
0.093	**1**	10.764
0.186	**2**	21.528
0.279	**3**	32.292
0.372	**4**	43.056
0.465	**5**	53.820
0.557	**6**	64.584
0.650	**7**	75.348
0.743	**8**	86.112
0.836	**9**	96.876
0.929	**10**	107.640
1.394	**15**	161.460
1.858	**20**	215.280
2.323	**25**	269.100
9.290	**100**	1,076.400

Area (continued)		
Square kilometres (km²)		**Square miles (mi²)**
2.59	**1**	0.39
5.18	**2**	0.77
7.77	**3**	1.16
10.36	**4**	1.54
12.95	**5**	1.93
15.54	**6**	2.32
18.13	**7**	2.70
20.72	**8**	3.09
23.31	**9**	3.47
25.90	**10**	3.86
38.85	**15**	5.79
51.80	**20**	7.72
64.75	**25**	9.65
259.00	**100**	38.61

Hectares (ha.)		Acres
0.41	**1**	2.47
0.81	**2**	4.94
1.21	**3**	7.41
1.62	**4**	9.88
2.02	**5**	12.36
2.43	**6**	14.83
2.83	**7**	17.30
3.24	**8**	19.77
3.64	**9**	22.24
4.05	**10**	24.71
6.07	**15**	37.07
8.09	**20**	49.42
10.12	**25**	61.78
40.47	**100**	247.1

REFERENCE SECTION

Temperature

| °C | -30 -25 -20 -15 -10 -5 0   5   10 15 20 25 30 35 40 45 |
| °F | -20   -10   0   10   20   30   40   50   60   70   80   90   100   110 |

To convert centigrade into Fahrenheit, multiply centigrade by 1.8 and add 32.
To convert Fahrenheit into centigrade, subtract 32 from Fahrenheit and divide by 1.8.

Fluid measures					
litres	imp. gal.	U.S. gal.	litres	imp. gal.	U.S. gal.
5	1.1	1.3	30	6.6	7.9
10	2.2	2.6	35	7.7	9.2
15	3.3	4.0	40	8.8	10.6
20	4.4	5.3	45	9.9	11.9
25	5.5	6.6	50	11.0	13.2

Tire pressure			
lb./sq. in.	kg/cm²	lb./sq. in.	kg/cm²
10	0.7	26	1.8
12	0.8	27	1.9
15	1.1	28	2.0
18	1.3	30	2.1
20	1.4	33	2.3
21	1.5	36	2.5
23	1.6	38	2.7
24	1.7	40	2.8

REFERENCE SECTION

BERLITZ DICTIONARIES

Berlitz two-way dictionaries featuring 12,500 concepts in each language with pronunciation shown throughout. Also include basic expressions and special section on how to read a foreign menu. An essential and practical aid for all travellers.

Danish	Italian
Dutch	Norwegian
Finnish	Portuguese
French	Spanish
German	Swedish

Ask your bookseller.

Say BERLITZ

... and most people think of outstanding language schools. But Berlitz has also become the world's leading publisher of books for travellers – Travel Guides, Phrase Books, Dictionaries – plus Cassettes and Self-teaching courses.

Informative, accurate, up-to-date, Books from Berlitz are written with freshness and style. They also slip easily into pocket or purse – no need for bulky, old-fashioned volumes.

Join the millions who know how to travel. Whether for fun or business, put Berlitz in your pocket.

BERLITZ®

Leader in
Books and Cassettes
for Travellers

A Macmillan Company

BERLITZ Books for travellers

TRAVEL GUIDES

They fit your pocket in both size and price. Modern, up-to-date, Berlitz gets all the information you need into 128 lively pages – 192 or 256 pages for country guides – with colour maps and photos throughout. What to see and do, where to shop, what to eat and drink, how to save.

AFRICA	Algeria (256 pages)* Kenya Morocco South Africa Tunisia
ASIA, MIDDLE EAST	China (256 pages) Hong Kong India (256 pages) Japan (256 pages) Nepal* Singapore Sri Lanka Thailand Egypt Jerusalem & Holy Land Saudi Arabia
AUSTRAL- ASIA	Australia (256 pages) New Zealand
BRITISH ISLES	Channel Islands London Ireland Oxford and Stratford Scotland
BELGIUM	Brussels

FRANCE	Brittany France (256 pages) French Riviera Loire Valley Normandy Paris
GERMANY	Berlin Munich The Rhine Valley
AUSTRIA and SWITZER- LAND	Tyrol Vienna Switzerland (192 pages)
GREECE, CYPRUS & TURKEY	Athens Corfu Crete Rhodes Greek Islands of Aegean Peloponnese Salonica/North. Greece Cyprus Istanbul/Aegean Coast Turkey (192 pages)
ITALY and MALTA	Florence Italian Adriatic Italian Riviera Italy (256 pages) Rome Sicily Venice Malta
NETHER- LANDS and SCANDI- NAVIA	Amsterdam Copenhagen Helsinki Oslo and Bergen Stockholm

*in preparation

PORTUGAL	Algarve
	Lisbon
	Madeira
SPAIN	Barcelona/Costa Dorada
	Canary Islands
	Costa Blanca
	Costa Brava
	Costa del Sol & Andalusia
	Ibiza and Formentera
	Madrid
	Majorca and Minorca
EASTERN EUROPE	Budapest
	Dubrovnik & S. Dalmatia
	Hungary (192 pages)
	Istria and Croatian Coast
	Moscow & Leningrad
	Prague
	Split and Dalmatia
	Yugoslavia (256 pages)
NORTH AMERICA	U.S.A. (256 pages)
	California
	Florida
	Hawaii
	Miami

NORTH AMERICA	New York
	Canada (256 pages)
	Toronto
	Montreal
CARIBBEAN, LATIN AMERICA	Puerto Rico
	Virgin Islands
	Bahamas
	Bermuda
	French West Indies
	Jamaica
	Southern Caribbean
	Mexico City
	Brazil (Highlights of)
	Rio de Janeiro
EUROPE	Business Travel Guide – Europe (368 pages)
	Pocket guide to Europe (480 pages)
	Cities of Europe (504 p.)
CRUISE GUIDES	Caribbean cruise guide (368 pages)
	Alaska cruise guide (168 p)
	Handbook to Cruising (240 pages)

DELUXE GUIDES
combine complete
travel guide, phrase
book and dictionary in
one book.
Titles available:
Amsterdam, Barcelona,
Budapest, Florence,
French Riviera, Madrid,
Mexico, Munich, Paris,
Rome, Venice.

SKI GUIDES
Top resorts rated,
where to ski, colour
maps:
Austria
France
Italy
Switzerland
Skiing the Alps*

BLUEPRINT GUIDES
Imaginative new large size guide with mapped itineraries,
special interest checklists, selected restaurant and hotel
recommendations, large-scale road atlas, all in full colour.

France, Germany*, Great Britain*, Greece*, Italy, Spain*.

MORE FOR THE $
Over $ 4'000 worth of discount coupons and gift certificates
from the finest hotels and restaurants for each country
covered.

France, Italy.

*in preparation

PHRASE BOOKS

World's bestselling phrase books feature all the expressions and vocabulary you'll need, and pronunciation throughout. 192 pages, 2 colours.

Arabic	Hebrew	Russian
Chinese	Hungarian	Serbo-Croatian
Danish	Italian	Spanish (Castilian)
Dutch	Japanese	Spanish (Lat. Am.)
Finnish	Korean	Swahili
French	Norwegian	Swedish
German	Polish	Turkish
Greek	Portuguese	European Phrase Book
		European Menu Reader

All of the above phrase books are available with C60 or C90 cassette and miniscript as a "**cassettepak**".

Cassette and miniscript only are also available in the major languages as a "**phrase cassette**".

DICTIONARIES

Bilingual with 12,500 concepts each way. Highly practical for travellers, with pronunciation shown plus menu reader, basic expressions and useful information. Over 330 pages.

Danish	French	Norwegian
Dutch	German	Portuguese
Finnish	Italian	Spanish
		Swedish

TRAVEL VIDEO

Travel Tips from Berlitz are now part of the informative and colourful videocassette series of over 80 popular destinations produced by Travelview International. Ideal for planning a trip, Travelview videos provide 40 to 60 minutes of valuable destination briefing and a Reference Guide to local hotels and tourist attractions. Available from leading travel agencies and video stores everywhere in the U.S.A. and Canada or call 1-800-325-3108 (Texas, call (713) 975-7077; (403) 248-7170 in Canada; 908-66 9422 in UK; (5) 531-8714 in Mexico City).